Feminism and Political Economy in Victorian England

Feminism and Political Economy in Victorian England

Edited by

Peter Groenewegen

Professor of Economics,
University of Sydney,
Sydney, Australia

Edward Elgar

Published by
Edward Elgar Publishing Limited
Gower House
Croft Road
Aldershot
Hants GU11 3HR
England

Edward Elgar Publishing Company
Old Post Road
Brookfield
Vermont 05036
USA

British Library Cataloguing in Publication Data
Feminism and Political Economy in Victorian England
I. Groenewegen, P.D.
305.420942

Library of Congress Cataloguing in Publication Data
Feminism and political economy in Victorian England / edited by Peter
    Groenewegen.
        p.   cm.
    Includes bibliographical references and index.
        1. Women—England—Social conditions.   2. Women—England
    —Economic conditions.   3. Women—Employment—England—
    History— 19th century.   4. Feminism—England—History—19th
    century.   I. Groenewegen, Peter D.
    HQ1593.F43   1994   94–2709
    305.42'0942'09034—dc20   CIP

ISBN 1 85278 928 X

Printed in Great Britain at the University Press, Cambridge

Contents

List of Tables

Notes on Authors

Barbara Caine is Associate Professor in History and Foundation Director of the Centre for Women's Studies at the University of Sydney. She has written widely on feminism and Victorian England, in particular her two books, *Destined to be Wives: The Sisters of Beatrice Webb* (Clarendon Press, 1986) and *Victorian Feminists* (Oxford University Press, 1992).

Peter Groenewegen is Professor of Economics and Director of the Centre for the Study of the History of Economic Thought at the University of Sydney. He has published widely on the history of economics, including most recently a *History of Australian Economics* (with Bruce McFarlane) and his *A Soaring Eagle: Alfred Marshall 1842–1924* (Blackwell, forthcoming).

Chris Nyland is Senior Lecturer in Economics at the University of Wollongong. He has published extensively on industrial relations and is currently researching the treatment of the 'women's question' in economic literature. His books and monographs include *Working Time and Work Intensity in the 1920s* (Flinders University, 1986) and *Reduced Work Time and Management of Production* (Cambridge University Press, 1989).

Gaby Ramia is a postgraduate student at the University of Wollongong. His honours degree thesis dealt with 'The Webbs, Women's Wages and the Legal Protection of Women Workers', providing the foundation for the chapter he co-authored for this volume.

Michael V. White is Senior Lecturer in Economics at Monash University. He has published widely on nineteenth-century economics, especially on the work of Jevons, in journals including *History of Political Economy*, the *Manchester School* and the *Economic Record*.

Acknowledgements

I am indebted to the participants of the original Workshop at which three of the chapters were initially presented, for giving the discussion such an enthusiastic response, and to the Centre for Women's Studies for acting as its co-sponsor. I am indebted to Mark Donoghue and Sue King for additional research for Chapter 6 on Clara Collet and for the Introduction; Valerie Jones for preparing the typescript and Sue King for assisting in the proofreading. The Australian Research Council provided funding assistance for the research on journal authorship used in the Introduction and granted a Senior Research Fellowship which enabled quicker completion of the editing and writing. I also thank Julie Leppard for her splendid editorial work which saved me from various errors and inconsistencies.

1. Introduction: Women in Political Economy and Women as Political Economists in Victorian England

Peter Groenewegen

It is well known that the women's question acquired tremendous importance in late Victorian England. The decades following the 1860s saw the gradual admission of women into universities, increased rights of married women with respect to property, a substantial victory won by women over the controversial contagious diseases legislation, the rise of the new working woman seeking economic independence and the growth of the suffragette movement. By the 1890s, the last full decade of the Victorian era, there was talk as the century drew to its close that this had been 'the woman's century' and the 1890s, the woman's decade (Rubinstein, 1988, p. xv). The decade heralded 'a revolt of the daughters and the birth of the new woman', a questioning of the ideal of marriage as the be-all and end-all of female existence, some criticism of the Victorian double standards in sexual morality and a gradual move of women into formerly male domains such as Royal Commissions, the higher echelons of public service and some of the professions. During this period, what was colloquially described as 'the women's question' also entered more firmly into the ambit of political economy and, more generally, that of the 'moral scientist'.

A happy conjuncture of research work made it feasible for the Centre for the Study of the History of Economic Thought at the University of Sydney to organize a Workshop on this subject in conjunction with its Centre for Women's Studies. This research encompassed Barbara Caine's completed study of Victorian Feminism, Michael White's ongoing research on Jevons, which had been looking at the attitudes of Jevons to married working women, and Peter Groenewegen's biography of Alfred Marshall in which Marshall's views on the women's issue in general were the subject of a separate chapter. Chapters 2, 3 and 4 of this volume are the immediate outcome of this Workshop, held during May 1992 and specifically designed to investigate attitudes to 'the women's question' by Victorian political economists and moral scientists. The authors explicitly included were John Stuart Mill, Henry Fawcett and Henry Sidgwick (discussed by Barbara Caine), W.S. Jevons (discussed by Michael White) and Alfred Marshall (discussed by Peter Groenewegen). These five men were all political economists of note, moreover they were all generally nurtured within the moral sciences, and in the case of four (Jevons only excepted) were actively involved themselves for at least part of their lives in aspects of the women's movement. In addition, and this is a particular aspect of Barbara Caine's discussion in Chapter 2, these four had wives likewise actively involved in women's emancipation, so that they presented particularly fascinating case studies of intellectual Victorians interested in this issue of growing importance. The discussion generated at the Workshop was such that publication to a wider audience was thought desirable by organizers and participants, something requiring an enlarged contents if this was to be successfully implemented.

The issues raised in the three papers prepared for the Workshop, dealing as they did with the nature of the treatment of women's issues in Victorian political economy, were sharpened by the coincident publication of Pujol (1992). This had addressed issues of feminism and anti-feminism in early (that is, pre-mid-twentieth century) economic thought. A mini-symposium on feminist theory and the history of economic thought organized for publication in *History of Political Economy* (Weintraub et al., 1993) further highlighted the importance of the issues addressed at the Workshop. The wide agenda opened up made it not difficult to find topics for two additional and supplementary chapters. Two of the participants at the Workshop, Chris Nyland and Gaby Ramia, had been examining the work of Sidney and Beatrice Webb on the rights of women within the economic sphere, and this became the topic addressed in Chapter 5. Two of the papers at the original Workshop had in addition focused some attention on the work of Clara Collet. Her late nineteenth-century research was particularly informative in the context of Jevons's participation in the debate over the effects of the employment of married women on infant mortality, a major part of Michael White's discussion, while her work had been reviewed by Mary Paley Marshall, the economist wife of Alfred

Marshall and, more importantly, she had been one of the Assistant Lady Commissioners for the Royal Commission on Labour whose report on women's employment featured extensively in Peter Groenewegen's discussion of Alfred Marshall's position on the sexual division of labour. Since her work is important and very neglected, a subject for a final chapter immediately suggested itself.

Although the two added chapters combined neatly with the conception of the original Workshop, because they deal with aspects of the political economy treatment of the women's issue in Victorian England, they nevertheless also widened the scope of the discussion. The focus on the work of Beatrice Webb (Potter) in Chapter 5 and that of Clara Collet in Chapter 6 provides insight into women *as political economists* during this period. The five chapters together therefore encompass both the treatment of women in Victorian political economy and the equally interesting and important topic of the growth and development of women political economists. The second of these topics is in itself a fascinating one since, as Barbara Caine points out in her chapter and others have stressed as well (Pujol, 1992; Weintraub et al., 1993), the women's perspective is often sadly lacking in these examinations of women's work. Beatrice Webb, who was even urged by Alfred Marshall to use her feminine insights into the question of women's labour (Webb, 1938, pp. 398–9) cannot of course be charged with such criticism. Clara Collet, who was widely regarded from the 1890s as *the* English expert on aspects of women's work and wages, issues which she treated invariably from a woman's perspective and the special insight acquired by an unmarried professional woman working in the public service (Board of Trade, Labour Department, then Department of Labour), started her social inquiries on this topic, like Beatrice Webb (Potter), in the team of researchers gathered by Charles Booth to investigate London life and labour and gained further experience with the Labour Commission.

To set the stage for this wider inquiry, thereby more generally introducing the topics covered in the following five chapters, the remainder of this opening chapter looks at the following: its first section presents some factual background to the debate on women's work concentrating on the shifting employment pattern and the relative wages earned by women workers; the next section discusses the treatment of women in the literature of political economy prior to the late Victorian period to which this volume is largely devoted, partly to supplement the introduction to this topic presented by Pujol (1992, Part I) and others (Madden, 1972; Folbre, 1992);   a third section then looks at the contributions made by women to political economy, especially during this period, in order to indicate that, contrary to popular belief, women contributed more widely to economic debate in relative terms in the initial years of the professionalization of the subject in England, than they have done ever since;   a final concluding section provides an overview of the contents of the remainder of the book in the context of the issues raised in the introduction.

WOMEN'S WORK AND WAGES IN THE VICTORIAN ERA

The reign of Queen Victoria from 20 June 1837 to 22 January 1901 precisely defines the Victorian era in English history.[1] It was a period of rapid change, political, social and economic, and this included changing attitudes to women's labour together with a hardening of more traditional views. During the 1840s the first Factory Acts were passed, specifically designed to protect women and children from the worst excesses of the factory system and the Industrial Revolution. In 1842, laws prohibiting the employment of women underground in mining were passed; in 1844 legislation regulated the hours of work for women and children. The year of revolution, 1848, regulated the work of women and children to a ten-hour maximum in the textile industry, ending a decade of reform of working conditions for women and children not to be resumed until the 1860s with the passing of the first Factory Inspection Act of 1867. In 1874 a Factory Act regulated a 56½ hour working week, followed in 1878 by further measures regulating working conditions and hours of work, generalizing a working week of 56½ hours to textile factories and 60 hours a week in what were considered less severely straining places of work (Jevons, 1882c, pp. 63–4). Favourable economic conditions in the early 1870s had, however, by then already resulted in considerable spread of the nine-hour day, though difficulties in enforcement made its universal application rather problematical. At the start of the Edwardian decade, in 1901, agitation of workers for the nine-hour day had been replaced by a general movement for 'the widespread adoption of Eight Hours as the standard working day in all branches of British Industry' (Webb and Webb, 1897, p. 352).

In the context of his wider discussion of factory legislation, Jevons (1882c, pp. 71–7) also raised the issue of the general desirability of making special legislative provision for adult women. Its basis was the generally 'conceded' ground 'that women are less able to take care of themselves than men' and that such regulatory measures were particularly appropriate to the case of 'married, or more strictly speaking, of child-bearing women'. As Michael White shows in detail in Chapter 3, Jevons was strongly in favour of the second of these measures as a means for reducing the rate of infant mortality in factory districts, while he was sceptical of the first proposition given the fact that, 'in the case of domestic service, ... women have known perfectly well how to advance their interests' and that, if 'liberty of the subject' were the only consideration in such matters, Professor Fawcett's opposition to factory legislation was 'unanswerable' (Jevons, 1882c, pp. 72–3). The issue of special provisions for women in factory legislation became a controversial one, dividing sections of the women's movement, and brought the Webbs initially on the side of special recognition of female characteristics in regulatory measures of conditions of work (as discussed in detail in Chapter 5).

Jevons's contribution to the subject is important because of its distinction between segments of the labour market in distinct groups. First of all, he clearly differentiated the treatment of adult males and females in line with Victorian practice. In connection with the female labour market, his work then distinguished the need to separate married women of child-bearing age from other women, and the labour of women in factories and workshops from that of women in domestic service. However, professional women were not mentioned in his discussion, nor did the right of women to work fall within the ambit of his inquiries. As a general qualification to the principle of *laissez-faire* some of his contemporaries were bringing to the question, Jevons implied the state had a duty of regulating female labour if this could be shown to be in the national interest. Only the right of individual labour to work unrestricted in a private shop or dwelling was to be excepted

Table 1.1: Labour force statistics 1841–1911 – females – (based on 1911 census categories): '000

	1841	1851	1861	1871	1881	1891	1901	1911
Public administration	3	3	4	7	9	17	29	50
Armed forces	–	–	–	–	–	–	–	–
Professional occupations and their subordinate services	49	103	126	152	203	264	326	383
Domestic offices and personal services	989	1135	1407	1678	1756	2036	2003	2127
Commercial occupations	1	–	–	5	11	26	76	157
Transport and communications of which:	4	13	11	16	15	20	27	38
Railways	1	–	–	–	1	1	2	3
Roads	1	3	3	3	2	2	1	3
Sea, canals and docks	–	3	1	1	1	1	1	1
Agriculture, horticulture and forestry	81	229	163	135	116	80	86	117
Fishing	–	1	1	1	3	1	–	–
Mining and quarrying, and workers in the products of mines and quarries	7	11	6	11	8	7	6	8
Metal, manufacture, machines, implements, vehicles, precious metals, etc.	14	36	45	46	49	51	84	128
Building and construction	1	1	1	4	2	3	3	5
Wood, furniture, fittings and decorations	5	8	15	26	21	25	30	35
Bricks, cement, pottery and glass	10	15	19	25	27	32	37	42
Chemicals, oil, soap, resin, etc.	1	4	3	5	9	17	31	46
Skins, leather, hair and feathers	3	5	8	10	16	20	27	32
Paper, printing, books and stationery	6	16	23	31	53	78	111	144
Textiles	358	635	676	726	745	795	795	870
Clothing	200	491	596	594	667	759	792	825
Food, drink and tobacco	42	53	71	78	98	163	216	308
Gas, water and electricity supply	–	–	–	–	–	–	–	–
All other occupied	41	75	80	106	78	89	75	98
TOTAL FEMALES OCCUPIED	1815	2832	3254	3650	3887	4489	4751	5413
TOTAL AS PERCENTAGE OF FEMALE POPULATION [a]	25.2	34.9	36.1	36.2	33.8	34.5	31.7	31.6
TOTAL AS PERCENTAGE OF TOTAL LABOUR FORCE [b]	26.3	30.2	30.9	28.7	30.5	31.0	29.1	29.5

Notes: (a) Sum of total occupied and unoccupied females – population of work age. (b) Sum of occupied males and females.
Source: B.R. Mitchell, Abstract of British Historical Statistics, Cambridge University Press, 1962, p. 60.

(Jevons, 1882c, p. 67). This issue is canvassed at length in the material that follows.

The growth and nature of women's work over the Victorian era and the Edwardian decade are illustrated in Table 1.1 on the basis of the industrial classification categories adopted for the 1911 census. These data show that it is difficult to generalize on the trends in women's employment over this period except with respect to specific industrial groupings. The percentage of women of working age employed, for example, rose to a maximum in 1871, reflecting the highly favourable economic circumstances of this period for employment in general, since the proportion of employed women relative to total labour force *fell* at the same time. From 1871, the census data disclose a gradual relative decline in the proportion of working women, and a remarkably stable proportion of employed women relative to the total workforce. The last proportion peaked in 1891, thereby warranting perhaps the opportunism expressed at the start of the 1890s which it described as the 'women's decade'.

The relative shifts in employment opportunities for women these data disclose are even more interesting, particularly in the context of the contributions made to this subject by Clara Collet discussed in Chapter 6. Table 1.2 presents the relative importance of some major occupational groups for the period. The relative shifts reflect a number of different factors. A number of temporary peaks in industries such as mining, metals and machinery, as well as furniture and wood working industries in 1871, reflect a scarcity of men's labour during this period of boom and hence a temporary increase in employment opportunities offered to women. Other rapid changes in the relative importance reflect technical progress and structural change. This is evident particularly in agriculture, where women workers shared in the steady decline of job opportunities. In paper, printing, books and stationery, they likewise shared rising employment opportunities as they did in the chemical, oil, soaps and resins industries particularly after 1891 and in the switch in relative importance of textiles and clothing, a phenomenon explicitly analysed by Clara Collet (below, Chapter 6). A rising share of women's employment in public administration became more significant from 1891. The rise in professional job opportunities recorded in Table 1.2 was largely associated with the growing teaching sector, while commercial occupations for women (including clerical staff and typists) accelerated from 1871, the year when they first became significant,

Table 1.2: *Relative employment opportunities for females in work*
1841–1911 (%)

	1841	1851	1861	1871	1881	1891	1901	1911
Public administration	0.2	0.1	0.1	0.2	0.2	0.4	0.6	0.9
Professional occupations and their subordinate services	2.7	3.6	3.9	4.2	5.2	5.6	6.9	7.1
Domestic offices and personal services	54.5	40.1	43.2	46.0	45.2	45.4	42.2	39.3
Commercial occupations	–	–	–	–	–	–	–	–
Transport & communications	0.2	0.5	0.4	0.4	0.4	0.4	0.6	0.7
Agriculture, etc.	4.5	8.1	5.0	3.7	3.0	1.8	1.8	2.2
Mining & metals, heavy industry	0.4	0.4	0.2	0.3	0.2	0.2	0.1	0.1
Wood furniture, fittings and decorations	0.3	0.3	0.5	0.7	0.5	0.6	0.6	0.6
Bricks, cement, pottery and glass	0.6	0.5	0.6	0.7	0.7	0.7	0.8	0.8
Chemicals, oil, soap, resin	–	0.1	0.1	0.1	0.1	0.2	0.7	0.9
Skin, leather, hair and feathers	0.2	0.2	0.2	0.3	0.4	0.5	0.6	0.6
Paper, printing, books and stationery	0.3	0.6	0.7	0.8	1.3	1.7	2.3	2.7
Textiles	19.7	22.4	20.8	19.9	19.2	17.7	16.7	16.1
Clothing	11.0	17.3	18.3	16.3	17.2	16.9	16.7	15.2
Food, drink and tobacco	2.3	1.9	2.2	2.1	2.5	3.6	4.5	5.7

Source: Calculated from Table 1.1

probably the result of scarce male labour in that year of high
employment. Yet despite these relative shifts in employment
opportunities for women, by the end of the period the dominant
employers of female labour in domestic and personal services, textiles
and clothing still provided seventy per cent of the jobs for women, as
compared with eighty per cent at the start of the Victorian era, with
much of the relative decline explicable from the very substantial decline
in the domestic service sector. There were marginal shifts in favour of
new employment opportunities, but few of these can be unambiguously

attributed to changing social attitudes on the issue of women's employment at the time.

The picture of changes in wages is even more complicated. A table in Wood (1903, p. 278) indicating wage growth for women from 1824 to 1900 shows an average increase of women's wages over this period of two-thirds, with very marked differences between the increases shown in particular sectors of industry. Wages in the cotton industry rose above average (73.9 per cent) but in woollens only by 52 per cent, a rate of increase shared by many other industrial sectors. The hosiery and silk industry experienced very fast wage growth, the latter more than doubling female wage rates. Average female wages peaked during the 1870s, on these data, lagging slightly behind the peak in male wages recorded around 1873. This conforms to the detailed wage study Clara Collet (1898a) conducted for the textile districts of Dundee, Ulster and Leeds. Highest female wage increases by the end of the period were in cotton, silk, hosiery, printing, pottery, boots and shoes, which experienced above-average increases. The data is of insufficient quality to give it a great deal of authority, but an abbreviated version of Wood's (1903) table is nevertheless reproduced as Table 1.3.

Subsequent work on female wages by Dorothea Barton (1919, 1921) revealed the impact of the First World War on women's wages and employment, a potential contribution of the war on female employment which Collet had commented on in 1915 with respect to professional women (Collet, 1915). However, Barton's data likewise show the difficulties in generalizing on this issue for the late nineteenth and early twentieth centuries for a variety of reasons, including regional variation. London wages for women (as for men) were invariably considerably higher in most trades, and smaller margins of difference applied to regional centres even in such unskilled female tasks as rag sorting (Barton, 1919, p. 523; Collet, 1898a, pp. 65–6). Comments on Barton's contribution by those present at the meeting of the Statistical Society at which it was given, illustrate the statistical problems with this topic. Bowley (1919, p. 545) described women's wage statistics as 'a very barren land', making comparisons virtually impossible when using proper statistical methods. Collet's comments (1919, pp. 646–9) show her consummate skills in drawing inferences from masses of statistical data, noted in Chapter 6 below. Stressing the ambiguities of the term, 'average wages', for trades where rates were fairly heterogeneous, Collet suggested concentration on the upper and lower confines of the

Table 1.3: Changes in average wages of women and girls (1833–1900, selected years). Calculated on the basis of 1866 = 100

	1833	1840	1850	1860	1870	1874	1880	1891	1900
Cotton	83	75	82	88	103	131	133	144	160
Wool	71	67	70	89	103	111	120	105	108
Shoddy	–	–	–	91	119	121	122	100	105
Worsted	71	80	–	84	–	133	–	110	115
Linen and flax	–	–	–	85	106	105	116	110	120
Jute	–	–	–	73	91	109	98	120	126
Silk	–	81	81	96	119	146	143	130	140
Lace	–	–	–	–	–	–	123	120	–
Hosiery	–	70	–	77	–	–	135	136	141
Average, textiles etc.	75	75	78	85	107	122	124	119	127
Printing	–	79	83	94	108	–	–	125	128
Pottery	–	–	–	97	102	111	108	135	142
Cotton printing and dyeing	–	–	–	94	–	135	126	–	–
Linen bleaching	–	–	–	64	103	124	–	–	–
Boots and shoes	–	–	–	99	101	–	130	131	136
Cotton bleaching	–	–	79	87	110	–	–	–	–
Agriculture (Northumberland)	79	100	100	100	119	160	149	–	–
Paper making	–	83	83	96	–	–	125	–	–
Average	74	76	79	92	108	122	124	123	128

Source: G.H. Wood (1903), p. 278.

middle half of the range of rates. This gave a better picture of the changes which were occurring. In addition, she pointed to another effect of the First World War, the sharp decline in domestic servants embracing one-servant, two-servant and three-or-more servant households. The favourable impact on servants' wages this had generated needed to be offset by the adverse impact of servant reduction on 'the home daughter, the home sister and home mother'.

Wood (1903, pp. 282–4) also sheds some light on relative wage growth for men and women workers. From 1860 to 1891 wages were growing considerably faster in the cotton, wool and shoddy industries and, more generally, for the whole of the textile industry. The data provided are once again difficult to interpret. However, they do permit the broad conclusion that in most of the textile industries women's wage growth from 1866 to 1891 outstripped that of men, a conclusion also applicable to the printing and associated industries. Two more general conclusions followed from this for Wood. There was no ground for believing that the Factory Acts with their preferential treatment for women had had a permanent effect in lowering women's wages, as many opponents of this legislation had so strongly argued. Second, the substitution of women for men from their initially lower levels of wages was a factor that needed to be taken into account, even though in this case the existing data provided no simple conclusions for such an inference.

The continuing relative paucity of data in this area suggests that considerable research is still required on the facts about women's work and wages for the Victorian period. This makes the contributions to this subject by statisticians such as Wood, Barton and Clara Collet all the more significant, because they gathered the raw material from which more systematic inquiries will probably have to start. The discussion of the women's issue with respect to the labour market in Victorian England is therefore still very frequently conducted on rather tenuous statistical evidence, though better than that available to most of the nineteenth-century commentators who pontificated on this subject in a manner best described as empirically blind.

TREATMENT OF THE WOMEN'S ISSUE IN EARLIER CLASSICAL POLITICAL ECONOMY

The paucity of the discussion of women's economic role is illustrated by the concentration of the literature on the exceptions which tended to prove the rule. Pujol (1992, Chapter 1) illustrates this approach by dwelling on the approaches of two of the classical economists, Adam Smith and John Stuart Mill, as well as on the feminine insights of the subject from Harriet Taylor and Barbara Bodichon. Although some of this treatment is in itself problematical, there are no ways of ascertaining from Pujol's argument whether these case studies were selected on the basis of a systematic search of the literature of economics in this period with a largely negative outcome, or whether it was simply the consequence of preconceived knowledge on the subject. A coinciding study (Folbre, 1992) suggests that other classical economists were involved in testing the rationality of economic man in bed or, more specifically, their conventional standards on the (female) monogamy and heterosexuality most classical economists espoused in discussions of population, combined with the view that contraception was both immoral and improper. The male political economist discourse on sexuality therefore tended to depart from its otherwise rational and secular view of the world. Exceptions came from the school of Bentham. These included James Mill and Francis Place and, in a later generation, the neo-Malthusians among the philosophical radicals, such as the young John Stuart Mill. The relevance of women when discussing the population issue was therefore explicitly acknowledged by at least some of the classical economists in a broad way.

Women, however, were also given specific treatment in a number of other issues in classical political economy. For example, J.-B. Say, in his discussion of consumption argued that 'the weaker sex is, from the very circumstances of inferiority in strength of mind, exposed to greater excess both of avarice and prodigality' (Say, 1970, p. 402n.). He illustrated this some pages later with a reference to Pliny's mention of Pauline, a Roman lady, adorned at a dinner by jewels worth 1,400,000 dollars (quadringenties sestertiuum) (Say, 1970, p. 477). In the same context, Mrs. Marcet (1826, p. 477) placed this story in the mouth of her young political economy student Caroline, who is then told by her governess, Mrs. B., that these jewels, now valued at £300,000, are but a 'trifling instance of profusion' in ancient times, and luxury all the more objectionable, because it derived from plunder (Marcet, 1826, pp. 477–8). An example of inequality in the female labour market is offered by McCulloch (1854, pp. 62–3) as an implicit indication of the irrationality in behaviour of a certain class of women forced to seek employment. McCulloch correctly indicated that female domestic servants comprised one of the largest divisions of the labouring population, and one 'best provided for' from a high rate of remuneration. This neither matched the level of education and attainment required for this occupation, nor its disagreeable nature from the need to conform 'to the rules and regulations' of employers. McCulloch therefore explained the high emoluments of servants in terms of dislike from a certain class of people to join the ranks of servants.[2] 'The daughters of professional people, decayed tradesmen, shopkeepers, and such like parties, ... have from infancy been taught to look upon domestics as a lower class' and therefore prefer the over-crowded occupation of 'needle-women' if they need to seek paid work. As a consequence, this particular trade frequently experiences distress. The doctrine of irrational economic woman was therefore applied by some classical economists to the labour as well as the goods market.

More interesting contributions to the treatment of women in classical economics come from Robert Owen and his followers among the so-called Ricardian socialists. In the first place, Robert Owen is unusual, because his discussions of labour are conducted in terms of its underlying segments of men, women and children, a subdivision also used by him when describing the poor (Owen, 1816, pp. 84, 86). The need for this subdivision is imperfectly explained by the remedies for distress Owen suggested in his famous scheme of factory colonies or 'parallelograms of labour'. This gave children preferential treatment with respect to hours of work and education, and, Owen indicated,

> It is proposed that the women should be employed –
> First, – In the care of their infants, and in keeping their dwellings in the best order.
> Second, – In cultivating the gardens to raise vegetables for the supply of the public kitchen.
> Third, – In attending to such of the branches of the various manufactures as women can well undertake; but not to be employed in them more than four or five hours in the day.
> Fourth, – In making up clothing for the images of the establishment.
> Fifth, – In attending occasionally, and in rotation, in the public kitchen, mess-rooms, and dormitories; and, when properly instructed, in superintending some parts of the education of the children in the schools.
> (Owen, 1817a, p. 263, 1817b, p. 195).

The sexual division of labour developed by Owen as a pre-requisite for his social utopia to relieve distress in the post-Napoleonic war period, became a natural aspect of the organization of society from its earliest development in the work of Hodgskin (1827):

> yet there is no state of society, probably, in which division of labour between the sexes does not take place. It is and *must* be practised the instant a *family* exists. Among even the most barbarous tribes, *war* is the exclusive business of the males; and they are in general, the principal hunters and fishers. The man takes to himself the perils and pleasures of the chase, and the woman labours in and about the hut. Different employments for the *sexes* may be traced in all communities, in every age of the world, and in every history, whether fabulous or true. In modern as well as

ancient times, in the most civilized as well as in the most barbarous societies, we find the men, as the rule, taking the out-door work to themselves, and leaving to the women most of the domestic occupations. This primary division of labour springs from sexual difference of organization, it has its foundation in the difference of our physical constitution, in the different parental duties required of the sexes, and is co-extensive with the existence of our race (Hodgskin, 1827, pp. 111–12).

Here political economy proclaims the sexual division of labour as the *sine qua non* of human existence, as an essential condition for the existence of the race. This viewpoint is found, albeit much more subtly, in Marshall's analysis of the subject at the end of the century. However, it is interesting that its clear enunciation comes in socialist writings, in strong contrast to the more egalitarian opinions on the women's issue later espoused by German and Russian (Marxist) social democracy.[3]

The romantic critics of political economy, Carlyle and Ruskin, likewise tended either to exclude women from their discourse or to place them on to a special pedestal as persons for worship by, and of specific service to, men.   Carlyle's strong attack on contemporary political economy, *Past and Present*, contains few references to women, and none in their role as fellow workers in the factory system he so much deplored.   They are mentioned for their special attributes as 'worshippers' (Carlyle, 1843, p. 48), as deserving widows rejected for charity by the spirit of the new poor law (Carlyle, 1843, p. 128) and as mothers and sisters always ready to assist man in his needs, as fetchers of milk and grinders of corn to use his example, which applied even in 'Black Dehomey' and hence demonstrated the universality of women's hearts 'richer than laissez faire' (Carlyle, 1843, pp. 181–2). Ruskin's (1862–63) *Essays of Political Economy*, later titled *Munera Pulveris* likewise ignored women's place in economic life. This omission of women from the public sphere enabled him to glorify them all the better as wives and mothers, whose morally guiding and educational functions were fully reconcilable with their equally essential, 'true wifely subjection' (Ruskin, 1865, pp. 110–25).[4]

During the mid-nineteenth century, women's economic role as seen by the fringe literature of political economy was often confined to that of helper or hindrance to her husband in the conduct of his life. Two examples can be given of this literature. First, the immensely popular guides to living such as *Self Help* and *Thrift* (Smiles, 1859, 1875) extolled the virtues and deprecated the vices of married woman in this direction;   condemning her potential for extravagant purchases, particularly in dress, and alternatively praising her skills in abstinence as crucial assistance for her husband's undertakings in business. In Smiles's homilies of the middle-class Victorian virtues, women such as Mrs. Chisholm are occasionally elevated with the far more frequent use of male examples, to models for good character. Smiles's praise of women in the household could implicitly be used by Brassey (1873, pp. 104–5) to justify his association of female manual labour with less civilized society. Drawing on examples from Russia, Brassey also showed that the employment of women in heavy work ended in the 'poverty which it is intended to alleviate', because of the lower wages from over-crowding such female entry into the workforce tended to produce. Both for their wages, their comfort and their offspring, society was better served if women stayed at home combining their domestic work with light labour for the market.

As the contents of the next five chapters show, the late Victorian era brought some improvement in the situation by diminishing the relative neglect of women's issues in political economy. The increased prominence of the topic, associated with the growth of women's employment, particularly in more visible industries like the professions and the public service, made it difficult to ignore the subject any longer. However, even if the debate was recognized by leading contemporary economists such as John Stuart Mill, Henry Fawcett and the later generation of William Stanley Jevons and Alfred Marshall, it was done in a limited and quite specific manner. The topic of woman's work rarely gained prominence in the textbook literature, irrespective of whether this was Mill's *Principles of Political Economy*, Fawcett's *Manual*, Jevons's *Theory of Political Economy* or Marshall's *Principles of Economics*, though Marshall did include the sexual division of labour as an important part of his framework. It became the subject for special contributions, directed at specific aspects of the debate, and frequently published in either the 'quarterlies' which filled such a prominent place in Victorian middle-class opinion making, or in the growing academic journal literature which came into its own at an accelerating rate from the 1890s. This exclusion from the textbooks remains a feature of the treatment of women's issues in modern economics practice, possibly something which will not be fully redressed until well into the coming twenty-first century.

WOMEN WRITERS ON POLITICAL ECONOMY

Although two of the subsequent chapters mention some famous political economy husband and wife partnerships – more specifically, those of Henry and Millicent Fawcett and Alfred and Mary Marshall – the first chapter by Barbara Caine also indicates that political economy was treated very much as a male domain and that this, to a considerable extent, explains the limited perspective on women's issues in its literature. It is equally well known that there have been few women contributors to that economic literature. The exceptions that prove this rule stand out as the prominent special cases they seem to be and invariably have tended to be treated in this way by later commentators. Thomson's (1973) *Adam Smith's Daughters* is a good example. It evaluates the pedagogic exercises catering for successive generations of nineteenth-century youth written by Jane Marcet, Harriet Martineau and Millicent Fawcett and as her other three examples takes the more original and significant work of Beatrice Webb (Potter), Rosa Luxembourg and Joan Robinson. In this volume, equally selective, Chapter 5 deals with Beatrice Webb's contributions to the women's issue; while Chapter 6 highlights the work of another late nineteenth-century woman social investigator with substantial political economy training, Clara Collet.

It is easy to explain this dearth of women economists by a variety of factors. It can be blamed on the maleness of the research programme of the subject, on long-standing sexist attitudes to women in academic, scientific and professional life and on the masculine subject matter of the 'public domain' of political economy, market and state, from which women have been equally effectively excluded. However, it is interesting, and surprising, to note that these types of arguments apply more strongly to contemporary economics practice, or to the economics after the Second World War, than to the developments which took place in the subject during the period of its embryonic professional development. The years from the late 1880s to the early 1920s saw a greater participation by women in political economy literature than appears to have been the case since then, when measured by their relative contribution to the English journal literature. Some statistical investigation[5] illustrates that, paradoxically though it seems, the late

Victorian and Edwardian decades were the heyday of women's contributions to the professional literature, and that, in particular for the *Economic Journal*, the number of women authors was quite substantial.

To set the stage for this discussion, another statistical index may be briefly mentioned. *The New Palgrave Dictionary of Economics* (Eatwell et al. (eds), 1987) contains twenty-nine entries devoted to women economists from a total of over 700 biographical articles. Most of these are in the small category. In addition, 37 women contributed entries to this standard reference work, but only a few of these female contributors produced more than four such entries. The last compares favourably with the seven women who contributed to the first edition of *Palgrave* as revised by Higgs (ed.) (1925).

The twenty-nine entries in the *New Palgrave* are, with the exception of Rosa Luxembourg, all drawn from Britain or the United States. British entries divided almost evenly between the nineteenth century (Maria Edgeworth, Clara Collet, Millicent Fawcett, Mary Marshall, Jane Marcet, Harriet Martineau, Harriet Taylor and Beatrice Webb) and the twentieth (Marian Bowley, Ruth Cohen, Barbara Hammond, Ursula Hicks, Helen Makower, Edith Penrose, Joan Robinson and Barbara Ward); while in the new world, twentieth-century contributors (Edith Abbott, Shirley Almon, Mary Bowman, Dorothy Brady, Eveline Burns, Selma Goldsmith, Margaret Reid, Anna Schwartz and Nancy Lou Schwartz) outnumber the nineteenth-century contributors (Sophinisba Breckenridge, Charlotte Gilman and Ida Tarbell) by three to one. While the nineteenth-century women in the United States tended to be social investigators with a feminist slant, the twentieth-century contributors were drawn very largely from statistics and econometrics, or else from applied areas of economics. Only Joan Robinson, and to a lesser extent, Helen Makower, made major contributions to theory.

The story told by contributors to the journals is rather different. On aggregate, there appears to have been a relative reduction in women contributors to the journals between the first third and last third of the twentieth century. For the five major English journals (*Quarterly Journal of Economics, Economic Journal, American Economic Review, Journal of Political Economy* and *Economica*) over the period 1886 to 1924, these constituted 5.6 per cent of the total; a count for 1966 of articles published in all journals included with the AEA Index of economic articles showed that little over three per cent appear to have been written by women.[6]

Given the subject matter of this book, a closer look at the women contributors to the economic journals of the earlier period is warranted. In line with the distribution of nationality of women included in the *New Palgrave*, contributions by British women were quantitatively more important (the 58 British authors comparing very favourably with the 61 who published in the United States, especially when taken relative to the total number of articles published). Of the 2028 authors listed over this period, 119 were women, that is, 5.9 per cent. Of these, 80 contributed only one article over the period in question; 16 wrote two articles and 23 in excess of two articles. The most prolific authors (in alphabetical order) were as follows:

1. Edith Abbott, 18 items, all in the *Journal of Political Economy* and concerned with women in industry;
2. Helen Bosanquet (née Dendy), 10 items, all in the *Economic Journal* and dealing with poverty, industrial conflict, housing and women in industry;
3. Sophinisba Breckenridge, 8 items, all in the *Journal of Political Economy* dealing with women, wages, and conditions of work.
4. Clara Collet, 9 items published in the *Quarterly Journal of Economics*, *Economic Journal* and *Journal of the Royal Statistical Society,* dealing with women's wages, cost of living and women in industry;
5. Amy Hewes, 6 items in the *Journal of the American Statistical Association*, *Journal of Political Economy* and *American Economic Review* and dealing with labour, wages and guild socialism.
6. Bessie L. Hutchins, 9 items in either the *Economic Journal* or the *Journal of the Royal Statistical Society* and largely concerning women in industry;
7. Anna Youngman, 9 items in the *Journal of Political Economy*, the *Quarterly Journal of Economics* and the *American Economic Review,* largely dealing with banking, trusts, credit theory and Federal Reserve Board policy.

These seven major female contributors to the journal literature reflect the composition of the output of their female colleagues. Items written by women tended to focus predominantly on issues related to women such as women in industry, women's wages, poverty, housing and pauper children. There were occasional articles on broader economic topics such as agriculture, prices, taxation, management, population, immigration, advertising and articles of a general historical bent. More theoretical articles, together with statistical contributions, tended to occur largely at the end of the period surveyed. They dealt with price indexes, production statistics, business cycle data and theory, trade statistics and international exchanges as the major topics covered. Interestingly, these articles were all published during the 1920s, almost all in the American journals.

The time profile of these contributions is also of interest. 44 items by women appeared in the years before 1900; the period up to 1910 produced a further 72, 46 were published in the years up to and including 1918, while the last six years of the period surveyed produced 78 articles. On an annual basis, there was a general increase over the four periods from 3.1 articles to 7.2, to 5.8, to 12, a significant rate of increase over this period, though this growth also reflects the growing number of journals, and hence articles, published per annum.

A final point of interest is that the *Economic Journal* was more receptive to female contributions, in all publishing 43 articles by women. This amounted to 6.9 per cent of the articles published in this period, reflecting the open-door policy to contributions from all sources which the *Journal* had adopted as its editorial policy on the urging of Alfred Marshall. This is totally ignored in Maloney's analysis of the contents of the early *Economic Journal* (1901–14). Moreover, these relatively large numbers of contributions are difficult to match with his title, 'Gentleman versus Players' (Maloney, 1990). In fact, apart from an unverified hypothesis about Mrs. Marshall's freedom to review books for the new journal (Maloney, 1990, p. 52), women get no real mention whatsoever in this centenary volume, either among its authors or its contents, despite the pioneering role the early *Journal* played in opening its pages to women contributors.[7]

The type of considerations raised in this section show that the subject of women writers on political economy needs far more discussion than it has so far received. Who were the women who wrote this literature? Where did they gain their education and their motivation? What caused shifts in their interests as reflected in the topics on which they contributed? Why did the female input into the economic journal literature seemingly decline during the twentieth century in relative terms? These are issues which both historians of economics and feminist theorists with an interest in female participation in science can do well to ponder, and even more fruitfully, actively study by looking at what was happening.[8]   There are almost certainly more neglected daughters of Adam Smith than Clara Collet during the Victorian, not to mention the later periods. A study of the journal literature, aided by analysis of the female composition of economics teaching staff and economics graduates, and perusal of similar data sources, can undoubtedly shed light on some of these mysteries. It can perhaps also explain why European women in particular stayed away from the dismal science during its formative period, with the single recorded exception of Rosa Luxembourg, perhaps for this reason as well very aptly described as the 'only man' in German social democracy.

AN OVERVIEW OF THE VOLUME

The five subsequent chapters present case studies devoted to topics raised in this introduction. All chapters look at the treatment of the 'women's issue' with special reference to women's work by Victorian political economists, the last two emphasizing the contributions to this topic by Victorian political economists and social investigators who were also women. It can perhaps best be left to the judgement of the readers whether these writers treated the subject in a superior way to their more famous male counterparts writing on this subject in the previous decades. If they wrote better on these subjects, there is some point in a sexual division of labour in writing political economy, as Alfred Marshall himself at some stage suggested (below, Chapter 4, pp. 96–7).

Barbara Caine in Chapter 2 addresses the 'central question as to who could, or should, speak on behalf of women, define the nature of their oppression, suggest solutions, and organise campaigns for their emancipation'. The cases she studied in this context, three men whose wives were actively involved in the feminist movement, and who in addition were prominent political economists, illustrate this issue perfectly for her. This applied to their conclusions in the broader political sphere as well as in the narrower, economic sphere of woman's right to work. Yet at the same time, her treatment of the one woman writer on political economy covered in the chapter, Millicent Garrett

Fawcett, illustrates that more is at stake than the sex of the writer: for Barbara Caine, it is 'the problematical status of women within the whole framework of political economy', that is of even greater importance. For her, it is political economy's intimate connection with the public sphere, 'the seat of masculine enterprise' which makes it impossible for women to get appropriate treatment within political economy as at presently constituted. 'It is only when one begins to interrogate and address the masculine assumptions behind these discourses that one is even able to see the omission of women and hence to think what it might mean to include them.' On this test, the feminist pioneers like Mill, Fawcett and Sidgwick, who wrote on political economy, can be seen only as failures.

Michael White addressed the views on women contained in the applied economics of Jevons, the marginalist theorist and statistician who sought to revolutionize thinking on the subject by his publication of a *Theory of Political Economy*. Women had no place in this text; they were no part of the subject's new theoretical foundations. However, as a case study in applied economics, especially in the context of labour market regulation, they constituted a subject of considerable importance. Jevons's analysis of the effects of working married women of child-bearing age is the major focus of White's chapter. In developing this theme, White shows that Jevons's treatment of the topic not only illustrates his tendency to support a 'generally punitive approach' to the 'lower classes', in which selective statistics as well as 'racist abuse' of the Irish played their part, but that in the analysis of this type of social question he contravened checks on good scientific behaviour he had methodologically set himself elsewhere. Even in a society where discriminatory views on women's nature and social role were well-nigh universal, Jevons's treatment of the issue stands out as exceptional from the manner in which he approached it.

Marshall's views on women's role in the economy are discussed by Peter Groenewegen in Chapter 4. This attributes Marshall's strong position on the need for women to stay at home, especially, but not only, if they were married women, to his beliefs about the dangers married working women posed to the efficiency of labour in general, to the family and to the future of the race. It therefore links Marshall's views on the women's issue to Marshall's longer-term hopes for economic development and progress, in which the family had a crucial and very specific nurturing role. Two sources for this perspective of the mature Marshall are identified. First is the empirical evidence he gathered on the subject through factory tours and from his work on the Labour Commission; the second is his strong belief in race progress, secured through heredity and good family environment, as founded on the evolutionary theory he was reading. However, the chapter also shows that the use he made of these foundations for his views on woman's role in society was often rather flawed, since when evidence was found to conflict with the picture he wanted, he tended to suppress or ignore it on this controversial topic.

The contribution of the Webbs to the economics of gender are discussed by Chris Nyland and Gaby Ramia in Chapter 5. After highlighting that the instrument the Webbs chose for this task was careful factual investigation rather than abstract theorizing, the main focus of the chapter is on their case for the use of the Factory Acts as a way of ensuring that adequate minimum standards are set to safeguard the interests and needs of working women. Sex-specific clauses in such legislation were argued by Beatrice Webb to have no detrimental consequences either on women's wages or on their employment, as the statistical evidence had tended to show. In their chapter, Nyland and Ramia also open up the dilemma faced on the women's issue by those who supported Fabian socialism and the rights of labour in general in combination with advocacy of the feminist demands for equality of the sexes, the full right of women to exercise their right to labour, and the right to vote. This conflict comes out in the Webbs' stand on factory legislation, and in their opposition to women's rights to undercut men's wages through unrestrained competition in the labour market. For Beatrice Webb, 'it was always imperative that women remained aware that their struggle was part of something greater', namely, the cause of socialism.

Peter Groenewegen's concluding chapter looks at the contribution of Clara Collet, female political economist and public servant, devoted to improving the opportunities for working women. After a biographical introduction, which raises the puzzle why Clara Collet's work has been so much neglected in contemporary literature, the chapter discusses two major concerns in Collet's work. The first subject deals with a relative minority in the female labour markets, working professional middle-class women. It raises issues of the need for such women to work, since not all can be assured, or do not necessarily want, marriage; the need to pay adequate wages for such women by abandoning implicit subsidy to their living costs and raising both the demand for, and the skills of, working women. Second, her statistical work on women's wages and women's work are examined. Collet designed such studies as vehicles for scrutiny of generally accepted prejudices on the subject and to expand the very limited information set on this important subject. The former objective is illustrated by her criticism of unwarranted conclusions from infant mortality statistics about the impact thereon of married working women; the latter by her careful investigation of the facts about women's work and the care with which she drew inferences from her own data. The essay concludes that knowledge and tolerance are essential parts of the armament of the social investigator and that Clara Collet's abundant endowment of both these qualities make her a person whose work deserves continuing study. This pioneer of the study of women's work and wages forms a fitting conclusion to this study of Political Economy and Feminism in Victorian England by pointing to both the value of, and the constraints implied in, this association, then and now.

NOTES

1. Thus of all the political economists being considered in this study, only Henry Sidgwick (1838–1900) falls neatly within the Victorian period. John Stuart Mill and Henry Fawcett are Victorian in the sense that they wrote their major works during the reign of Queen Victoria; Jevons, Marshall, the Webbs and Clara Collet are Victorians in the sense that they received their basic training in political economy either during the mid-, or the late-Victorian period, and that, in the case of Jevons, they wrote all of their economic work during the Victorian era.
2. McCulloch (1854) may therefore be the source for Jevons's (1882c) remark on the advantageous position in the labour market of domestic servants, as mentioned previously (p. 5), and below, Chapter 3, pp. 68–9.
3. And also by French socialism, for example, Fourier (1901, p. 77): 'Social advances and changes of periods are brought about by virtue of the progress of women towards liberty, and the decadences of the social order are brought about by virtue of the decrease of liberty of women.' Fourier benefited here from the position on progress developed by Condorcet (1795) which also emphasized the association between liberty for women and the higher stages of civilization, as Turgot had done before him to a lesser extent. More generally, this was the stance of writers from the Enlightenment on the issue with the notable exception of Rousseau.
4. Arnold Toynbee, the 'co-operator, Poor Law Guardian and Church Reformer' is another of these romantic Victorian political economists, and one particularly inspired by Ruskin. He likewise tended to ignore women as a specific entity in his writing on political

economy, especially that on the Industrial Revolution. His political economy teaching at Balliol, Oxford, inspired a generation of philanthropists concerned with the needs of the poor of East London and elsewhere, and raised the interest of men and women in charitable social work.

5. This statistical research was done by my research assistant, Sue King, as part of a longer research project which includes investigating the growth of the journal literature over the twentieth century, and which is funded by the Australian Research Council. The next paragraphs draw heavily on her findings, a contribution here gratefully acknowledged.

6. Female authorship unfortunately cannot always be easily established, and with respect to 129 names no sex could be unambiguously assigned. In the unlikely event that all the doubtful cases are females, the women authorship rate doubles to 6 per cent; more realistically, if 20 per cent are assigned as female, then the proportion of women authors rises to 3.7 per cent, and is still well below the 5.6 per cent recorded for the 1886–1924 period.

7. The index to Hey and Winch (eds) (1990) lists the following women, with number of page references placed in brackets: Margaret Bray (2), Clara Collet (2), Phyllis Deane (2), Millicent Fawcett (1), Patricia James (2), Elizabeth Johnson (3), Peggy Joseph (1), Mary Marshall (1), Joan Robinson (1) and Beatrice Webb (4).

8. After the book was in press, Bob Coats drew my attention to the work of Dr. Barbara Libby on the subject. I am grateful to Dr. Libby for kindly sending me the papers on women economists in the United States (Libby, 1984, 1987, 1989, 1990) to which reference should be made to answer at least some of the questions raised in this paragraph.

2. Feminism and Political Economy in Victorian England – or John Stuart Mill, Henry Fawcett and Henry Sidgwick Ponder the 'Woman Question'

Barbara Caine

The importance of men's support for the nineteenth-century English women's movement has long been recognized. Indeed the presence of a supportive father has been suggested as a common feature in the background of most prominent feminists, many of whom also drew strongly on the help and support of husbands (Banks, 1986, p. 28). The twentieth-century question whether it is possible to consider men as 'feminists' (Delmar, 1986, pp. 9–14) was rarely asked in the nineteenth. Women's very lack of political and legal rights made male support imperative in all Victorian feminist campaigns, whether they were for the entry of women to universities, the ending of organized prostitution, the granting of political rights or the expansion of paid work. Not only did women lack direct access to the public and political forums where these matters were discussed and decided, they had even to fight to speak in public at all.

In this chapter, the focus is on three prominent men, all of whom were well known as supporters of the nineteenth-century English women's movement: John Stuart Mill, Henry Fawcett and Henry Sidgwick. Mill was the most vocal amongst them as a critic of the subordination of women, and his *Subjection of Women* was one of the central texts in Victorian feminism. He was the first to raise the issue of women's suffrage in parliament, he supported the campaign for the higher education of women and he was a powerful opponent of the Contagious Diseases Acts. Henry Fawcett accepted Mill's feminist views as part of his broader discipleship, going on to support the suffrage cause, to assist in the attempt to have women admitted to universities and, in his capacity as Postmaster-General, to introduce into the post office clerical work for women. Like Fawcett, Henry Sidgwick was also influenced by Mill and turned his attention to the question of women's education partly as a result of Mill's *Subjection of Women* and partly in response to the general concern about women's education evident amongst progressive liberal clergymen such as F.D. Maurice (Sidgwick and Sidgwick, 1906, p. 204). Sidgwick's involvement with the women's movement was narrower in scope than that of Mill or Fawcett, coming as it did through his enormous and passionate interest in educational reform in general and in reform of Cambridge in particular. Sidgwick was one of the founders of, and perhaps the moving spirit behind, Newnham College, one of the first Women's Colleges to be established at Cambridge. He was also very much involved in the whole debate about how a university education for women should be constituted.

For all of these men, involvement in the feminist cause had a personal as well as a public dimension. Each of them married women who were deeply engaged with feminist issues or with the women's movement and, in each case, marriage seems to have involved a close companionate relationship in which deep affection was combined with mutual respect. Although later writers have disputed it, Mill was only too keen to acknowledge his intellectual debt to his wife, although not specifically in terms of his ideas about women (Mill, 1975, pp. 143–51). Moreover his description of an ideal marriage 'in the case of two persons of cultivated faculties, identical in opinions and purposes, between whom there exists that best kind of equality, similarly of powers and capacities with reciprocal superiority in them – so that each can enjoy the luxury of looking up to the other, and can have alternately the pleasure of leading and being led in the path of development' was assumed to be a depiction of his own marriage. It became the marital ideal for many Victorian feminists (Mill, 1975, p. 541). In a sense, one could see the Fawcetts as exemplifying this ideal. Henry Fawcett married Millicent Garrett, one of the leaders of the campaign for women's suffrage. Fawcett seems to have been determined to marry a feminist, having already proposed to two others (including his wife's sister) before being accepted by Millicent Garrett (Rubinstein, 1988, p.

165). At the time, she was only twenty while he was already both an MP and Professor of Political Economy at Cambridge. But in a way unusual in Victorian marriages, and facilitated obviously by his blindness, he made his knowledge available to his wife and assisted her in becoming a competent political economist. Millicent Garrett Fawcett in turn combined the duties of being his wife, companion, political assistant and even sometimes amanuensis with the pursuit of her own intellectual interests and with a very active engagement in the suffrage movement and strong support for several other campaigns (Rubinstein, 1988, p. 170).

Sidgwick's marital involvement with feminism, like his overall involvement with the women's movement, was of a rather different kind. Although his wife, Eleanor Balfour, supported women's suffrage, she was not engaged in feminist debates in quite the same way as either Harriet Taylor or Millicent Garrett (Sidgwick, 1913). Eleanor Balfour was also one of the early students at Newnham College, becoming very active on the College Council after she left and finally being appointed its principal in 1880. Thus while Sidgwick was not as intimately involved in the day-to-day concerns of the women's movement as Mill and Fawcett, he, far more than they, had to come to terms with some of the autonomy and the professional status being demanded by the women's movement – and achieved by some women. For some years, Henry Sidgwick had the quite extraordinary experience for a middle-class Victorian gentleman of having to reside at his wife's place of work. It would appear that he accepted this situation – and carried out the role of principal's husband – with considerable grace and charm (Sidgwick, 1938, pp. 118–19).

The importance of all three men to the Victorian women's movement was widely recognized during their own lifetimes. As one would expect, Mill has received the most recognition, his centrality within the women's movement being widely proclaimed by a number of Victorian feminists. Millicent Garrett Fawcett, in her capacity as a suffrage leader, for example, frequently paid Mill fulsome tribute:

> There can be no dispute that Mr. Mill's influence marks an epoch in the women's movement. He was a master and formed a school of thought. Just as in art, a master forms a school and influences his successors for generations, so the present leaders and champions of the women's movement have been influenced and to a great extent formed by Mr. Mill (Fawcett, 1888, p. 4).

But while Millicent Fawcett, like many twentieth-century feminist scholars, examined and applied some of Mill's specific ideas about women, she never explored in any detail the extent to which his concern about women and his ideas about sexual difference are expressed or reflected in his general social, economic or political writings. This chapter poses the question with regard to Mill, and also to Fawcett and Sidgwick. Raising this question allows one to shift the focus away from the specific utterances of these men about women and to ask how central their concern with women's oppression was for them and how closely connected it was with their other social and political views. It serves also to raise a more general question about nineteenth-century political and economic discourses and about the extent to which their structures and assumptions permit the recognition of sexual difference and of the need to consider women separately from men.

How then does one assess the ideas of Mill, Fawcett and Sidgwick on 'the woman question' and to what extent is their concern about and involvement with the cause of the advancement of women reflected in their general writings? In view of what Stefan Collini (Collini et al., 1983, p. 311) refers to as 'its privileged place for those exploring things political in the nineteenth century', this chapter largely concentrates on their works on political economy, but occasionally refers to their other social and political writings as well.

The long-standing English tradition in which political economy was considered to be not merely an abstract science, but rather 'a fragment of a greater whole; a branch of Social Philosophy', meant that many of its nineteenth-century treatises embraced discussions of history, society and politics alongside their exposition of the laws of the production of wealth (Collini et al., 1983, p. 311; cf. Mill, 1971, pp. 141–8). Mill in particular emphasized the broad scope of his inquiry by taking as the title of his book *Principles of Political Economy with some of their Applications to Social Philosophy*, including within it detailed discussions on government which were not part of his own definition of political economy at all (Collini et al., 1983, p. 311). While Fawcett did not claim so wide a scope, he made it clear that he was delimiting the field himself because otherwise 'the range of the subject would be practically unlimited' (Fawcett, 1863, p. 511). Sidgwick, too, adopted much of Mill's approach. He was concerned to establish in precisely what ways political economy should be regarded as an art and in what ways as a science, but in his lengthy discussion of the art of political economy, he spanned a huge range of social and moral questions. In the eyes of some recent scholars, he was the only other nineteenth-century English figure who could compare with Mill in his command of the whole field of moral sciences (Collini et al., 1983, p. 280).

Turning to the texts themselves, there are several points worth noting. Firstly there are some interesting differences in position on how to view the situation of women between Mill and Fawcett, on the one hand, and Sidgwick on the other. In part these differences reflect a wider shift in liberal thinking about government intervention, individual rights and social responsibilities across the second half of the nineteenth century. They also point to the differing approaches to and beliefs about women and the appropriate way to approach 'the woman question' amongst the three men – and to the problematic status of women within the whole discourse of political economy.

The contrasting views about women amongst these three men indicate the extent to which the assumptions about liberal individualism which were so central for Mill and Fawcett had been called into question by the 1870s. Thus both Mill and Fawcett approach the question of women's work through a discussion of *laissez-faire*, insisting on their right to work and to have the same freedom from legislative intervention as they demanded for men. Both insisted that women were not and should not be treated as children, but should be recognized as being 'as capable as men of appreciating and managing their own concerns' (Mill, 1848, p. 126). Factory legislation which limited women's hours of work or excluded them from particular occupations was particularly repugnant to them. Mill followed the line of argument evident in the writings of a number of Victorian feminists by his insistence that the desire to limit women's paid employment was directly connected with their subordination to men – and the requirement that they also provide unpaid labour in the home.

> If women had as absolute control as men have over their own persons and their own patrimony or acquisitions, there would be no plea for limiting their hours of labouring for themselves, in order that they might have time to labour for the husband, in what is called by the advocates of restrictions, *his* home. ... For improving the condition of women, it should on the contrary, be an object to give them the readiest access to independent industrial employment, instead of closing either entirely or partially, that which is already open to them (Mill, 1848, p. 126).

The imposition of restrictions on women and on the areas in which they could find employment served for Mill, as it did for Fawcett, to ensure that the occupations open to women were overstocked – and poorly paid. Mill saw this as the main reason why there was so great a difference between men's and women's wages while in Fawcett's view, it was one of the chief reasons why women swelled the ranks of paupers, dependent for their survival on relief. For both Mill and Fawcett, concern over matters of individual liberty and women's rights as citizens were clearly central here.

In his *Principles of Political Economy*, as in his *Subjection of Women*, Mill argued that granting women the right to work and indeed the same rights of citizenship as men would not only improve the situation of women but would contribute to the overall development and improvement of society. In the *Principles of Political Economy* he argued this case primarily in regard to the question of population and poverty. If women were given all the rights of citizens, they would be in a position to voice their own concerns about the whole question of reproduction and, or at least so Mill suggests, would be firmly in favour of limiting family size (Mill, 1848, p. 321; cf. Bladen, 1974, pp. 242–3).

Writing some thirty years after Mill, Sidgwick had far less concern with the question of women's rights as individuals and far more concern about the needs of the society and the role of government in dealing with its overall well-being. He made clear his own recognition that while English exponents of political economy had generally advocated *laissez-faire* principles in regard both to production and distribution, such advocacy was not always appropriate nor was it in fact an integral part of political economy. On the contrary, he insisted,

> the investigation of the laws that determine actual prices, wages and profits, so far as these depend on the free competition of individuals, is essentially distinct from the inquiry how far it is desirable that the action of free competition should be restrained or modified – whether by the steadying hand of custom, the remedial intervention of philanthropy, the legislative or administrative control of government, or the voluntary combinations of masters and workmen (Sidgwick, 1887, p. 23).

He was himself inclined to accept a much larger sphere for the legislative or administrative control of government than either Mill or Fawcett and to accept the need for individual rights to be sacrificed in order to meet a public need. Like Mill, he listed the protection of persons unfit through age or mental disorder to take care of their own interest as one of the necessary functions of government. But he derived arguments from this premiss which Mill would never have accepted. The most important groups requiring protection were children – and Sidgwick argued that the protection of children might be either direct through protective legislation or indirect, through 'regulation of the sexes, so far at least as to make generally adequate provision for the care and nurture of children' (Sidgwick, 1887, p. 426). When spelt out, this meant the possibility of indirect action to ensure the care of children by placing 'restrictions on the labour of married women (or women who have borne children) so far as these appear necessary in order to secure the proper performance of their maternal functions (Sidgwick, 1887, pp. 431–2). Hence for Sidgwick the question was not, as it was for Mill and Fawcett, whether women were denied autonomy and treated like children in being made subject to factory legislation. Rather, he took up the question addressed by contemporary political economists like Jevons and Marshall on how best to meet the needs of children for proper care and education (Marshall, 1890, pp. 592–3, 730–31; Jevons, 1882a, pp. 37–53).[1]

Sidgwick's approach to the question of women's labour reflects both his greater sense of the scope of government intervention in the lives of individuals than Mill was prepared to countenance and his much more ambivalent approach to the overall question of the status of women. In his *Elements of Politics*, he expanded on the earlier discussion in ways which demonstrate very clearly his own hesitancy about challenging existing beliefs or assumptions about the nature of women and about their entitlement to political rights. The framework which Sidgwick adopted in his attempt to 'introduce greater clarity into the language and ideas held about politics' was one with a notably conservative tendency: he took as his starting ground broadly accepted assumptions and propositions concerning human motives and tendencies and subjected them to detailed – although not critical – analysis.

Working within this broad framework, Sidgwick took as one fundamental assumption Mill's statement that 'each person is the only safe guardian of his own rights and interests', but insisted on applying this only to adult males. Sidgwick was, as he said, well aware that Mill himself would have applied it to adult females as well, but he was not himself prepared to do so in this text because 'it is not clear that the common sense of mankind considers women generally to be the safest guardians of their own pecuniary interest' (Sidgwick, 1891, p. 9). Mill was of course well aware that his beliefs about women were different from those of the majority – but he regarded the common sense of mankind as wrong, and as inimical both to the interests of women – and to the well-being of mankind as a whole. Although derived in some measure from Bentham, Sidgwick's reworking of utilitarianism avoided the criticism of existing institutions which was so central to Bentham just as he avoided any kind of attack on commonly accepted beliefs which was so much part of Mill's approach. His own method served very clearly to reflect his own much more hesitant and conservative approach (Collini et al., 1983, pp. 290–95).

The conservatism of his approach is also evident in his discussion of women's suffrage. While Mill argued that the complete legal and political equality of men and women was the only sure way to improve the situation of women both within the immediate confines of the family and within society as a whole, Sidgwick looked rather for the minimum possible change demanded by principles of justice and equity. Hence while he could see 'no adequate reason for refusing the franchise to any sane self-supporting adult otherwise eligible, on the score of her sex alone', he was not at all persuaded that married women either needed, or should be given, the franchise. Sidgwick was not so much echoing the earlier argument of James Mill that married women were virtually represented by their husband as arguing that their enfranchisement was likely to be ineffective.

> If a husband is not abnormally wanting in domestic affection and the sense of domestic duty, the interests of his wife are tolerably safe in his hands; while if he is so wanting he is likely to have little scruple in exercising on her a kind of intimidation which law is powerless to prevent; so that she will derive little benefit from enfranchisement, except through deception that is likely to be demoralising. Even apart from intimidation, a wife's political judgement is likely to be biased by the desire of domestic harmony, prompting her to avoid political disagreement with her husband. Moreover, according to the customary division of labour between husbands and wives, the experience of the latter will, generally speaking, be of less value as a preparation for the wise exercise of the franchise (Sidgwick, 1891, p. 370).

Important and interesting as these differences are, what remains most noticeable when one searches the work of Mill, Fawcett and Sidgwick is the very small space that questions about sexual difference or about the situation of women occupy in their published work. The omission is most striking in regard to the question of women's work. From none of their writings does one gain any suggestion of the numbers of women actually engaged in paid work in agriculture, in industry, in home-based work or in domestic service. On the contrary, the general picture presented is one in which women are not engaged in paid labour, but are primarily dependents.

On the rare occasions when women's paid labour was mentioned, it was presented always as something which was unusual – and as a problem. Mill is particularly interesting here, because in his few brief discussions on women and work in his *Political Economy*, he adopts two somewhat contradictory positions. On the one hand, Mill was extremely critical of any form of legislation designed to limit hours or to exclude women from paid work. He saw this as an indication that women were not regarded as independent adults, able to safeguard their own interests. He also felt that paid work for women would help solve the population problem, arguing that it could not be solved until women were able to work and not forced to devote their lives, and hence to find their only source of income, from being wives and mothers. But at the same time, Mill was not in favour of married women engaging in paid work, believing that the care of a home and a family would more than fill their time. Fawcett devoted even less space to women than did Mill, omitting any mention of them in the early editions of his *Manual of Political Economy*, and discussing them only in relation to 'the Poor Law and its Influence on Pauperism' in later editions. Within this context, he followed Mill in attacking the ways in which industrial legislation closed occupations to women and tended to lower wages, seeing all of this as an 'encouragement to pauperism'. Sidgwick's political economy, too, gave women very limited attention, discussing them mainly in regard to the question of how best to meet the needs of children.

How does one explain the absence of detailed discussions of women from these texts, given the lengthy and sustained involvement of all three men with campaigns for the emancipation of women? One could see their lack of discussion as something which illustrates both how limited their concern with the problems of women actually was – and how very problematic male involvement was for feminism. And this is certainly a point that needs to be addressed. Within the nineteenth century, while all three of these men were acknowledged by women active in feminist causes, their participation in the women's movement was subject to criticism. Even Mill did not escape this. Although some regarded him as an heroic champion of feminism, he was not universally seen in this light. Josephine Butler was one prominent Victorian feminist who was more than a little critical, arguing that his views on women – especially those expressed in *The Subjection* – were not particularly advanced. 'On the contrary they are but the somewhat tardy expression of a conviction which has been gaining strength in society for the last twenty years'.[2] Emily Davies agreed, making it quite clear that, in her view, Mill's importance for the women's movement derived from the fact that he was the most eminent man publicly to identify himself with the cause, rather than from the strength or novelty of his ideas. And some recent research suggests that Mill's participation created real problems for the women's movement. Working with his step-daughter, Helen Taylor, he attempted to impose his own views about the nature and the conduct of the suffrage movement on the women who had begun this agitation, allowing almost no scope for dissension.

The nature of Sidgwick's involvement with women's emancipation also warrants critical discussion. As his wife recognized, his taking up of the question of women's education in the late 1860s and early 1870s had much to do with his own immediate needs and concerns. Having just relinquished his Cambridge fellowship, in part as a protest against the intellectual and religious constraints imposed by the University, he felt the need to take up some practically useful project contributing to university reform. His promotion of a scheme to establish a college for women was the result not so much of an overall commitment to the emancipation of women as a form of active social work whereby he could demonstrate his ideas on educational reform (Sidgwick and Sidgwick, 1906, p. 205; Sidgwick, 1938, p. 58). His participation within the movement for the higher education of women was always controversial. His refusal to accept that women should undertake the same education as men once at university was almost violently opposed by some women active in the campaign for access to higher education. Hence while Sidgwick took a major role in setting up Newnham College, it offered women a special education without access to Cambridge degrees. Sidgwick regarded the whole movement for women's education in the 1870s and 1880s as being a tentative and experimental phase from which 'we may do the cause as much good by failing in an intelligent and cheerful manner as by succeeding'. It is hardly surprising that Emily Davies, the most important of the English feminists fighting for higher education, and a woman who devoted most of her life to this cause, regarded Sidgwick as a 'viper gnawing at her vitals' (Caine, 1992, pp. 89–92; McWilliams-Tullberg, 1975, pp. 89–96).

What was ultimately at issue here was the central question as to who could, or should, speak on behalf of women, define the nature of their oppression, suggest solutions, and organize campaigns for their emancipation. As this evaluation of the work of Mill, Fawcett and Sidgwick suggests, these influential men who supported the women's movement, assumed absolutely that by virtue of their standing, their training, their intellects – and even their sex – they understood the overall situation of women and the best ways of improving it better than women did themselves. Where they disagreed with their female partners in relation to the woman question, they showed no inclination to change their views. Nor were they able to recognize the importance of women's participation in their own emancipation, or their desire to define their world themselves (Caine, 1978, pp. 52–67).

Mill offers a particularly interesting illustration of this. Although later commentators have argued that Mill's discussion of women owed a great deal to his wife, and he himself emphasized his debt to her in regard to much of his general work, he did not accept that he owed any of his insight into the situation of women to her (cf. Pujol, 1992, pp. 20–35). On the contrary, he argued, it was his pre-existing concern about women's oppression which drew her to him. But their views on some questions were quite different, most notably their views about women's work. While Mill believed that women should not be legally excluded from undertaking paid employment, he shared the view that women should not generally undertake such employment with the majority of other Victorian economists. Harriet Taylor totally disagreed. Mill's *Principles of Political Economy* echoes the debate evident in a set of early essays they wrote for each other in which Harriet Taylor argued that women's economic dependence was a fundamental cause of their subordination (Mill and Taylor, 1970, pp. 22–3, 67–87). Mill simply could not accept this, fearing as he did the effects on wages if women entered into the labour market in competition with men. He could not accept Taylor's view that, even if the entry of women into the labour market served to depress wages so that the wages of a man and a woman taken together should only equal what the man alone had been able to earn, 'the advantage to the woman of not depending on a master for subsistence may be more than equivalent'. Nor could he accept it as desirable 'as a *permanent* element in the condition of the labouring class, that the mother of the family (the case of single women is totally different) should be under the necessity of working for subsistence, at least elsewhere than in their place of abode' (Mill, 1871, p. 490).

Henry Fawcett's refusal to accept his wife's initial enthusiasm for the campaign to oppose the Contagious Diseases Acts is an analogous case. On this subject, Fawcett tended to agree with Mill's approach, and to support Mill both in his insistence on the need to give women's suffrage first place amongst feminist campaigns and to prevent any connection between this and the campaign against the Contagious Diseases Acts. Fawcett added his voice to Mill's successful prevention of Millicent Fawcett becoming involved in the Contagious Diseases agitation. Ironically, within a very few months of his death, Millicent Fawcett threw herself with gusto and ferocity into those very campaigns centring on prostitution and on the sexual exploitation of women of which her husband had so strongly disapproved (Strachey, 1931, p. 107; Caine, 1992, pp. 225–7).

But while one can see the participation of these men within feminism as problematical, this does not of itself explain why they devoted so little space to women in their general writing. Moreover, if one looks at the writings of some of the women interested in political economy, one can see a pattern very similar to that evident in the work of these men. Millicent Garrett Fawcett offers an interesting illustration. She was regarded by some as the leading woman economist of her day and she was even informally proposed for election to the Political Economy Club by Sir Charles Dilke. Mill did not support the suggestion – and ultimately it was not acted upon (Rubinstein, 1988, p. 77).

Millicent Fawcett wrote a series of *Tales in Political Economy* and a book on *Political Economy for Beginners* as well as assisting her husband in preparing the third edition of his *Manual of Political Economy*. She drew frequently on the precepts of liberal economics in her many speeches and papers dealing with the emancipation of women, arguing for example, that the demand to remove the barriers which closed paid employment was simply another aspect of the free trade argument. But when she wrote on political economy, women are largely absent from her texts. Her own *Political Economy for Beginners* fails to mention women's employment – although she was clearly aware of its importance and subsequently wrote a series of essays on social and political subjects which discussed it extensively. Under her influence, Henry Fawcett likewise took up the question of women's employment, particularly in the battle against special industrial legislation for women.

The case of Millicent Fawcett, like those of Mill, Henry Fawcett and Sidgwick, clearly illustrates that the application of economic ideas to the situation of women was seen in a very partial way. All these Victorian political economists recognized the relevance to the situation of women of specific precepts which were central to their economic and political or social thought. However, they failed to acknowledge that this involved the need to incorporate, or the possibility of incorporating, sexual difference into their overall framework rather than single or isolated applications of particular ideas.

This relative lack of reference to, and discussion of, women seems, in my view, to be closely connected with the problematical status of women within the whole framework of political economy. Although originally evolved from a broader field of economics which included domestic economy and household management, political economy's later development moved far from these original foundations. These origins had been noted by Sidgwick. 'It was because a monarch or statesman was conceived to have the function of arranging the industry of the country somewhat as the father of a family arranges the industry of his household, that the Art which offered him guidance in the performance of this function was called Political Economy' (Sidgwick, 1887, p. 14). By then, however, political economy addressed itself to the public sphere while domestic economy remained in the private. In its expansion, the contrast was evident from the very form of the discourse: political economy took the form of a science dealing with the operation of laws, whereas domestic economy remained the art of managing household resources.

The connection between political economy and the public sphere is absolutely fundamental. Indeed, in the view of Jurgen Habermas (1984, p. 20), the transformation of the economics handed down from antiquity into political economy was in itself a major reflection both of the development of the market and of the demarcation of a bourgeois public sphere. In the writings of political economists, the public sphere was a fundamentally gendered one, the seat of masculine enterprise and activity which contrasted with the private world of family and home – the proper location of women and children (cf. Rendall, 1988, pp. 44–73; Pujol, 1992, p. 87). Habermas's own position fits rather neatly into the framework adopted by the political economists; while recognizing that there was always a connection between the intimate sphere of the family and the market, he nonetheless accepted the basic liberal assumption that the public sphere was unproblematically masculine, involving the possibility that the *homme* was also the *citoyen*, simultaneously a property owner and one concerned to protect the stability of the property order (cf. Pujol, 1992, p. 87).

This sense of a gendered public sphere and of a world of work composed of men was reinforced by the terms of political economy. Its preoccupation with the accumulation of wealth and with production, distribution and exchange went along with an emphasis on industry and on manufactures. This meant that it focused attention on new locations and patterns of work: on factories and workshops which were predominantly male places of work rather than on the continuation of domestic and small-scale production in which women were engaged (for example, Alexander, 1983). As a result, not only is the actual work of women ignored, but so too are the arguments found in much recent work on the early stages of industrialization concerning the importance of women's paid work in providing the capital, the techniques and the sources of labour for industrialization (Berg, 1988; Roberts, 1988).

The very terminology used within political economy helped both to down-grade women's work and to render it invisible. The largest category of women's paid work in the nineteenth century was domestic service – classified within political economy as 'unproductive labour'. Mill went to great pains to stress that 'unproductive' did not necessarily mean 'useless', as the terms 'productive' and 'unproductive' referred not to the production of utilities, but to the production of wealth. But it is interesting to see that his list of those whose labour did produce utilities – and hence was necessary, if not technically speaking 'productive' – was largely composed of men. He regarded as especially necessary and useful, that labour which was 'employed in conferring on human beings qualities which render them serviceable to themselves and others' and this included the labour of educationists, moralists, physicians and all involved in the medical profession. He includes the wages of domestic servants as 'partly productive and partly unproductive', but all discussions and elaborations of this category are directed towards male professions. There is no discussion of women's unpaid labour and little of that for which they were paid.

The omission of women is evident in every aspect of political economy: in its language, its assumptions and its subject matter. If one shifts the focus away from the discussion of women as objects of discussion and turns to an analysis of how gender functions in the whole framing of the political economy, it becomes immediately clear that one is dealing with a discourse in which not only the writer, and the reader, but also the employer and the labourer are implicitly and even sometimes explicitly male. The tradition of authorship into which each writer carefully placed himself, stating his position in regard to Smith, Malthus, Ricardo and so on, served both to expand the tradition and to enhance the status of individual authors. The eminence of the writers of political economy was closely connected with its immediate target: statesmen and men of affairs. This male public world of intellect and politics meshed neatly with its subject matter: its scientific investigation of economic laws, its concern with the behaviour and activities of entrepreneurs and labourers. There is no question that these terms apply specifically to men. Thus, in Sidgwick's view, for example, any approach to the question of wages needed to take into account the amount required to support not only the labourer, but his family including his wife, his children, and even his mother (Sidgwick, 1887, pp. 310–12).

The nature of both public and private spheres has been the subject of much interest amongst recent historians, many of whom have stressed the extent to which an absolute division between public and private in the late eighteenth and nineteenth centuries operated at an ideological level rather than reflecting actual economic and social developments. The male public world of paid work was heavily dependent on the paid and unpaid work of women undertaken both in the workplace and in the home – to say nothing of the dependence of industry and commerce on the inheritances and other financial support of women (Davidoff and Hall, 1989). Of course all political economists from Adam Smith onwards knew only too well that the public world and the world of paid work were not entirely masculine: and conversely that the private sphere did not and could not encompass the lives of all women. Women often did have to contribute to the income of the family – or lacked families entirely and had to support themselves. But both of these cases were dealt with as exceptions and as problems. The fact that the public world was seen in such masculine terms made women's entry into, or participation within, it necessarily both problematical and exceptional.

Mill himself was acutely sensitive to this emphasis within political economy on male activities and male work practices and to its complete exclusion of women and of women's experience. In a passage which seems to echo the anger of Harriet Taylor, he argued that some of the conclusions of political economy offered illustrations of 'how little the ideas and experiences of women have yet counted for, in forming the opinions of mankind'. The experiences of women served, for example, to question the views of Adam Smith concerning the advantages arising from the division of labour. Alongside Smith's insistence on the advantages of specialization, Mill argued that it was necessary to place the advantages and benefits that arise from versatility and change. Rather than resulting in dilatoriness and the wasting of time, Mill argued that the ability to move from one occupation to another might give workers a freshness of spirit that would improve their efficiency. The general activities of women served to illustrate his point.

> Women are usually (at least in their present social circumstances) of far greater versatility than men, ... There are few women who would not reject the idea that work is made vigorous by being protracted, and is inefficient for some time after changing to a new thing. ... Women are in the constant practice of passing quickly from one manual, and still more from one mental operation to another, which therefore rarely costs them either effort or loss of time, while a man's occupation generally consists in working steadily for a long time at one thing or one very limited class of things (Mill, 1848, pp. 133–4).

But despite this, 'women are not found less efficient than men for the uniformity of factory work, or they would not generally be employed for it, and a man who has cultivated the habit of turning his hand to many things, far from being the slothful and lazy person described by Adam Smith, is usually remarkably lively and active' (Mill, 1848, pp. 153–4).

Having castigated mankind in general for excluding the insights and experiences of women, Mill himself failed to abide with this precept and addressed such matters in only the most cursory way. Although he noted the omission of women from the general discussion of the experiences of mankind, he did not devote any time to exploring the consequences of this omission or its ramifications. Indeed, in many situations, Mill refrained from pursuing even from his own sense of how discrimination against women might work. In his discussion of wages, for example, Mill posed the question why the wages of women were generally so much lower than those of men. In his answer, he considered, but dismissed the possibility that custom and 'the present constitution of society' offered the explanation. Hence he admitted that,

When an employment (as is the case with many trades) is divided into several parts, of some of which men alone are considered capable, while women and children are employed in others, it is natural that those who cannot be dispensed with, would be able to make better terms for themselves than those who can (Mill, 1848, p. 471).

Believing, however, that women in factories earned as much as men, Mill argued that this proposition failed to explain the actual situation of women in employment. To the contrary, the principal reason for their low wages in his view related to the peculiar employment of women:

The remuneration of these is always I believe, greatly below that of employment of equal skill and equal disagreeableness carried on by men. The explanation of this must be that they are overstocked: that although so much smaller a number of women than of men support themselves by wages, the occupations which law and custom make accessible to them are comparatively so few, that the field of their employment is still more overcrowded (Mill, 1848, p. 472).

Because the wages of women need only to be sufficient to support one individual, whereas those of men need to support children and sometimes a wife, Mill went on to argue that the wages of women could be depressed more than those of men.

What is particularly interesting here is the way in which Mill, having briefly considered the need to consider the specific circumstances of women and the overall ways in which 'the present constitution of society' affects their options and their wages, falls back on one of the broader general propositions of political economy to explain why they are so badly paid. Hence the issues that have come to the fore recently in discussions of women's wages, particularly the ways in which terms like 'skilled' are used in discriminatory ways and the ways in which the level of female participation in any field determines its level of remuneration, are not discussed. Mill clearly recognizes that they are issues: his insistence that, in his view, women are paid less than men, even when they are engaged in occupations involving 'equal skill and equal disagreeableness' makes this clear and differentiates him from a number of nineteenth-century commentators, notably Sidney and Beatrice Webb for example, who argued that women's wages reflected their overall lack of skill, training and commitment.[3] But Mill failed to pursue the argument by asking whether others would accept his sense that women's skills are unrecognized and hence removes this as a question that needs analysis.

It is ironic that, in the very moment of indicating an underlying recognition of some of the specific issues involved in the question of women's wages, Mill should himself reinforce the sense that paid work for women was atypical and that woman's appropriate place was as the wife of a wage earner. His discussion of productive and unproductive labour, of the ways in which market forces would tend to keep women out of paid work, and of the antagonism between concern for family and concern for the public good served to enhance the merits and virtues of the public sphere at the same time as they underlined the exclusion of women from it.

Mill's acceptance of this sexual division of labour and of the separation between the public and the private spheres has been criticized frequently, showing as it does his own acceptance and even endorsement of the patriarchal framework evident in liberal political thought. But in terms of his economic thought, even more than his political thought, this emphasis on the public sphere and the relegation of women to the private sphere and to the family ensures their invisibility. The reason for this lies partly in the way in which the private sphere itself was defined and understood. For although the private sphere is often taken to be gendered, as a female sphere and the location of femininity, it is not really in any way symmetrical with the masculine public sphere. Indeed, as both Carole Pateman (1989, pp. 125–60) and in a very different way Habermas (1984) have shown, it was not ever actually constituted in and of itself, but rather covered those people and those aspects of male life that are omitted from the public world. The private is the world of family, home, reproduction. It is therefore not specifically a female sphere, although women are central to it. Men, after all, not only lived in, but were economically and legally the dominant ones within the home and family. Political economy added to the definition of the public world in its political aspect the values of being both productive and progressive. Hence women's relegation to the private sphere simultaneously removes them from the focus of analysis and removes any specificity from them. It defines them primarily as being dependent and hence like children.

That the private sphere is not in any specific or meaningful way a female one is evident in all the discussions of women in Mill, Fawcett and Sidgwick. Indeed, their discussions of women, for all their differences, also contain this marked similarity. For all of them, the status of women and the question as to how they should be thought about or discussed is problematical – and differs according to the particular characteristics of women and their specific location. Every discussion about women centred on the question of dependence and independence and hence of their status: were they to be seen and treated as being like men, as Mill and Fawcett urged – and as Sidgwick too urged in regard to single women. But how then to think about the majority of women who married and devoted a large amount of their lives to the care of families, a form of unproductive if useful labour, even for those like Mill, who were concerned about the quality of human capital? Were these women like children, or at least to be defined primarily in terms of their obligation to care for children – as Sidgwick urged.

In one sense, one could argue that their responses to this question are very different with Mill and Fawcett emphasizing the need to see women as autonomous adults who are similar to men and who should therefore be treated in the same way as men in terms of industrial legislation while Sidgwick argued rather in terms of difference and the primacy of maternity. But on closer inspection, one can see that Sidgwick accepted Mill's approach – when it came to single women. He saw single women as entitled to the franchise and as entitled both to the franchise and to be free of legislative restrictions in regard to employment. And Mill too believed that the situation and circumstances of single women were quite different from those of married ones. While he did not accept legislative restrictions on the employment of either group, he concurred absolutely with Sidgwick in regarding it as undesirable that married women should engage in paid work. Hence for both of them, when talking about women one is dealing not with one category but at least with two, married and single. The categories depend on whether specific women are single and hence independent, and like men, or whether they are married, and hence (like children) dependent on men.

For Mill as for Sidgwick, the belief that the majority of women would and should immerse themselves in family life had serious political as well as economic consequences. As we have seen, Sidgwick believed that 'the customary division of labour between husbands and wives' in which women took over the care of the home and family was not much value as a preparation for the franchise. Indeed, it was for him an argument for restricting the franchise to single women. Ironically, although Mill was a much stronger advocate of the enfranchisement of women than Sidgwick, and felt that being enfranchised would be very beneficial to women, even in their domestic and marital relations, he did agree with him that domestic and familial life was not in itself of any value in terms of training for public activity. Unlike many women active in Victorian feminist debates who argued that women's nurturant capacities, their care of homes, of children, the sick and the aged gave them particular insights and views which deserved representation, Mill shared with both Fawcett and Sidgwick a belief that independence was a necessary condition for representation and that education and activity within the public sphere was the only proper basis for claiming rights within that sphere (Caine, 1992, pp. 35–40).

Hence the only women who could participate fully in the public sphere were those who had forgone or had outgrown familial responsibilities. What seems never to have been explored or developed by the political economists under consideration was the question of how to think about women – as adults who contributed both to the domestic and to the wider economy, but in ways different from men. The structures which political economy set up revolved around the notion of independent male workers – and of dependents: their wives and children.   Until or unless political economy could incorporate an analysis of sexual difference and of the implications of the sexual division of labour it could not seriously address the situation of women. Within its framework, women were not really a separate category at all: they were defined entirely in relation to men;   as wives, as mothers – or as spinsters. Each had different needs and hence was thought about in different ways. It is only when one begins to interrogate and address the masculine assumptions behind these discourses that one is even able to see the omission of women and hence to think what it might mean to include them.

NOTES

1 Discussed in Chapters 3 and 4 below.
2. Josephine Butler to the Rt. Hon. H.A. Bruce, 8 June 1869, N.U.W.S.S. Papers, M50/2/36, Manchester Library.
3. The Webbs' views on this subject are discussed below, pp. 112–13, 137–40.

3. Following Strange Gods: Women in Jevons's Political Economy *

Michael V. White

> We in England – the poor people – have been lectured by great men from John O'Groat's to Lands End upon what we ought, and ought not to do ... but it was reserved for Mr. Jevons to suggest a law that married women, when child-bearing, should not be allowed to work if they liked. Verily my countrymen have begun to follow strange gods (W. Darbyshire, January 1882).[1]

> [L]egislation with regard to labour has almost always been class-legislation. It is the effort of some dominant body to keep down a lower class, which has begun to show inconvenient aspirations (W. Stanley Jevons, 1882).[2]

INTRODUCTION

In early 1866 W. Stanley Jevons became something of a public name when his book, *The Coal Question*, was used in Parliament by W.E. Gladstone and J.S. Mill to support the government's budgetary policy. Following the ensuing 'coal scare' the government appointed a Royal Commission to inquire into the British coal industry and the extent of coal supplies. In the last year of his life Jevons attempted to repeat that success[3] with his article 'Married Women in Factories', which was published in the *Contemporary Review* (Jevons, 1882a; reprinted in Jevons, 1883, pp. 156–79). The paper argued that 'child-bearing women' with children under three years of age should effectively be prohibited from obtaining paid employment outside the home because such employment led to 'excessive' child mortality rates. While Jevons's argument was part of the debates which laid the groundwork for subsequent discussion of the 'family wage' (cf. Rose, 1991), he indicated that his 'real purpose' in writing the article was to have a 'comprehensive [public] inquiry', such as a Royal Commission, constituted to inquire into the causes of child mortality in the 'manufacturing districts' (Black, 1973–81, V, pp. 165, 167; Jevons, 1883, pp. 175–6).

Jevons had written the article while preparing his *The State in Relation to Labour* (*SIRTL*) for publication. That book, which appeared later in 1882, summarized the argument (Jevons, 1882c, pp. 70–75), referring the reader to the *Contemporary Review* for a more detailed explanation. Although a good deal of attention has been paid to *SIRTL* so as to analyse Jevons's approach to policy, his discussion of the paid employment of married women and associated issues has either been ignored or given cursory attention (Peart, 1990b, p. 291; Bowman, 1989, pp. 1126, 1127). Surprisingly, this 'neglect' of Jevons is evident in the recent stimulating study by Michèle Pujol, *Feminism and Anti-Feminism in Early Economic Thought*. Pujol 'trace[s] back to the origins of the neoclassical school of thought the particular biases in methodology and discourse which characterize the school's treatment of women and their place in a capitalist economy' (Pujol, 1992, p. 1). Yet Jevons, who produced the first English statement of marginalism (or 'neoclassicism') in *The Theory of Political Economy* (1871) is not mentioned. In this regard, the significance of Jevons's 1882 discussion of the employment of married women is that, when coupled with other aspects of the analysis in *SIRTL*, it helps to explain what role women were given in his marginalist analysis although there is no mention of them in the *Theory*.

Jevons's arguments are relevant for considering Pujol's assessment of later economists' treatments of a 'family wage' and of equal pay for women, as well as a number of issues raised in her chapter on Alfred Marshall.[4] Pujol refers to Marshall's 'argument that infant mortality is directly linked to women's employment', noting that the claim was not supported by any specific data and that no attempt was made to consider whether any other variable(s) could explain the mortality rate. At this and other points in his *Principles*, Marshall departed from his 'positivist [epistemological] posture' (Pujol, 1992, p. 126). By contrast with Marshall, Jevons did produce a statistical analysis to support the claim about mortality rates and women's employment. Examination of this aspect of his 1882 article will provide a specific example of the way in which he constructed arguments, including statistics, in an attempt to influence public debate and policy. Moreover, the public discussion of

Jevons's proposals gives some indication of his place in a spectrum of opinion at the time concerning the issue of women's employment.

The chapter is presented in four sections. The first three consider the 1882 paper, outlining its argument , the responses to it and Jevons's use of statistics. Drawing on the preceding discussion, the next section then considers the more general question of what role women were given in Jevons's political economy by examining the *SIRTL* and *The Theory of Political Economy*.

POLICING THE WORKING-CLASS FAMILY

Today, historians point to a complex of factors to explain the high infant mortality rates in nineteenth-century Britain:

> Most infant deaths were due to nurtural deficiencies: maternal exhaustion and malnutrition producing sickly offspring; and unhygienic conditions; wrong feeding, and a damp foetid atmosphere producing respiratory infections; whilst maternal venereal infection, and contamination of the bloodstream with alcohol or poisonous abortifacients would have been responsible for many of the 'congenital defects' as vaguely classified in the official returns (Rose, 1986, pp. 7–8).

If poverty coupled with alcoholism (cf. ibid., pp. 12–13 and Chapter 19) are now seen as the principal culprits, they were also critical in Jevons's account, albeit with a particular twist. For Jevons's discussion of the paid employment of 'child-bearing women' drew on his more general explanation for poverty and pauperism which he outlined in two Presidential Addresses delivered to the Manchester Statistical Society in November 1869[5] and to Section F (Economic Science and Statistics) of the British Association for the Advancement of Science in September 1870.[6] He argued there that the prevailing extent of poverty and pauperism was due to an absence of the 'spirit of self-reliance ... [which] is the true remedy of pauperism'. Although the 'poorer classes' were 'supplied with easily earned wealth', they remained 'too ignorant, careless, improvident or vicious, to appreciate or accumulate the wealth which science brings'. Because of this failure, any further increase in real wages of the 'working classes', through remission of their taxation, would be wasted because it would be spent merely on a 'higher scale of living. ... It is only with an increase of education and temperance, that the increase of wages will prove a solid advantage' (Jevons, 1883, pp. 196–200, 205).

This was not the only problem. While the working classes wasted their wages, especially through drinking, and failed to save for times of adversity, the 'upper classes' facilitated this by providing charities which undermined the Poor Law, creating and perpetuating 'a class living in hopeless poverty' which thus existed on 'gross fraud' (ibid., pp. 197–200).[7] As Jevons explained in his 1878 primer, '[m]uch of the poverty and crime which now exists' was due to 'mistaken charity in past times', which had 'caused a large part of the population to grow up careless, and improvident, and idle' (Jevons, 1910, pp. 9, 10). Consequently, his programme to reduce poverty and pauperism had three principal components. The first was compulsory education for children; the second was the 'repress[ion of] drunkenness'; the third was the control of private charities by bringing them under the control of the Poor Law, coupled with vigilance to ensure that there was no 'relaxation' of 'the vigour of ... application' of the Poor Law itself (Jevons, 1883, pp. 186–92).

As will be shown below, the significance of the employment of 'married women in factories' within this framework was not simply that it led to a deterioration of conditions within the home, but also that it provided the male of the family with both the income and the time to indulge in dissipative activities which had further deleterious results for the home and the workplace. In 1870, however, Jevons was prepared to accept that the high mortality rate of children was not due to their mothers working in 'the mills'. Because the 'excessive' mortality rates applied to both adults and infants, 'Manchester mothers are thus exonerated from the charge of neglect' (Jevons, 1883, p. 208). It is not clear when Jevons changed his position on this point. In 1875, when lecturing to students at Owens College, he observed it was 'said' that an important cause of 'the increase in child mortality' in England was 'mothers going to work in the day' (Black, 1973–81, VI, p. 59). It is possible that, but unclear whether, Jevons agreed with the argument at that stage, but there is no doubt that he was firmly convinced of its validity by 1882. His shift on this matter followed the debates which surrounded the passage of the 'Factories (Health of Women etc.)' Act (1874), which set the maximum number of hours women and children could work in textile factories (56½ per week). In the early 1870s, a number of unions covering skilled male workers obtained reductions in working hours and other unions, with less bargaining power, then attempted to have legislation introduced to reduce 'ordinary time' in their industries. It was considered unlikely, however, that Parliament would legislate in that manner. In part as a tactical device, emphasis was then placed on the need to further reduce the hours of women and children, one argument being that the policy would reduce the high rates of child mortality. This tactic was fraught with difficulty because, 'once the debates were underway in the House of Commons, [male unionists] lost control of the discourse about the working mother problem'. They were blamed for sending their wives to work because of their 'moral failings' (Rose, 1991, pp. 36, 38, 45). When the Act was passed, it excluded outwork and family-run domestic industries from its coverage and proposals to ban (for varying periods) the employment of women with young children from employment outside the home were also rejected. In 1882, Jevons attempted to reopen that debate in part by using its language and terms of reference.

Although he acknowledged that his argument applied to 'the employment of child-bearing women away from the home' in virtually any occupation, Jevons's focus was on 'the lower-class population of the manufacturing districts' (Jevons, 1883, pp. 157, 160). He proposed that 'radical' legislation should be introduced with the aim of the *'ultimate complete exclusion of mothers of children under the age of three years from factories and workshops'* (ibid., p. 172 OE).[8] This was for three reasons. First, such employment resulted in high child mortality rates because the children were 'farmed out' to 'old women' minders who were effectively killing them with a poor environment and diet, while sedating them with 'Godfrey's Cordial', a 'compound of opium treacle, and infusion of sassafras'.[9] At the same time, because the parents gave their children to 'strangers', they became 'more or less careless and indifferent about them' which led to 'intentional infanticides' in 'no small number of cases', especially in the case of illegitimate children (ibid., pp. 157, 162–3, 165–6, 176). The second reason was that, even if the children survived, they were subsequently inefficient workers and a threat to social order. They became adults who are 'physically and morally weak, and in most instances lapse into pauperism and crime' (ibid., p. 163). The third reason was that such employment led to 'improvident and wrongful marriages': 'dissolute men allure capable young women into marriage with the idea that the wives can earn wages, and enable their husbands to idle away their time'. Hence, in 'too many cases it is the woman's power of earning wages which constitutes her hold upon the paramour' (ibid., pp. 161, 172). The 'character' of the 'lower classes' was thus a crucial part of the explanation for infant mortality rates, a problem for which existing legislation was quite inadequate. For example, the 1872 Infant-Life Protection Act was, in an unfortunate phrase, 'a dead letter' (ibid., p. 171).[10] Nor was it possible to use 'day nurseries' as advocated by the Manchester and Salford Sanitary Association (as discussed subsequently). If used on a large scale, the nurseries would actually 'increase the evil' because they would lead to the spread of infectious diseases and, because there were no adequate means of inspecting them, they would become 'the scenes of fearful abuses' (ibid., p. 170).

Jevons's proposed legislation would work through a series of penalties on parents. Since men were principally to blame for sending women with children under three to work 'regularly', any such 'able-bodied husband, or reputed husband' would incur an (unspecified) 'moderate pecuniary penalty', as would anyone caring for the children, 'whether it appears to be done for profit or not'. Employers would have to provide evidence on women they employed and would be fined if they employed those whose names appeared on a list, to be supplied by factory inspectors, of women 'fined, or otherwise known to have broken the law'. (This seems to entail that women as well as men would be fined, although that was not made clear.) Apart from that measure, employers 'cannot be burdened with the duty of inquiring into the nature of a woman's home duties'. However, any woman giving a false name or address would be 'more severely punished' (ibid., pp. 173–4). The actual implementation of the law would be carried out by police surveillance, aided by informers among the 'operative classes': 'I fancy that an active police officer would soon discover infractions in the law; for the carrying of infants along a public street to a nursing home is a thing evident to anybody, and the officer would only need to follow the woman to the factory, and he would have all the evidence needed' (ibid., p. 174).

Jevons acknowledged that there could be some problems with the implementation of the legislation. For example, he had no idea how 'reputed' husbands and married couples were to be identified.

Moreover, because the legislation would initially cause much disruption, Jevons was prepared to allow that there could be some licensing of *crèches* on or near factory premises. These would, however, have to be financed by employers, be closely supervised by the government and their existence understood to be a 'transitional measure' only. Widows, deserted wives or women whose husbands were 'disabled' by illness or sickness, could, at most, continue employment if there was a *crèche*, although this would apply only for a maximum of two children. In all other cases, women would have to find outwork ('home employment') and, since this would involve 'small earnings', they would have to apply for 'poor-law relief'. Although Jevons speculated that, in 'the long-run, it would pay for the State to employ them as nurses of their own children', it was clear that for the foreseeable future these women would be subject to the decisions of the local Guardians (ibid., p. 175).[11]

The results of the policy would be a reduction in both the infant death-rate and, initially, the growth rate of production. Jevons acknowledged that this would bring 'some trouble and distress for a few years' as household incomes were reduced (ibid., p. 178). However, after a decade, employers would be supplied with a more efficient workforce of 'vigorous young mill-hands' (ibid., p. 175) and an idyllic family life would prevail as there would be

> almost incredible blessings to the people, and to the realm. Many a home would be a home, which cannot now be called by that sweet name. The wife, no longer a mere slattern factory-hand, would become a true mother and housekeeper. And around many a Christmas table troops of happy chubby children would replace the 'wizened little monkeys' of girls, and the 'little old men' of boys, which now form the miserable remnant of families (ibid., pp. 178–9).[12]

DEBATING EXPERTISE IN MANCHESTER

While Jevons's article attempted to reopen questions raised in the debate over the 1874 Factory Act, it was also symptomatic of a significant change in attitudes towards the more generalized problem of child abuse. Since the 1860s, doctors had become 'disillusion[ed] with the voluntary principle as it applied to problems of public health' (Behlmer, 1982, p. 35). This was evident in pressure for direct government inspection of 'baby-farmers' and in the passing of the Contagious

Diseases Acts (1864) to control the spread of venereal disease. The Acts allowed for the licensing and inspection of brothels in garrison and dockyard towns with the forcible detainment (by the police) and examination of any woman suspected of being a prostitute. Behlmer argues that, by the 1880s, the disillusionment with 'the voluntary principle' had resulted in a 'discontinuity' on policy towards child abuse in that 'the domestic relations of parent and child were [no longer regarded as] immune to government regulation' and that the protection of children 'took precedence over the claims of parenthood' (ibid., pp. 12, 16). Jevons's surveillance proposals for 'child-bearing women' provide one illustration of that discontinuity, while reflecting also the disillusionment with the failure of the Liberal Government, elected in 1880, to amend the Infant Life Protection Act. Although pressure had been applied by the *British Medical Journal* and the Metropolitan Board of Works, no action was taken – 'only scandals were likely to stir the government and the next batch of shockers [that is, infanticide court cases] did not come until 1888' (Rose, 1986, pp. 112–13).

Of course, such interventionist proposals did not meet with unanimous approval. As has been noted in another context, examination of debates on such matters 'enables one to identify tensions, cleavages, and the notion of struggle during a particular moment in historical time' (Worsnop, 1990, p. 21). Fortunately, there is a record of 'tensions and cleavages' regarding Jevons's proposals for, immediately after his article was published, it received high praise in a leader in the *Manchester Guardian.* Noting the local relevance of the topic which had 'often been discussed in our columns', the leader concluded, 'here, then, is a man who has a just claim to advise us on this most difficult and serious matter'. Jevons had certainly achieved his objective in stimulating public debate, at least in Manchester. For there was a subsequent correspondence in the *Guardian,* consisting of fifteen often lengthy letters which included a reply by Jevons to some early critics.[13]

Since almost all of the correspondents were apparently 'middle class', we do not know how those directly affected might have reacted to Jevons's proposed policy. Lewis has argued, however, that the 'ideal' of the 'male-breadwinner family model ... with its concomitant sexual divisions' was '*shared* by working-class men and women'. Nevertheless, there was 'resentment' by working-class women 'whenever state policy threatened either their management of the fragile family economy or their domestic authority' (Lewis, 1986, pp. 102–3 OE). Jevons's arguments were based on the 'male-breadwinner model' and this was assumed also by the *Guardian* correspondents. It is notable, however, that there was little attempt to argue that the Manchester working class was responsible for the infant mortality because of a weakness of 'character'.[14] And there was surprisingly little emphasis on working-class 'intemperance' to explain infant mortality. Indeed, what is striking about the correspondence is that, even with the male-bread-winner assumption, there was an overwhelming rejection of Jevons's proposal to disrupt the 'fragile economy of family life'.

Jevons was criticized in part because of the hardship his policy would create with reductions in family income. Necessarily coupled with this was the fear of the Poor Law Guardians. One correspondent, complaining that Jevons was unfamiliar with conditions in Manchester, wrote of the 'terrible ordeal' which the 'heartless' administrators forced on any woman seeking 'parochial relief'. Not only were the administrators of little help in enforcing maintenance payments if a woman was deserted but, in such cases, as well as those where the male of the household had died, was unemployed or ill, resort to the Poor Law would usually mean the separation of the children from their parent(s).[15] Such fears were well justified, coming in the wake of the general tightening of Poor Law provisions in the 1870s. The Manchester Board of Guardians was known particularly for its punitive approach with the 'Manchester Rules' (1875) prohibiting out-relief for 'single men and women, widows with one child, deserted wives with or without families and the wives of prisoners and soldiers' (Kidd, 1985, p. 54). Thane (1978) has shown more generally how women were effectively punished under such a strict regime.

Although Jevons's proposals were overwhelmingly rejected, there was an interesting division between the male and female commentators as to who had the appropriate expertise to deal with the problem of child mortality. Jevons had argued that the Manchester and Salford Sanitary Association (M&SSA) supported the extensive use of *crèches* to reduce infant mortality (see above). Thomas Horsfall, a member of the M&SSA, then attempted to distance the Association from that proposal, arguing that infant mortality was due in large part to environmental conditions such as unhealthy small houses, the lack of clean playgrounds and soot and smoke in the air (*MG*, 4 January 1882, p. 8;

11 January 1882, p. 7). However, the first of the women correspondents, Ursula Bright, focused on other matters. Bright was one of a group of prominent Manchester feminists who opposed legislative measures such as the Contagious Diseases Acts, compulsory registration of baby nurses, and protective labour legislation which discriminated between women and men. They argued that such legislation 'consigned women (particularly married women) to the home, excluded them from the world of work and public life, and dealt with them as if their most important characteristics were their sexual and reproductive capacities'. This was linked closely with the restrictive electoral franchise which assumed that the proper place of women was in the home, bearing and raising children (Shanley, 1989, p. 79). In her letter to the *Guardian*, while noting the problems of Poor Law provision and of how married women were 'to live' if their employment was effectively prohibited, Bright thus argued that it would be better to introduce measures to reduce intemperance and hence 'begin with the fathers, at least until we are willing to give votes [to women] which may serve as some protection to the mothers against paternal legislation whose intended kindness may prove somewhat killing in its operations'. This was not, however, to be a universal female franchise, but rather one for the propertied elite, 'legally qualified women, married or single ... [They should have] the right to vote for members of Parliament, just as it is possessed by men, married or single' (*MG*, 4 January 1882, p. 8).

It has been noted that after 1900 explanations of infant mortality in terms of working-class mothers' ignorance or incompetence 'gained widespread currency' (Dyhouse, 1978, p. 251). But this point formed the pivot of the female interventions in the *Guardian* in 1882. Even Bright, who emphasized national parliamentary politics, argued also that infant mortality was due in part to ignorance 'among poor mothers as regards feeding and clothing and general management of children'. The argument was then developed by Dr. Anna Dahms. Having graduated in Paris, Dahms was the eleventh woman to be registered as a medical practitioner in Britain and, in 1882, was physician to the Ancoats Dispensary for women and children (Black, 1973–81, V, p. 166n.). While acknowledging that the necessity for women to work in factories was one part of the problem, she insisted that the 'cardinal point' was the ignorance of mothers as to 'proper nourishment' of their children. To address this problem was 'the work of women and of women only', with a 'mission ... organised by true and noble-minded women' who could deal with 'tact' with 'our ignorant sisters'. Knowledge was required on matters such as the benefits of mothers' milk (as opposed to that of animals and milk 'manufactured in a chemist's laboratory'), which would entail 'permanent exhibitions ... in every district', with mothers' meetings where children could be examined. Within a quarter of a century, 'a generation of women will grow up who will not need a policeman to tell them that their place is not in factories or workshops of any sort. They will know better already' (*MG*, 9 January 1882, p. 6).

In opposing Jevons's proposed policy, Bright and Dahms were attempting to wrest control of the terms of the debate away from male officials, such as Horsfall, who dominated local organizations such as the M&SSA. That this control was the subject of some dissension is indicated by Dahms's criticism of Horsfall in her letter and by a subsequent letter, signed 'Lucretia', from a member of the 'Ladies Sanitary Association'. Supporting Dahms, she called also for control over the sale of Godfrey-type syrups and for the establishment of day nurseries, a policy which, as noted above, Horsfall had downplayed. 'Lucretia' also noted the need for diagrams in instruction since 'with these people "seeing is believing"' (*MG*, 10 January 1882, p. 8).[16] It was then left to Arthur Ransome, the chair of the M&SSA, to attempt to repair some of the damage by defending more strongly the use of 'day nurseries, and the teaching of the artisans' wives by our sanitary mission women' (*MG*, 13 January 1882, p. 7).

Jevons's response (*MG*, 12 January 1882, p. 5) was basically intransigent. While he acknowledged that there were some problems with the Poor Law which 'ought to be remedied' by legislation, he continued to insist that it would be a good thing if family incomes were reduced. Contrary to Bright, intemperance was not in itself the cause of infant mortality. Nevertheless, the two matters were linked by high incomes and the increasing 'leisure' of the male 'manufacturing and mining classes' in the north of England, which were made possible by the employment of mothers in mills and factories:

> It is easy to declaim about the poverty of the people and the difficulty of paying ... house rent. ... But a careful review of undoubted facts shows that there are more healthy children and less drunkenness where there are lower earnings. The inference is that higher wages are not conducive to the good of a certain part of the population while their state of civilisation is at its present standard. Now of all the

ways of earning higher family earnings the worst undoubtedly is that of sending the mother to the mill.

Moreover, the problem of living conditions, with small houses, lack of clean playgrounds and a polluted atmosphere, was a side issue for the matter at hand: 'Small and unsanitary though the dwellings may be, it is difficult not to see that a well-kept small dwelling differs *toto caelo* from an ill-kept one. Now, whether women are to have votes or not, there can be no doubt that the proper place of a good housewife is in her house.' This reference to votes for women followed Bright's letter, which elicited the information that Jevons thought that 'every woman who can vote for municipal elections ought to have a parliamentary vote', although this was declared irrelevant for the matter under discussion. Jevons displayed a marked insensitivity here by referring to her as 'Mrs. Jacob Bright' (she was married to Jacob, brother of John, Bright), although she had signed herself Ursula Bright, with no mention of her marital status.

Jevons's insensitivity was shown in another aspect of his reply. During the debates on the 1874 Factory Act, it had been argued that, faced with a ban on factory employment and the rigorous application of the Poor Law, women would be likely to resort to prostitution (Cooke-Taylor, 1882b, pp. 437–8). This was not mentioned explicitly in the *Guardian* correspondence, possibly because it was considered indelicate. That this was the case was suggested by Dahms's comment on Jevons's proposed use of the police: 'Anybody familiar with the movement for the suppression of another grave social evil will know what little benefit and gratitude the State derives by entrusting supervision of its laws to police officers' (*MG*, 9 January 1882, p. 6). While euphemistic, this was clearly a reference to the use of the police to enforce the Contagious Diseases Acts. (Dahms had reason to be euphemistic because there was a great deal of male hostility to the 'impropriety' of women discussing the Acts (Shanley, 1989, p. 85).) In his reply, however, while claiming to agree to a significant extent with Dahms, Jevons continued to insist that 'the temporary intervention of the policeman' was required. Jevons's blithe dismissal of the fear generated by the association between the police and the implementation of the Contagious Diseases Act serves as an indicator of the manner in which he approached the question of the employment of working-class women.

THE MORTALITY RATE STATISTICS

Jevons's 'selection', while in his mid-thirties, as President of Section F of the British Association for the Advancement of Science signalled the 'recognition of his work on statistics, since his Presidential Address was on that topic and was published in the Journal of the Statistical Society' (Stigler, 1982, p. 354). It is appropriate to note in this context that Jevons used that 1870 Address to comment on a current controversy over infant death statistics in a way which provides an interesting counterpoint to the position he adopted in 1882.

In arguing that the excessive child mortality rate in Manchester was not due to mothers working outside the home (see above), Jevons referred to a paper by Joseph Baxendell which concluded that 'the stigma which has often been cast upon the mothers belonging to the working classes of Manchester is most undeserved ... [I]n fact, infants and young children are better cared for, and attended to, in Manchester than in any other leading manufacturing town in England' (Baxendell, 1870b, p. 179). In presenting statistics to support this claim at the April 1870 meeting of the Manchester Literary and Philosophical Society, Baxendell affected some surprise at his results. However, the paper drew on a theme which Baxendell had outlined in previous papers to the Society. The high Mancunian mortality rates could be explained by 'meteorological causes' because variations in rainfall were linked statistically to the incidence of fatal disease. Since the working-age population was 'exposed to the vicissitudes of the weather', its mortality rate was more devastating than that for children under five years. Indeed, meteorological causes 'far exceed those arising from defective drainage, ill-contrived privies and water-closets, crowded dwellings, and an insufficient supply of good water'. Therefore, rather than continuing to spend 'enormous sums of money' on sanitary improvements, finance should be redirected towards the study of the effects of 'the atmosphere' upon disease (Baxendell, 1870a, pp. 162–63, 164).[17]

There had been increasing Mancunian concern with increased child mortality rates in the 1860s, with the M&SSA arguing in 1867 that the official statistics were 'comparatively useless as a basis for legislation for sanitary purposes' (Rose, 1986, p. 124; see also Chapter 14). As might then be expected, Baxendell's claim and use of statistics met with some resistance. There was a lengthy and often acrimonious debate in the correspondence columns of the *Manchester Guardian* between late May and early July 1870. The key point at issue was the peculiar way in which Baxendell had calculated mortality rates by expressing infant deaths as a fraction (per thousand) of deaths for all ages of the population. Although Baxendell was able to show that infant deaths alone could not explain the high total mortality rate in Manchester, critics such as A. Ransome and W. Royston from the M&SSA explained the bizarre results which followed from Baxendell's method of calculation, noting that the more appropriate procedure was to calculate deaths as a proportion (per thousand) of those living in the relevant age group. On this basis, Manchester had the second highest mortality rate both for those over five years (equal with Liverpool) and for those under five (equal with Newcastle) in a sample of eighteen 'large towns'.[18]

Some months later, speaking as President of Section F at the British Association, Jevons summarized the debate by noting that Baxendell had produced statistics 'tending to show that the mortality of Manchester was not due to any peculiar excess in the rate of infantile mortality'. While Ransome and Royston had criticized those results, 'it still turns out that the adult mortality of Manchester is as excessive as the infantile mortality. Manchester mothers are thus exonerated from the charge of neglect' (Jevons, 1883, pp. 207–8). If Jevons had some sympathy for Baxendell's 'naturalistic' explanation of the mortality rates, his summary of the debate was misleading. Baxendell had argued that Manchester infants and young children had a lower mortality rate than 'in any other large manufacturing town' (see above) and this claim had been shown to be incorrect. Jevons thus used his position as President of Section F to create the impression that Baxendell had, in the main, been correct, a manoeuvre adopted subsequently by the President of the Manchester Literary and Philosophy Society.[19]

By 1882, Jevons had reversed his position on the responsibility of working mothers for the high child death-rates. It is somewhat ironic, therefore, that his claim that the employment of 'child-bearing women' caused 'much' of the 'preventible deaths' of 'certainly 30,000 infants, and perhaps as many as 40,000 or even 50,000' per annum (Jevons, 1883, pp. 158, 160) used the same statistical basis which Ransome and Royston had advocated in 1870. Despite the importance which Jevons attached to his statistical results, however, critics argued that they were produced by a number of questionable procedures and that they failed to support his argument.

Following the publication of Jevons's 1882 article, it had been suggested in the *Manchester Guardian* that the statistics he used showed that 'factory towns, as such, do not appear one fraction worse than the towns in which there are no factories, as Manchester people understand them'.[20] If this could be shrugged off as Mancunian parochialism, such was not the case for a critique of Jevons's article by R.W. Cooke-Taylor, which appeared as a letter in the *Pall Mall Gazette* (Cooke-Taylor, 1882a). Jevons was quick to respond to this, acknowledging that the letter 'certainly requires an answer from me' (Jevons, 1882b, p. 11) and Cooke-Taylor then replied with a lengthy critique in the *Contemporary Review* (Cooke-Taylor, 1882b). Because of its more detailed argument, the latter article can be used to assess Jevons's analysis.

The basis for Jevons's argument was a series of statistics on child mortality rates for twenty 'large towns' published in the 1880 and 1881 Annual Reports of the Registrar-General of Births, Deaths and Marriages. The rates were calculated per one thousand living children. Table 3.1 reproduces the full information, to which Jevons referred, from the Reports. Jevons took the lowest average rate for 1873–77, that of Portsmouth, as a minimum 'standard' and used that rate to calculate the 'excess mortality' for 1878. This amounted to 24,000 children for the towns in Table 3.1. He failed to explain how he had arrived at the much larger number of 40,000 or 50,000, but it was apparently a 'guesstimate' since he noted that the statistics did not include 'a multitude of small towns'. Jevons claimed that there was no reason to regard Portsmouth as 'exceptional' and that it could serve as a benchmark because it was not a 'factory town'. Indeed, Jevons followed the Registrar-General in claiming that its low mortality rate could be explained by it being a naval and garrison town (Jevons, 1883, p. 159). However, as Cooke-Taylor (1882b, p. 430) noted, not only was this a 'somewhat strange' argument, but Jevons failed to mention that Plymouth, also a naval and garrison town, had a high mortality rate.

If the rationale for the benchmark was arbitrary, Jevons also had to explain the case of Liverpool. That city had the highest mortality rate, occupying the 'place of dishonour ... the infants (under five years of age) are decimated annually!' (Jevons, 1883, p. 158). (As Table 3.1

shows, this was strictly the case only for 1878, but Jevons dismissed the significance of the 1879 figures as the result of 'the unusual healthiness' of that year.) The problem, however, was that Liverpool was a seaport with, as Jevons acknowledged, 'no great textile factories' (ibid., p. 167). This was characterized as an 'anomalous' case which had to be explained by another variable (see below). However, as Cooke-Taylor explained, Liverpool was not anomalous because Plymouth and Sunderland were also seaports with high mortality rates (Cooke-Taylor, 1882b, pp. 430–31). This point was not evident in Jevons's article because, instead of reproducing the full tables from the Registrar-General reports, he cited statistics only for selected towns in 1878. As Table 3.1 shows, where Jevons's selections are marked by asterisks, Plymouth and Sunderland were not included in his list.

Despite the arbitrary way in which Jevons explained the significance of the towns with the lowest and highest mortality rates, the statistics simply failed to support his argument that it was factory towns with women employees which explained 'much' of the excess mortality. He had no figures on the employment of women in 'factories and mills'. Yet, of the twelve towns he selected, the worst was Liverpool, followed by Sheffield and Birmingham. As Cooke-Taylor noted, in the latter two cases, 'women are not employed at "mills"'. Taking the full list in Table 3.1, of the seven towns with the highest rates, three were seaports and only one (Oldham) could be classified as 'a factory town' (Cooke-Taylor, 1882b, p. 430).

The analysis in Cooke-Taylor's *Pall Mall Gazette* letter was by no means as telling as that published later in the *Contemporary Review* and, to some extent, the letter misunderstood Jevons's arguments. Nevertheless, Jevons's response indicated that he realized his statistical case was vulnerable: 'I have come to the conclusion that the complexity of the subject [i.e. mortality statistics] is too great to admit of sure inference'. A further indication of the recognized vulnerability is that Jevons then attempted to switch attention away from the statistics: 'The real proof of the pernicious effects of the employment of the mothers of young children away from home is not to be found in complicated statistical tables, but in the direct testimony of medical men and others, who see the effects and can positively support their existence' (Jevons, 1882b, p. 11). Jevons had indeed referred to such 'testimony' in his

Table 3.1: Mortality rates (per 1000 living) of children under
five years of age for twenty 'large towns'

Town	1878	Mean Annual 1873– 77	1879	Mean Annual 1876– 79
* Portsmouth	59.4	59.6	41.6	60.7
* Brighton	65.8	–	–	–
* Bristol	66.2	–	–	–
* Newcastle	73.2	82.9	71.5	77.5
* Wolverhampton	74.8	74.7	62.5	73.9
* London	78.6	72.8	75.9	74.1
Bradford	80.3	90.0	–	88.2
* Leicester	82.9	90.2	80.0	87.7
* Nottingham	82.9	84.6	82.1	85.2
Manchester	83.4	92.3	75.5	88.8
Leeds	84.6	88.6	71.7	87.4
Norwich	84.7	68.2	67.4	73.6
Glasgow	86.2	91.5	–	–
Plymouth	89.1	–	–	–
Oldham	92.0	84.0	69.6	86.5
Sunderland	93.0	72.5	65.5	76.2
* Salford	93.8	94.2	88.0	94.1
* Birmingham	95.2	86.1	74.9	87.4
* Sheffield	95.9	79.2	68.0	82.6
* Liverpool	103.6	96.3	88.4	99.7
Mean	83.2	82.8	72.1	82.7

* Jevons's selections.

Sources: *Forty-First Annual Report of the Registrar-General of Births, Deaths and Marriages in England*, H.M. Stationery Office, London, 1880, Table XXXIX, p. xxvi. *Forty-Second Annual Report of the Registrar-General of Births, Deaths and Marriages in England*, H.M. Stationery Office, London, 1881, Table 67, p. cxi.

original article, using, in particular, one of two 'classic Victorian "proofs" of the adverse effects of female factory employment' (Rose, 1986, p. 9). An examination of Jevons's argument on this point will provide a further striking example of how he presented the significance of certain types of evidence.

To establish that the excess mortality was not due to the environmental conditions of 'town life', Jevons cited a study, by Dr. H.J. Hunter, of the increase in child mortality in a number of agricultural districts bordering the North Sea.[21] The study had been published as an Appendix in the 1863 report of the Medical Officer of the Privy Council (Privy Council, 1864, pp. 454–63) and, as the more detailed discussion of it in *Capital* (Marx, 1974, p. 376) suggests, it was regarded as providing decisive evidence on the effects of married women's employment. After questioning 'about 70 medical practitioners ... [and] other gentlemen acquainted with the condition of the poor', Hunter reported that 'nearly all' agreed that the increased mortality rate was due to the increased employment of married women in field work-gangs which followed the draining of previously marshy ground (Privy Council, 1864, p. 455). Hunter added his own observation that the work gangs of women.

> are to be met morning and evening on the roads, dressed in short petticoats, with suitable coats and boots, and sometimes trousers, looking wonderfully strong and healthy, but tainted with a customary immorality and heedless of the fatal results which their love of this busy and independent life is bringing on their unfortunate offspring who are pining at home (ibid., p. 456).

The imagery here is fascinating regarding the dress of the women and their 'customary immorality' which the trained eye of Hunter could observe.[22] In a subsequent sympathetic discussion of Hunter's report, Hewitt argued that the significance of the study was that it 'refuted' the argument that the excess child mortality in Lancashire was 'adequately explained by the overcrowded conditions of the towns' (Hewitt, 1958, p. 113). This conclusion now seems unsatisfactory.[23] Nevertheless, Hewitt's qualified approach which suggested that the study indicated that some factor other than overcrowding was influencing the results, was quite different from that of Jevons. He concluded that, because the study showed that the increase in child mortality was 'not due to the bad sanitary condition of the courts and streets' of towns, it provided 'in fact, *a true and complete induction, pointing to the employment of women away from their homes as the efficient cause of their children's decadence'* (Jevons, 1883, p. 164 OE).[24] Jevons thus argued that one case 'proved' that married women's employment was the cause of 'much' (this virtually became 'all' in his argument) of the excess mortality in factory towns. If this epistemological claim that one example established a 'perfect induction' appears bizarre, it was consistent with his treatment of statistics on child mortality. Determined to establish that the employment of 'children-bearing women' was the 'efficient cause' of excess child mortality, Jevons used arbitrary methods of calculation and selection of statistics, failed to consider carefully what other factors might be involved in mortality rates and was apparently oblivious to the point that, in any case, his statistics failed to support his argument.[25]

While Jevons's response to Cooke-Taylor's *Contemporary Review* article cannot be known since the article was published after his death,[26] Jevons did indicate that he was sensitive to the initial criticism of his use of statistics. Despite his claim, when replying to Cooke-Taylor, that the 'real proof' for his argument was 'not to be found in complicated statistical tables' (see above), Jevons then attempted to repair his case on precisely that basis. In February 1882, after failing to obtain any help from the (London) Statistical Society in pressuring the government for a public inquiry on child mortality, he contacted the National Association for the Promotion of Social Science. The result was that Jevons was to continue his campaign by presenting a paper to the Association's meeting in September (Black, 1973–81, V, pp. 168–9, 173–4). He then spent a good deal of time producing new statistics for the paper because, as he told his brother in July, he was going to use it to 'overthrow my critics'. Using figures from the census and the Registrar-General's reports, Jevons claimed he had established that 'the mortality of children under five years of age is proportional to the percentage of women over twenty years employed in industrial occupations' (ibid., p. 200).

Just what those figures did show is unclear because Jevons drowned a month later and the paper was never finished (H.A. Jevons (ed.), 1886, p. 448).[27] It should be noted, however, that a subsequent paper on the same topic by Clara Collet was to show problems of 'spurious correlation' which clearly never occurred to Jevons. Because of the inadequacy of the census statistics, Collet used figures from a range of statistical sources to show that, for the years 1889–93, while there was a weak correlation of the type Jevons had suggested, the results were skewed by the class composition of the towns. (Infant mortality rates were greater where there was a smaller proportion of the 'servant-owning class'.) If a more appropriate comparison was made between working-class districts, there was little relationship between infant mortality rates and the proportion of married women in paid employment. Moreover, even with a high proportion of married women in factories, it did not necessarily follow that these were women with children below one year old, 'or even that the children of mothers at work are more neglected than those of unemployed mothers in the same position' (Collet, 1898b, pp. 230–40; see also Dyhouse, 1978, p. 263).[28]

The relevance of comparing this approach with that of Jevons's is that it indicates precisely how Jevons's dogmatism meant that he simply failed to consider alternative explanations and take due care with the statistical material. While it would be useful to have his response to Cooke-Taylor's detailed analysis, there is some evidence that, regardless of the quality of any criticism, Jevons would not budge once he was determined to argue a particular case. This evidence concerns his response to a critique of the statistics he had used in his 1870 Presidential Address to Section F of the British Association and to which he referred again in 1882 to explain the 'anomalous' case of Liverpool.

Referring to the 'excessive mortality in great towns' such as Manchester, Salford, Liverpool, Glasgow and Dundee, Jevons argued that the explanation was the presence of 'a poor Irish population': 'the great towns which are unhealthy agree in containing a large proportion of Irish, and agree in nothing else which I can discover'. Presenting a series of statistical tables which he claimed gave his argument an 'almost ... conclusive character', Jevons added that his explanation would 'relieve us from some perplexity, give us more confidence in sanitary measures, and point out exactly where most attention is needed' (Jevons, 1883, pp. 208–9, 213–16). A refutation of this argument appeared almost immediately. In a paper presented to the Manchester Statistical Society, T.R. Wilkinson showed that the statistics Jevons had provided could not support his conclusion (Wilkinson, 1871). Despite this devastating critique, Jevons continued to repeat and to amplify his claim in the 1870s (Black 1973–81, VI, p. 59; Jevons, 1879, p. 640). He returned to the Irish theme in the 1882 *Contemporary Review* article where he argued that, until 'statists' understood that 'the different towns and counties of England are to a great extent peopled by races of different characters, it will prove impossible to understand the profound statistical discrepancies which they exhibit'. Although an 'opposite opinion' had been expressed by Wilkinson, '[r]enewed and very careful inquiry has ... quite satisfied me as to the correctness' of the argument given in 1870 which explained the 'anomalous' high mortality rate in Liverpool (Jevons, 1883, p. 159). It is extraordinary that, without meeting Wilkinson's argument or producing any new statistical evidence, Jevons continued to repeat his racial claims about the Irish while characterizing Wilkinson's paper as simply an 'opposite opinion'.[29]

Unlike Jevons, Wilkinson did not rely simply on official mortality statistics. His paper also reported the results of detailed studies of the Manchester slums which were used to reinforce his argument that mortality rates would be greater in the large towns where 'the population is more densely packed' and where sanitary conditions were unsatisfactory. Kidd (1985) and Seed (1982) have emphasized that the Manchester middle class did not speak with one voice on poverty, a number of private charities 'undermining' the punitive approach of the Poor Law Guardians. Such divisions were reflected by Jevons and Wilkinson in the early 1870s. While Jevons attacked the 'character' of the 'lower classes', denounced the sentimental private charities and blamed the Irish for high mortality rates, Wilkinson concluded his paper with the following:

> the high rate of mortality in large towns is caused by an increasing proportion of the very poor to the whole population, rather than by a large proportion of poor Irish ... [T]he commonest labourers, the means of whose daily living is precarious, those also who prey upon society in various ways, as well as those multitudes of people who continually attend to the roughest drudgery of the world, remain mostly in the centre of our cities, where if not by their labours, their sufferings, and their sorrows, at least by the voluminous records of their deaths, they make themselves known to society (Wilkinson, 1871, p. 55).

The relevance of examining Jevons's statistical treatment of mortality rates is illustrated by one historian's reference to Jevons's 'missionary fervour' and 'earnest social concern and commitment' which was 'balanced by three vital checks: (1) a genuine strenuous concern to find out empirically about the lives of the poor and those to whom he was aspiring to do good; (2) an insistence on the discipline of careful empirical testing, as far as possible; (3) a fundamental cautious and critical fallibilism regarding the principles of science' (Hutchison, 1982, p. 373). As examples of this 'philosophical caution and critical fallibilism', Hutchison (ibid., p. 374) cites Jevons's statements in his *Principles of Science* that an analyst should exhibit a 'perfect readiness to reject a theory inconsistent with fact'. Indeed, 'the more a man loves his theory the more scrupulous should be his attention to its faults' and he should suspend 'judgement when the data are insufficient' to support an argument (Jevons, 1887, pp. 586, 592). Clearly, however, Jevons's treatment of mortality statistics and his general approach to the question of 'married women in factories' violated all of Hutchison's 'vital checks' as well as those principles of good scientific behaviour which Jevons enunciated in the *Principles of Science*.

UPSTAIRS, DOWNSTAIRS: WOMEN IN THE MARGINALIST ECONOMY

Jevons supported the admittance of women to degrees at tertiary institutions[30] and regarded as 'tyrannous' any attempt by government or professional associations to bar women (other than those with children under three) from 'access to employment' (Jevons, 1882c, p. 120; 1883, pp. 160, 172). Such barriers to 'negative freedom' would apply principally to members of the 'middle' and 'upper' classes, but there is no evidence that Jevons had any substantive interest in analysing labour market conditions for these women. So far as female participation in the paid labour force was concerned, Jevons was driven by a class perspective. The politically and hence analytically relevant questions concerned female employment in 'the operative and handicraft classes' (Jevons, 1882c, p. 1) with particular attention paid to married women. His most detailed discussion can be found in the *SIRTL* where Jevons argued that wages were 'governed by – that is to say, manifest – the laws of supply and demand' which were explained theoretically by his version of marginal productivity theory (ibid., pp. 90–96, 153). The laws ensured that, ultimately, all labour market participants were rewarded according to their (marginal) contribution to production:

'Cases, of course, constantly occur where the labourer is quite ignorant and indifferent as to what is to be the result of his labour. ... But even this ignorance will not necessarily deprive him or his class from receiving in the long-run their due share' (ibid., p. 96). The labour market which illustrated this 'model' was that for domestic servants, which accounted for nearly half of female employment at the time. Jevons argued that in domestic service women 'have known perfectly well how to advance their interests' without trade unions. No legislation was required to regulate that market because the 'common law, which in this case means little more than custom, has been found sufficient to secure the rights and interests of adult women as well as men' (ibid., p. 69).

Since the laws of supply and demand ensured that all labour market participants ultimately received their due reward, union-organized strikes to increase money wages were both unnecessary and futile. Indeed, Jevons's preferred wage bargaining situation was between 'individual workmen and employers' (ibid., p. 153). Once again, the market for domestic servants illustrated this claim because, 'by the natural operation of the laws of supply and demand, and by their own good sense these employees have been greatly advanced in earnings and other advantages' (ibid., p. 118). Indeed: 'Domestic servants ... arrange their terms of hiring in perfect independence; there are no strikes and no lockouts. If an employer offers too low terms, servants are not to be found. There is the freest competition among good servants for good places, and among employers for good servants. The general result is quite satisfactory' (ibid., p. 153).[31]

Jevons argued that 'there is no ground whatever for legal limitation' on the work hours of adult men (ibid., p. 66). However, while the conditions for female domestic servants were 'quite satisfactory' and required no legislation, Jevons supported existing legislation restricting the work hours of women in manufacturing, mining and shipping. Indeed, he advocated extending the restrictions to the agricultural sector, retail shops and warehouses. Moreover, 'child-bearing women' with children under three years, were to be effectively prohibited from 'factories and workshops' (ibid., pp. 68–75, 81–7). The grounds for distinguishing different types of women's employment need to be clarified.

Two common avenues for analysing legislation were not open to Jevons. It had been argued that adult male labour hours could not be regulated because it was an interference with personal 'liberty'. Jevons thought that, in general, there was 'a certain considerable probability that individuals will find out for themselves the best paths in life, and will be eventually the best citizens when left at liberty to choose their own course' (Jevons, 1883, p. 176). However, he could not rely on 'some supposed principle of liberty' to oppose restrictions on male hours because the 'same principle, if it existed, would apply to adult women' (Jevons, 1882c, p. 65). Another common rationale for restricting the employment of women 'seems to be ... that women are less able to take care of themselves than men' (ibid., p. 68). The argument that women were not 'free agents', because of pressure from husbands or a 'natural instinct to preserve the family', had passed into legislation with the 1874 Factory Act (Rose, 1991, pp. 36, 41). But Jevons could not use this approach because, if it was accepted as a general principle, he could not explain the highly satisfactory outcome in domestic service. Jevons's argument was thus couched in different and utilitarian terms. As he explained in the first chapter of the *SIRTL*, which set out his general approach to legislation, any policy measure ought to be judged by the criterion of whether it 'will conduce to the greater sum of happiness ... without ulterior consequences' (1882c, p. 12). Consideration of legislation thus had to proceed on a case-by-case basis. It was on this ground that Jevons approved, although he did not clearly explain, the banning of women from work in mines and collieries because the 'conditions of employment' were different from those in domestic service (ibid., p. 69).

In the case of adult males, legislation to reduce work hours would have adverse effects by reducing the rate of production. Nor would it have any positive effects because 'It is an economic fallacy to suppose that any adequate counter-balancing advantage can, as a general rule, arise out of this loss, except of course the recreative, sanitary, or intellectual advantages (if any) to the workman for his enjoyment of more leisure time' (Jevons, 1882c, p. 66). Of course, for Jevons, the increased leisure time would actually be spent in a wasteful and destructive fashion (see above), the effects of which could already be seen with the trend to reduced work hours. Even worse, that reduction produced the 'great evil' of the employment of 'child-bearing women in factories and workshops'. Where 'the mother can earn her own living' (and these women were 'not uncommonly ... unmarried'), there was increased child mortality, and the 'immorality and intemperance not unnaturally produced by the destruction of home influences'. Because of male greed and laziness, the 'operative or handicraft classes' were sacrificing 'the interests of a future generation to the apparent good of the present'. Hence it would be a great social benefit to reduce their family incomes: 'It must not necessarily be assumed that the amount of earnings is the measure of the advantages enjoyed. Those who know not how to spend well are often injured rather than bettered by higher earnings' (Jevons, 1882c, pp. 70–72). In 1868, Jevons had argued that the male 'working-classes' should 'abstain' from agitation for legislation to reduce work hours until satisfactory legislation had been passed which would restrict both the employment of their children and provide for their compulsory education (Jevons, 1883, pp. 110–16). Duty to their children should thus override the pursuit of self-interest through the reduction of work time. In 1882, with the requisite legislation in place, Jevons continued to oppose reductions in male work hours because it would still mean that they were neglecting and hence failing in their duty to their families. Criticism of legislated reductions in male work hours was thus part of the same perspective that advocated the effective prohibition of women with young children from paid employment.

For Jevons, then, the ideal employment for 'lower-class' women with families was domestic service, where they could work a sufficient number of hours to supplement the male's income. This would simultaneously reduce the deleteriously high incomes such families currently received and prevent women from 'neglecting a young family and destroying the home'. Removed from the 'slavery' of having to work long hours outside and inside the home, they would be free to carry out their principal responsibilities (Jevons, 1882c, pp. 72–4). Clearly, all this assumes the male bread-winner model which was supplemented by the claim that economic independence for working-class women (i.e. the ability to 'earn their own living') would produce great 'evil'. It may appear odd, then, that given the importance which Jevons attached to this argument, *The Theory of Political Economy* (*TPE*) makes no mention of work hours policy and has no explicit reference to women and their 'appropriate' employment. It is possible to show, however, why the question of work hours policy was not discussed and how the male (working-class) bread-winner model was assumed in that statement of marginalist economics.[32]

When Jevons discussed the distinction between 'moral philosophy' and the science of political economy in *TPE* (Jevons, 1871, pp. 27–32), he announced that he had 'no hesitation in accepting the Utilitarian theory of morals' and a tautological explanation of the motives for human behaviour: 'all forces influencing the mind of man are pleasures and pains' (ibid., pp. 27, 31). These motives could, however, be graded in a 'hierarchy of feeling', ranging from the 'mere physical pleasure or pain ... arising from ... bodily wants and susceptibilities' to 'mental and moral feelings of several degrees of elevation' which involved questions of ethics and 'duty' (ibid., p. 29). As Jevons noted in his 1875 lectures at Owens College, consideration of ethics fell within the domain of *'Moral Philosophy'*, which discussed 'the character of men and the effects of action on their characters' (Black, 1973–81, VI, p. 8 OE). The science of political economy and therefore *TPE* dealt only with the 'lowest rank of feelings' which drove the pursuit of wealth: 'The calculus of utility aims at supplying the ordinary wants of man at the least cost of labour. Each labourer, in the absence of other motives, is supposed to devote his energy to the accumulation of wealth. A higher calculus of right and wrong would be needed to show how he may best employ that wealth for the good of others as well as himself' (Jevons, 1871, p. 32). Provided that a policy question could be decided using the accumulation of wealth as the only criterion, a political economist could pronounce on the desirability of that policy within the domain of 'science'. The question of 'free' international trade fell within that category and so Jevons advocated a free trade policy in *TPE* (Jevons, 1871, pp. 134–9). However, a policy question which required reference to other criteria could not be adjudicated within the domain and an example of this was the legislation of work hours.

Jevons made clear in *TPE* that a 'scientific' marginalist analysis could explain the work hours of different races and classes. For example, 'A man of a lower race, a negro for instance, enjoys possessions less, and loathes labour more; his exertions, therefore, soon stop.' This same behavioural characteristic was evident in the 'general tendency to reduce the hours of labour at the present day' by the English working class (labourers, artisans and white-collar employees). Those workers aimed at a target real income and, with increasing real wage rates, preferred greater 'ease' to the effort involved in obtaining greater wealth by working the same hours as before. By contrast, the 'learned professions' (solicitors, barristers, physicians, architects and engineers) 'generally' worked 'more severely' as their income increased. Indeed, the 'rich man in modern society is supplied apparently with all he can desire, and yet he labours unceasingly for more' (Jevons, 1871, pp. 176–8). Despite this argument, the language of which indicates that Jevons opposed the contemporary 'tendency' to reduce work hours, he avoided making an explicit statement on legislation in that regard. This was because the policy question involved analysing how economic actors spent their leisure. The use of leisure time, however, was not part of the economic domain because it involved questions of ethics (and therefore duty) as it entailed analysing the effects of the use of leisure on character building or dissipation. Jevons made clear that this question fell outside the domain of *TPE* with the example he used to explain how the domain of political economy could be overridden in the calculus of human actions where questions of duty were involved. The first of these were to family and friends: 'it is a man's duty, as it is his natural inclination, to earn sufficient food and whatever else may best satisfy his proper and moderate desires. If the claims of a family or of friends fall upon him, it may be desirable that he should deny his own desires and even his physical needs their customary gratification' (ibid., p. 30).

While this discussion of the domain boundary helps explain why Jevons did not explicitly discuss legislation to control the work hours of men and women in *TPE*, it indicates also that he was assuming that labour was supplied to the economy by families where the male dominated decision-making. This did not entail that women were incapable of the 'civilised' (subsequently called 'rational') behaviour which maximized the accumulation of wealth. For given the constraint of the males' decision on the amount of hours to be supplied, working-class women could choose their employment so as to equate the marginal utility and disutility of work. Just as importantly, the example shows that, consistent with Jevons's other published work, it was working-class behaviour which dominated much of his thinking about the economy, so that questions involving the employment of middle-class women or single women in general were treated as being of relatively peripheral importance.

It has been argued that economists basically characterize the different domains of 'the economic' and 'the non-economic' with a series of mutually exclusive couples: the public and private, the market and the household, self-interested and altruistic behaviour, male and female actors (Folbre and Hartman, 1988, p. 185). If some aspects of contemporary economic analysis seem to escape this characterization,[33] its set of differences is not adequate to characterize the first English appearance of marginalist economics in the work of Jevons. For example, while 'the economic' is clearly constituted as the domain of self-interested behaviour in *TPE*, it does not preclude the participation of women. Again, while the analysis of altruistic behaviour fell outside the domain of 'economic science', it could (or should) be undertaken by both men and women.

A different account could begin by noting that, for Jevons, a woman's principal 'duty' was to 'the home', particularly if there were young children ('There are no duties which are more important in every respect than those which a mother is bound by with regard to her young children' (Jevons, 1883, p. 172)). At the same time, all women were not precluded from 'the economic' ('It is very desirable that women who have no such domestic duties should have the freest possible access to employment' (ibid)). This is clearly a 'gendered' discourse because such women were principally to work in a restricted range of occupations and, to this extent, Jevons regarded the proper place of women as being in the home, whether their work was paid or unpaid. Moreover, he assumed in *TPE* that labour supply decisions, so far as total hours worked were concerned, were made by the male in the household. At the same time, *TPE* cannot be analysed simply through a male/female dichotomy because Jevons's economic analysis and policy proposals were driven by a perceived need to control the dangerous working classes (that is, the 'lower orders' or 'masses'). Further, men and women were discussed also in terms of their race, whether it was the 'lower race of negroes' or that of the Irish. This class and race perspective, which is made clear in Jevons's analysis of the paid employment of 'child-bearing women', is missing from virtually all of the commentary on Jevons's 'scientific' analysis and his policy proposals.[34]

CONCLUSIONS

Jevons's criticisms of, and proposed attack upon the economic independence of working-class women clearly differentiated his approach from that of J.S. Mill, as set out in *The Subjection of Women* (cf. Green, 1992, pp. 25–6; Pujol, 1992, pp. 24–5). This was consistent with Jevons's verdict that the *Subjection* was marked by 'extravagant' if not 'grotesque' views:

> Both Mill & Hobbes were marked by a like wrong headedness, & tendency to the adoption of extreme and sometimes grotesque views. The extravagant statements to be found in Mill's 'Subjection of Women' are hardly to be equalled out of Hobbes' Essay on Human Nature in his Leviathan.[35]

It should be noted, however, that, in criticizing Mill, Jevons avoided the mire inhabited by some other critics. In 1871, for example, the Drummond Professor of Political Economy at Oxford, Bonamy Price, launched a bitter attack on Mill. Two years after the publication of *The Subjection of Women*, Price claimed that Mill, 'however unconsciously, [is] introducing into England the theories and practices of the Communists and Socialists of France'. He traced this political failing to a weakness of Mill's character: 'the feminate passionateness of his nature, the quickness with which his feelings are excited, even on the most abstract subject' (Price, 1871, p. 32). [36]

One reason for the different approaches of Mill and Jevons is that Jevons was deeply influenced by the work of Charles Darwin, although this was read through the filter of Herbert Spencer's version of 'evolution' (Jevons, 1890, pp. 290–94). That a 'natural selection' perspective was never far from Jevons's work is indicated by a note which he wrote in early 1882: 'The fact is that natural selection is now acting almost to the extent of exterminating those classes of which the mothers resort to the mills'.[37] It appears, moreover, that in explaining the 'natural' duties of women in the sexual division of labour, Jevons followed Darwin who argued, in *The Descent of Man* (1871), that women were intellectually inferior to men. Jevons was certainly very impressed by that text and, in his attack on Mill's discussion of the 'pliability' of human nature (Jevons, 1890, p. 292), cited Darwin's criticism of Mill which has since been interpreted (Albury, 1975;

Richards, 1983) as a critique of *The Subjection of Women*.[38] It might be thought that, because Jevons supported the admission of women to tertiary degree courses, he would have dismissed such a claim. However, this conclusion cannot necessarily be drawn because both Darwin and T.H. Huxley supported the admission of women to degree courses, but argued that it would have little effect because of women's inferior capabilities (Albury, 1975; Richards, 1983).

If Jevons's approach was similar to that in the *Descent,* it might be concluded that the following characterization of Darwin applies just as well to Jevons: 'To label him a sexist may be technically correct and emotionally satisfying to those who oppose all manifestations of sexual discrimination, but it is mere rhetoric in the context of a society in which almost everyone was a sexist – who held discriminatory views of women's nature and social role' (Richards, 1983, p. 99). In the case of Jevons, however, it must be emphasized that his policy proposals on 'married women' used a series of arguments which met with strong opposition even from those who accepted his basic assumption on the sexual division of labour. Moreover, his dogmatic arguments were based on a highly selective use of statistics and racist abuse of the Irish, where there was also clear dissent from his position. What is striking about Jevons is his generally punitive approach to the 'lower classes' in which women with young children were a special target.

NOTES

* This is a revised version of a paper presented to a symposium on 'Victorian Political Economists and Moral Scientists and the Women's Issue', at the University of Sydney, May 1992. I would like to thank Geoff Harcourt, Gillian Hewitson, Michael Roberts and participants at the seminar for comments and suggestions. Thanks also to the John Rylands Library, University of Manchester, for permission to quote extracts from the Jevons Archive.

1. 'Married Women in Factories', letter in *The Manchester Guardian,* 14 January 1882, p. 5.
2. Jevons, 1882c, pp. 33–4.
3. The exercise was a 'success' only in establishing Jevons's public name as an economist. The report of the Royal Commission focused on the question of absolute coal supplies which was not the principal concern of *The Coal Question.* The reason for this was, in part, that Jevons's text was principally used as a parliamentary diversionary tactic in 1866 (White, 1991).
4. This chapter (8) was originally published as (Pujol, 1984).

5. 'Inaugural Address as President of the Manchester Statistical Society on the Work of the Society in Connection with the Questions of the Day', reprinted in Jevons, 1883, pp. 180–93.

6 Jevons, 1870, reprinted in Jevons, 1883, pp. 194–216.

7. For the more general context of these remarks, see Roberts 1991, pp. 227–9.

8. OE = original emphasis.

9. See Hewitt, 1958, Ch. 10, for the use of such 'preservatives'.

10. For discussion of the inadequacies of the Act, see Rose, 1986, Chapter 12.

11. Bowman (1989, pp. 1127, 1132) describes Jevons's policy as 'mothers of small children should be ... excluded from the workplace and supported by the state'.

12. The phrases 'wizened little monkeys' and 'little old men' were taken from an 1863 report on child mortality by Dr. H.J. Hunter (see below). Hunter reported that 'surgeons' had used the phrases to refer to the effects of opiates, in Godfrey-type cordials, on children (Privy Council, 1864, p. 460). Jevons argued that the extent of the opiate sales was due to 'excessive competition' between retailers (Jevons, 1883, p. 165). Marx, who also cited Hunter's phrases, took a wider perspective: 'we see here how India and China avenged themselves on England' (Marx, 1974, p. 376).

13. 'Married Women in Factories', *Manchester Guardian*, 2 January 1882, p. 5 (hereinafter *MG*). The subsequent correspondence on Jevons's article appeared principally under this heading. Jevons's letter is reprinted in Black, 1973–81, V, pp. 163–7.

14. The exception was a letter from a clergyman, T.A. Lacey (*MG*, 13 January 1882, p. 7).

15. Letters from W. Darbyshire, *MG*, 7 January 1882, p. 5, and 14 January 1882, p. 5. See also Black, 1973–81, V, p. 162n.

16. See also the letter by 'Janet', *MG*, 13 January 1882, p. 7.

17. An earlier paper had drawn attention to the importance of studying and explaining changes in the amount of ozone in Manchester, in part because of its importance in 'a sanitary point of view'. Baxendell linked changes in ozone to sunspot patterns and therefore to solar radiation, while calling for help from chemists in explaining more local effects in relation to cloud cover (Baxendell, 1869, pp. 24, 31). Jevons then provided a commentary on Baxendell's paper which drew on his work in chemistry and meteorology while in Australia (Jevons, 1869).

18. Jevons's copies of the *Guardian* correspondence (which consisted of eighteen letters between 5 May and 7 July) are in the Jevons Archive, John Rylands Library, University of Manchester, JA6/38/21–26. The calculations by Ransome and Royston, which appeared in two letters on 14 June (p. 6) and 29 June (p. 6), showed that using Baxendell's 'new' method, towns with the highest general mortality rates were presented in a more favourable light than those with the lowest rates.

19. Comments by E.W. Binney in the *Proceedings of the Manchester Literary and Philosophical Society, Session 1871–72*, **11** (1), p. 2.

20. Letter from W. Darbyshire, *MG*, 14 January 1882, p. 5.

21. This was the first 'classic Victorian proof' of the evils of women in factory employment. The second was the decline in the Lancashire infant death-rate during the cotton famine consequent upon the American Civil War. This was explained as the result of mothers losing employment outside the home and hence 'staying at home to breastfeed their babies'. However, as Rose notes, this was a peculiar argument since 'half-starved' mothers could hardly produce adequate breast milk (Rose, 1986, p. 9). Rose's preferred explanation is that falling incomes meant reduced 'maternal alcohol consumption', although the only reference given for this is a Presidential Address by J. Burns, reported in the *National Conference on Infant Mortality* (1906) (ibid., pp. 9, 188).

22. When discussing Hunter's study, the report of the Privy Council's medical officer referred to the 'vast quantity of reckless fornication' in the work gangs (Privy Council, 1864, p. 36).

23. It has been argued recently (Rose, 1986, p. 10) that cottage 'overcrowding' (with a consequent high illegitimacy rate) and the widespread use of opium ('traditionally a palliative against the once widespread fen malaria') produced the high infant death rate. This followed 'overlying' – the suffocation of the child when sleeping in bed with one or two adults. For discussion of overlying in connection with alcoholism in towns, see ibid., pp. 180–81.

24. Jevons's use of an 'efficient' cause entails a 'substantive' notion of cause and effect as compared with a 'contingent' notion of cause as a succession of events (cf. Smith, 1973, pp. 98–9).

25. It is interesting to compare Jevons's account of excess child mortality with that of Marx (Marx, 1974, pp. 372–9). Using a number of the same official reports as Jevons, Marx argued also that married women's factory employment increased mortality rates. However, he explained this as the result of manufacturing sector employers changing the (age and gender) composition of their workforce. The employers were able to do so because of their superior bargaining position, a point which was supported in Hunter's study (Privy Council, 1864, p. 456). For Marx there was no suggestion that the increased employment of married women left their men able to drink more and work less hours. This was because, with the increase in women's paid employment, there was also an increase in family expenses (some work previously done in the home was replaced with purchased commodities). Hence, the increase in market expenditure 'balances the greater income' (Marx, 1974, pp. 373, 379). My attention was drawn to Marx's comments by Sandra Peart (1990a, pp. 39n.–40n.) and Chris Nyland (1987).

26. The article was 'in type' when Jevons drowned (Cooke-Taylor, 1882b, p. 428). Taylor was initially able to respond quickly to Jevons because, in part, he was repeating a number of general arguments he had used in the mid-1870s debate over the employment of women in factories (Cooke-Taylor, 1875).

27. A number of notes, which appear to be Jevons's calculations from this period, can be found in the Jevons Archive (JA6/38/1–64), although it is difficult to see what his precise argument was going to be. However, one note indicates that Jevons was attempting to formulate a statistical 'law': 'let x = per cent of mortality of children under five years. y = per cent^{age} of women over 20 employed in industry[.] then x = y/3' (JA6/38/6).

28. For the background to Collet's paper see Dyhouse, 1978, pp. 252–3. For biographical information on Collet, see below, Chapter 6.

29. The remainder of this section draws on White, 1993b.

30. In March 1877, Jevons was one of the signatories to a Memorial requesting the Governors of Owens College, Manchester, to admit women to lectures and examinations (Manchester Association for Promoting the Higher Education of Women, *Memorial to the Governors of Owens College,* March 1877). At an 1879 public meeting in Manchester, a letter was read from Jevons on the same topic. Based on his experience at University College, London, Jevons argued that the presence of women at lectures 'decidedly raises the tone of behaviour of the men students' and that there were no adverse effects on the 'standard of instruction' ('The Manchester and Salford College for Women', *Manchester Guardian,* 9 October 1879, p. 6).

31. For a different subsequent assessment, see Best, 1979, pp. 121–6.

32. The following paragraphs draw on White, 1993a.

33. For example, without further clarification, it does not seem able to account for the neoclassical 'economics of the family' or work on the 'economics of altruism'. The adequacy of such work is, of course, another matter.

34. Pujol argues that Marshall's use of the family as the unit for 'consumption, welfare decisions or income levels' necessitated jettisoning the basic depiction of the neoclassical economic actor, which was based on 'individualistic rational behaviour' (Pujol, 1992, p. 122). Using the case of Jevons, I have argued elsewhere (White, 1993a) that it is misleading to claim that early English marginalism was based on 'theoretical individualism'. It is easy to show that the same applies to Marshall. It might be noted that, if the latter category provided the basic 'model', it would be difficult to explain the implicit use of the household and the explicit use of class and race categories in *TPE*.

35. Jevons Archive, JA6/5/43, Part V. Characteristically, Jevons could not help adding that 'I am far however from wanting to assert that Mill can permanently stand in so high a rank as Hobbes ...' These notes appear to have been written c.1880–82.

36. For similar comments, see Anonymous, 1871, pp. 231, 261.

37. Jevons Archive, JA6/44/14. The note is scribbled on the back of an envelope with a December 1881 postmark.

38. 'Mr. J.S. Mill speaks, in his celebrated work, *Utilitarianism* (1869, p. 46), of the social feelings as "a powerful natural sentiment," and as "the natural basis of sentiment for utilitarian morality;" but on the previous page he says, "if, as is my own belief, the moral feelings are not innate, but acquired, they are not for that reason less natural." It is with hesitation that I venture to differ from so profound a thinker, but it can hardly be disputed that the social feelings are instinctive or innate in the lower animals; and why should they not be so in man? Mr. Bain and others believe that the moral sense is acquired by each individual during his lifetime. On the general theory of evolution this is at least extremely improbable' (Darwin, 1871, I, p. 71).

4. Alfred Marshall – Women and Economic Development: Labour, Family and Race*

Peter Groenewegen

INTRODUCTION

When Marshall's *Principles of Economics* first appeared in 1890, one perceptive reviewer noted that its rich contents among other things pinpointed the case for women staying at home.[1] That case made its first appearance in Book II dealing with 'some fundamental notions', in the chapter devoted to defining 'necessities', with special reference to 'the efficiency of an ordinary agricultural or of an unskilled town labourer'. Along with a 'well-drained dwelling with several rooms, warm clothing, with some changes of underclothing, pure water, a plentiful supply of cereal food, with a moderate allowance of meat and milk, and a little tea, &c, some education and some recreation', Marshall lastly listed 'sufficient freedom for his wife from other work to enable her to perform properly her maternal and her household duties' among the necessities of the labourer. If deprived of any of these things, the efficiency of the labourer suffered in the same way as that of a horse 'not properly tended' or a steam engine with 'an inadequate supply of coal' (Marshall, 1890, p. 123; 1920, pp. 69–70). Clearly an aspect of the quality of labour supply, Marshall pursued the matter further under that heading. After approvingly quoting Roscher's finding that the Jewish population of Prussia has increased faster than the Christian, though its birth–rate has been lower because 'Jewish mothers seldom go away from their homes to work', Marshall commented on the fiscal illusion inherent in families thinking and acting 'as though the family income was increased by all that the mother earns when she goes out to work'. Marshall's explanation was as follows:

a little consideration would often show that the things she can buy with her earnings are of far less importance for the health and happiness of the family than the mere material services she could have rendered them if she had stayed at home, to say nothing of her moral influence in educating the children, in keeping the household in harmony and making it possible for her husband to be cheered and soothed in his evenings at home. This fact is getting to be understood by the better class of artisans and their wives; and there are not now very many mothers with young families at work in English and American factories (Marshall, 1890, pp. 252–3; 1920, p. 199).

Although, as shown subsequently, Marshall's perspective on the role of the wife in the family had clear implications for wage determination, through its effect on labour supply for example, the issue of the woman's role had a far wider dimension in his thought. It arose, as Edgeworth succinctly put it, from the leading part family life was to play in 'Marshall's ideal State'. This aspect of Edgeworth's reminiscences of Marshall is so instructive on Marshall's general views on the women's issue, that it can be quoted at length.

The central figure would be the wife and mother practising pristine domestic virtues. But her interests were not to be confined to the family circle. At the opening of his remarkable discourse on the future of the working classes 1873 – comparable with Mill's chapter on that subject – Marshall asks 'Whether the quick insight of woman may not be trained so as to give material assistance to man in ordering public as well as private affairs.' Nothing that I have heard him say or have read in his writings leads me to believe that he answered this question in the negative. He had in his own home a proof that all the virtues and graces of domestic life could be combined with ability to assist in the preparation of the greatest modern treatise on the economic interests of men.

Concerns for the practice of family duties was the ground of Marshall's opposition to the granting of degrees to women (1896). Without offering an opinion on this issue, I may point out that his arguments were deduced from principles which with general approbation he applied to another issue, that which is raised by Socialism. Again and again he has expressed sympathy with the generous aspirations of the socialists, while declining to follow them far on untried abrupt paths. In a similar spirit he urges the Cambridge Senate to begin with half measures, to wait for experience before taking a step of doubtful policy but great magnitude.

It was not only in the matter of education that Marshall deprecated the identical treatment of men and women. In the most intimate of talks which I have had with him he expressed himself as opposed to current ideas which made for shaping the lives of men and women on the same model. In this connection he expressed strong dissent from some of Mill's treatment of sex as an 'accident'. Some loss of individual liberty, Marshall thought, should be risked for the sake of preserving the family. He regarded the family as a cathedral, something more sacred than the component parts. If I might complete the metaphor in my own words so as to convey the impression which I received: whereas the structure as it stands is not perfectly symmetrical, the attempt to make it so might result in pulling it down (Edgeworth, 1925, pp. 72–3).

Rather than looking at the whole of Marshall's views on the women's issue, some of them analysed in detail by Rita McWilliams-Tullberg (1975, 1990, 1991), this chapter examines Marshall's views on the role of women in the investment process leading to human capital creation, on the determinants of women's wages and on the role of women in the workforce. In addition, it focuses on two issues guiding the mature Marshall in his decided views on the role of women in society. One relates to his interest both as a Labour Commissioner, and more generally, as social investigator eager to discover facets of women's labour impinging on their nurturing role in the family. The second relates to his 'social Darwinist views' on marriage, heredity, race progress and social progress. The chapter therefore explores aspects of Marshall's thought which have tended to be ignored in the literature so far (for a partial exception, see Pujol, 1984; 1992, Chapter 8) although they all have an important bearing on what he himself used to call 'the high theme of economic progress' (Marshall, 1920, p. 461, cf. p. xv).

WOMEN'S WORK BEST CONFINED TO THE HOME

Work, work, work,
From weary chime to chime;
Work, work, work,
As prisoners work for crime,
Band and gusset and seam,
Seam and gusset and band,
Till the heart is sick and the brain benumbed
As well as the weary hand.

Oh! but for one short hour,
A respite, however brief!
No blessed leisure for love or hope,
But only time for grief!
A little weeping would ease my heart,
But in their briny bed
My tears must stop, for every drop

Hinders needle and thread.
(cited in Marshall, 1873, p. 109).

The interest in the plight of the needle-woman revealed by Alfred
Marshall's choice to quote from this poem in his first published paper on
economics in 1873 was an interest in the conditions of women's work
not sustained in his later published work. Even in that first paper the
inferences Marshall drew from the poem immediately eliminated its
gender references. Its subsequent contents dwelled on the situation of
the working classes as a whole and, more particularly, the consequences
from certain types of work for men:

> Surely we see here how work may depress, and keep low 'the working classes.'
> Man ought to work in order to live: his life, physical, moral, and mental, should be
> strengthened and made full by his work. But what if his inner life be almost
> crushed by his work? Is there not then suggested a terrible truth by the term
> working man, when applied to the unskilled labourer – a man whose occupation
> tends in a greater or less degree to make him live for little save for that work that is
> a burden to bear? (Marshall, 1873, p. 108).

In fact, Marshall's subsequent economic writing reveals relatively little
interest in the condition of working women and associated issues such
as women's wages. The *Economics of Industry*, written jointly with his
wife, Mary Paley Marshall, herself a married working woman, is the
major exception to this.[2] This is not to say that women had no place in
Marshall's scheme of things economic: their crucial role in the family,
particularly that associated with the nurture of young children, was
frequently stressed in his major published work.

References to women as paid workers are, however, surprisingly
infrequent in the pages of the *Principles*. The following remarks exhaust
his comments on women's work *per se*. In the context of the division
of labour, women managing machine looms are said to have work far
less monotonous and calling for much greater judgements than that
associated with the former hand-loom weaver (Marshall, 1890, p. 316;
1920, p. 263). As an important industrial locational factor, textile works
and other factory employers of women and children are claimed to be
frequently situated in iron districts, because in their absence
employment can only be found in such regions for 'strong men' and
average family earnings are consequently low (Marshall, 1890, p. 333;
1920, p. 273). In the chapter devoted to general influences of economic

progress, women's factory work is equated to that of children in terms of required skill, ranking below that of 'men of ordinary capacity' (Marshall, 1890, p. 724; 1920, p. 682).[3] Last, but not least, social progress is associated by Marshall with the interest of 'the coming generation ... in the rescue of men, and still more in that of women, from excessive work; at least as much as it is in the handing down to it of a good stock of material wealth' (Marshall, 1920, p. 694).[4]

Progress is also associated in the *Principles* with the relative improvement of women's wages. 'The wages of women are for similar reasons [their ability to handle machines and raised skills from the spread of education] rising fast relative to those of men. And this is a great gain in so far as it tends to develop their faculties; but an injury in so far as it tempts them to neglect their duty of building up a true home, and of investing their efforts in the personal capital of their children's character and abilities.' (Marshall, 1890, pp. 727–8; 1920, p. 685). Apart from the reason stated in this passage, soon to be elaborated, higher relative wages for women were not necessarily a good thing in Marshall's view because of their potential effect on the family wage. Marshall provided some views on the connection between the family wage and the individual (male) wage in the context of minimum wage legislation for men and women workers:

> This last consideration seems to have been pushed on one side largely under the influence of a faulty analysis of the nature of 'parasitic' work and of its influence on wages. The family is, in the main, a single unit as regards geographical migration: and therefore the wages of men are relatively high, and those of women and children low where heavy iron or other industries preponderate, while in some other districts less than half the money income of the family is earned by the father, and men's wages are relatively low. This natural adjustment is socially beneficial, and rigid national rules as to minimum wages for men and for women, which ignore or oppose it, are to be deprecated (Marshall, 1920, p. 715 n.1).[5]

Marshall remained rather sceptical of the minimum wage notion for the whole of his life. The fact that only Australasia provided practical guidance on its operation at this stage was one reason. Moreover, he feared that minimum wage legislation would not be made effective and hence that its great potential benefits would not be fully secured. Such benefits included the contribution minimum wage legislation could make to removing much hardship for the most disadvantaged class of the population which he described as 'the residuum' (Marshall, 1920, pp. 714–15).

Two issues need to be more fully explored here. In the first place, Marshall's notion of a family wage has an occasional ambiguity. Often it implies a number of wage earners in a family. A note in the *Principles* (Marshall, 1890, p. 45 n.1, and for its subsequent revisions, see Marshall, 1961, Vol. 2, p. 733) implies five wage earners in an artisan's family, sharing the increases in earnings to which the text refers. More generally, as in the last passage from the *Principles* quoted, family wage is defined as the aggregate earnings of a husband, wife and children employed. On other occasions, a family wage is identified with the necessaries to maintain a family in adequate comfort. A minimum family wage would then be designed to secure a satisfactory standard of comfort for the breadwinner in the household and its dependent members. Such a minimum family wage would therefore have been the most satisfactory means for securing Marshall's objectives of ensuring an adequate standard of life for the working classes without the necessity of sending wives and young children to work. However, and this is the second point, Marshall never seriously entertained the thought of adopting a minimum wage. In fact, he endorsed the Labour Commission's view that minimum or maximum rates of pay should not be legislated as a matter of principle. Marshall failed to link women's work explicitly at any time with economic necessity, perhaps generalizing here from his own middle-class experience where working wives and daughters indulged a desire to work from motives other than financial need. This indicates a further limitation to his analysis of this segment of the labour market by a failure to distinguish between the different types of need which made particular classes of women enter the labour market.

Marshall's reference to locational aspect in the family wage returned to a theme in women's wage determination which he had first broached in *Economics of Industry* (Marshall and Marshall, 1879, p. 175). Its more detailed analysis of the reasons for low female wages in England, not repeated in such a clear and succinct form in the later *Principles*, is worth quoting in full:

> In England many women get low wages, not because the value of the work they do is low, but because both they and their employers have been in the habit of taking it for granted that the wages of women must be low. Sometimes even when men and

women do the same work in the same factory, not only the Time-wages, but also the Task-wages of the women are lower than those of the men. In so far as this inequality is due to custom, it will disappear with the progress of intelligence and of the habits of competition. But more of it than at first sight appears, is due to causes that are likely to be permanent. Employers say that if a man and a woman are equally good workers, the woman is of less service in the long run. For although she is generally more anxious than a man is to merit the approval of the employer or overlooker, – she does not give up her whole mind to her work in the same way as a man does: her work is more liable to be interrupted than that of a man, and she is less likely to continue at it during her whole life: partly for these reasons, her thoughts are occupied more about her home and less about the place in which she works than his are, and she has on the whole less persistence, and less judgment and resource in cases of difficulty. Thus though the accuracy with which women follow their instructions is very serviceable in some branches of the work, the employer often prefers to have men, because he can select from them foremen and overlookers as well as workers in those branches of the business in which discretion is wanted. Again many kinds of work which are generally regarded as light, occasionally require the use of great physical strength, and perhaps the working overtime in special emergencies; and for such work women are at a disadvantage. Thus the occupations for which women are well fitted are few, and therefore overcrowded and badly paid. And this influences custom and general opinion, and causes women to be underpaid when they are doing difficult work well (Marshall and Marshall, 1879, pp. 175–6).[6]

At this stage, the Marshalls expected part of the unequal pay problem to disappear with the progress of science, machinery and education, combined with some learning from French experience where much more of the work of business management was then in the hands of women as compared with England. The *Principles* later only pursued the argument with respect to the influence of machinery on the quality of work and of education in raising skills and breaking down prejudice with respect to wages and labour conditions in general and without reference to unequal pay between men and women. Moreover, the Marshalls' proud report that the largest and most successful brass works in Birmingham employed a woman as general manager, an example which needed to be more widely followed (Marshall and Marshall 1879, pp. 176–7), was not reproduced in the *Principles*.

As already indicated, the Marshall of the *Principles* did not approve of high wages for women if this interfered with the crucial role women played in the family. In the first place, the female nurturing role benefited the level of 'general ability' in the nation. Such 'general ability', was a key factor in securing a productive and inventive work force for the nation. It 'depends largely on the surroundings of childhood and youth' and here 'the first far the most important influence is that of the mother', followed in turn by that of the father, of household servants and of the school. In this context Marshall noted Galton's statement, that 'all great men have had great mothers', is an exaggeration, since this remark can only show:

> that the mother's influence does not outweigh all others; not that it is not greater than any one of them. He [Galton] says that the mother's influence is most easily traceable among theologians and men of science, because an earnest mother leads her child to feel deeply about great things; and a thoughtful mother does not repress, but encourages that childish curiosity which is the raw material of scientific habits of thought (Marshall, 1890, p. 263, n.1; 1920, p. 207, n.1).[7]

There are in addition longer-term influences of the responsible mother on labour supply. A beneficial effect of high wages on the death-rate may be diminished if mothers as a consequence neglect their duties to their children, while the strictly necessary consumption for the reproduction on a steadily improving workforce requires that adults take good care of their children (Marshall, 1920, p. 529).[8]   Other more detailed references to the importance of this essentially female role in the nurture of children as an investment in human capital can be given. A striking example occurs in the following remarks:

> If we compare one country of the civilized world with another, or one part of England with another, or one trade in England with another, we find that the degradation of the working-classes varies almost uniformly with the amount of rough work done by women. The most valuable of all capital is that invested in human beings; and of that capital the most precious part is the result of the care and influence of the mother, so long as she retains her tender and unselfish instincts, and has not been hardened by the strain and stress of unfeminine work.

> This draws our attention to another aspect of the principle already noticed, that in estimating the cost of production of efficient labour, we must often take as our unit the family. At all events we cannot treat the cost of production of efficient men as an isolated problem; it must be taken as part of the broader problem of the cost of production of efficient men together with the women who are fitted to make their home happy, and to bring up their children vigorous in body and mind, truthful and cleanly, gentle and brave (Marshall, 1890, pp. 592–3; 1920, p. 564).[9]

Although in this context of the nurturing role in families, it is perhaps tempting to replace Marshall's emphasis on women's duties in the family with that on the mother alone, this was not what Marshall had in mind and kept to the forefront of the discussion. His was a wide notion of female family responsibility, that is, covering both mothers and daughters. He clearly explained this in his evidence to the Committee on Higher Education in Wales and Monmouthshire during December 1880. In the context of higher education for girls, Marshall indicated that 'the number of girls who can leave home [for higher education] is really very small' because 'the best women generally speaking are women whose families require part of their time; generally they have duties to perform to their fathers and mothers and sisters and brothers that take up some part of their time, and while a woman can give half her time for six years much more easily than a man can, she cannot give her whole time for three years as easily as a man can.'[10]   Follow-up questions showed that Marshall was thinking here of college-aged girls, 17 to 23 years old, and that the best of these girls, as 'the bright lights in their families' are indispensable to these families because they not only make the 'home cheerful' but 'educate younger brothers and sisters', a matter which his experience as Principal at Bristol University College had brought home to him.[11]   A further reason for Marshall's mature opinion on the nurturing role of girls in the family can be found in his own upbringing and family experience, in which his mother, his Aunt Louisa and his sisters Agnes and Mabel Louisa, played a particularly important role.[12]

Not directly as workers but indirectly as nurturers and shapers of the future labour force were women important in Marshall's vision of a future civilized and developed society. High wages and improved methods of production were therefore useful in his scheme of things as catalysts to free women, young and old, from the drudgery of factory and domestic service to enable them to concentrate all the better on their family responsibilities. Such views were of course not novel in the late nineteenth century. They were echoed, for example, by Sidney Webb's evidence to the Labour Commission, which indicated that, rather than prohibiting the employment of married women, 'the proper policy is to hasten the advent of such a social development in which mothers of families should be released from their present necessity of working for their living.'[13] Webb, however, advanced the notion of a high minimum wage to cater adequately for dependents, a solution which Marshall was unwilling to consider from principle. In this way, the *Principles* presented his vision of woman's future cogently, clearly but selectively when elaborating the national as well as the social and economic benefits which could be derived from it. Part of that selectivity arose from his obfuscation of the different motives which took women into paid employment and his tendency to confine solutions to the problems to ones to which he could in principle give approval. For Marshall, this ruled out legislated minimum family wages such as Webb endorsed, and generated a tendency unduly to treat working women as a homogeneous group independent of marital status or social class.

AN EMPIRICIST ON WOMEN'S WORK

In early 1891 Marshall was appointed to serve on the Labour Commission, set up by the Government of the day to investigate conditions of labour and industrial relations which could shed light on the causes of industrial disputes.   Marshall's membership of the Commission involved him in attending its hearings and by assisting in the drafting of its *Final Report*, an involvement in its work which Marshall described in the final years of his life as the most educational experience he had ever enjoyed (Marshall, 1919, pp. vi–vii).   The Commission saw its role as fact gathering, and among the mountain of material it published was an extensive report on women's labour prepared for it by four assistant lady Commissioners, and generally praised as one of the better outcomes from the Commission's work (Webb, 1894, pp. 2–3, 21; Collette, 1989, pp. 13–14).

Little concrete evidence in the form of written material remains on what type of influence the Commission had on Marshall's thinking (Groenewegen, 1994). However, his active participation in the taking of evidence suggests that he used that opportunity of contact with working leaders, unionists and employers in part to further his knowledge about the influence of women's work on the manner in which working women could fulfil their household responsibilities. This corroborated views earlier expressed on the subject in the *Principles*. Marshall's tours of factories in the previous decade, as far as ascertainable from the notes taken by his wife on these occasions, were an earlier source of information on this subject. In combination, they provided part of the empirical foundation for the mature views on woman's socio-economic role which Marshall developed in his *Principles*, in conjunction with the inspiration on this subject he gained as an educationist.

Marshall's membership of Committee B of the Commission, devoted largely to labour conditions in transport, enabled him to enquire at some length about the consequences for children's upbringing from women working on barges. Part of his questioning concerned the 'unwomanly nature' of the work on barges, in terms of its form and the hours of labour, part of it consisted in ascertaining facts on the educational opportunities for the children of married couples employed in this segment of the transport industry. Its aim was to discover whether suitable methods of inspection could be found to ensure that barge children received adequate education or whether it was feasible to end women's labour on the ships. On both scores the answers Marshall received tended to be in the negative (Royal Commission on Labour 1892, pp. 300–301, 305; 1893, p. 22). In addition, Marshall sought more general information on the attitudes of male workers to women's employment, for example, in the upholstery-making industry; and on the prohibition in certain trades against the employment of married women (Royal Commission on Labour, 1893a, pp. 220–21).

At a more general level, Marshall learned much on the subject from the Commission's Reports on the Employment of Women and Women's Labour Conditions (Royal Commission on Labour, 1894a, pp. 478–82, 507–10).[14] In the matter of wages, these corroborated the vast differential between male weekly wages and those paid to women and girls. This ranged from an almost threefold difference in the silk industries and the potteries to a little less than double in the retail trade, in textiles and footwear. The gradual and general rise in women's wages over time, the *Principles* proclaimed, likewise found support in the statistical investigations of the Commission, particularly when interpreted in real terms. However, these data also indicated that in the three decades before 1890 the growth in male wages far outstripped the most favourable wage growth for women, contrary to the drift of the general trend in this differential Marshall had reported in the *Principles* (Marshall, 1890, pp. 727–8, 1920, p. 689).[15]

Marshall's hostility to the work of married women in factories would have been strongly reinforced by the information gathered on this subject through the Commission. Considerable evidence was collected on the deleterious effects on the health of children of married women who worked; both from 'careless nursing' on the part of working mothers and from the 'injudicious treatment' children received from their minders while the mothers were at work.   Medical officers corroborated this evidence. Among the worst consequences of the all too frequent inexperience, youth and negligence of the child-minders, were excessive use of sleeping draughts for quietening their charges, accidents from burns or scalds, and exposure to the influence of bad weather. Partly from its long and irregular hours, work at home in the 'sweated' trade carried dangers with it for the sleep of the children, as well as of ill-health for the women engaged in it.   In addition, making home the workplace entailed other sanitary hazards. The Commission also found that heavy and dangerous work in the chemical and white-lead industries, as well as in nail- and chain-making, by affecting both mothers and their future offspring was doubly bad. Finally, the picture it painted of sanitary conditions in many workplaces, and the particular dangers from the nature of employment in specific industries, demonstrated that many of the employment opportunities for women were highly unsuitable for those involved in the rearing of children. The summary evidence reported on this issue to the Commission therefore explains the dangers to the future generations Marshall diagnosed as the major cost of working women. The appropriate remedy for such evils could be found, of course, equally well in better factory legislation combined with improvement in its enforcement, as in active discouragement of the employment of married women. This was a point Marshall invariably failed to make.

The Final Report of the Commission (Royal Commission, 1894b) was rather cautious on the issue of employment of married women. Since Marshall signed it without reservations, he must have agreed with its thrust.   The Commission listed four objections against the employment of married women. The first of these concerned complaints that married women competed unfairly with unmarried women, since their husbands' wages enabled them to work for lower rates than their unmarried female competitors. More relevant to Marshall's views on the impact of working married women on domestic duties, the Commission reported considerable evidence that in this situation, 'homes are made comfortless, and children and husbands neglected'. This not only came from oral evidence presented by workmen, it was confirmed 'in some instances' from 'the personal inspection made by the Lady Assistant Commissioners'. Heavy labour for women at a time when they were close to childbirth was likewise condemned in the case of specific industries such as nail- and chain-making, as were the dangers of employment of married women in white-lead works and potteries because of the effects of absorbed poison and dust to both themselves and their children. Finally, the employment of mothers in factories was condemned as generally harmful to their children. In particular, medical evidence was cited to support a period of non-work for three months after childbirth in the interest of lowering infant mortality in specific factory districts. The Commission did not see more legislation as the answer to most of these complaints. Two reasons were given: the presence of young children in the family often created an economic necessity for the woman to work; second, married women were said to prefer factory work to escape the monotony of a life exclusively devoted to domestic duties. Few other recommendations on the subject of women's labour were presented by the Commission to ameliorate these distressing conditions, with the exception of suggestions for improvements in factory inspection (Royal Commission of Labour, 1894b, pp. 93–4, 107–9).[16]

Marshall's work on the Labour Commission only reinforced his views on the longer-term detrimental consequences of women's work in factories in 'unwomanly' occupations. After all, he had published such views with little variation from the first edition of the *Principles* in 1890. Much of the data on which these views had been formed were gathered during the tours of inspection of factories the Marshalls tended to organize as part of their English summer vacations during the 1880s and after. These followed a pattern Marshall himself appears to have initiated when he first became interested in social questions during the late 1860s. An 1883 visit to the Worcestershire pottery industry produced notes (in Mary Paley's handwriting), commenting on the substantial employment it offered to women, 'largely in unskilled, mechanical tasks' while their 'apprenticed work' was confined to 'low grade painting and transferring'. The notes also indicated that women did most of the unsanitary work, such as 'scrubbing of the biscuit pottery' with its high risk of respiratory illness from inhaling the ensuing dust, and dipping pottery ware into glaze containing lead. Nevertheless, women continued in their place of employment in the potteries after marriage because they found the work on the whole pleasant and healthy, except from the dust and heat of the kilns.[17] More detailed notes have been preserved of a similar tour in the summer of

1885, taking in Cumbria and the Lake District. Its evidence was mixed on the issue at hand, reporting as it did on the suitability of women for factory work, but also on some of its consequences: 'dirty children' and women's tasks concentrated in 'dirty and disagreeable work'.

> Barrow: rapid growth. Saw large steel works and beautiful factory girl. Is factory life or domestic service best (i) for the girl (ii) for the race? Wonderful floating dry dock. Saw varieties of ore. Bessemer process.

> August 15. Lancaster. Charming, rather conservative looking old town but good deal of manufacture chiefly furniture. Beautiful park with wonderful air and view. Visited Gillows. Machines for cutting square furniture. Advantages of large production make it worthwhile to have excellent design. No women employed except for sewing upholstery. The most artistic woodcarvers are Irishmen. Deaf and dumb wood carvers.

> August 25–27. Preston. Fine enterprising town. Most beautiful hotel we have seen. Aug. 26. Visited Horrocks spinning and weaving mills. Went in trams and walked in working people's quarter. Children dirty. Excellent houses and furniture nearly universal. Favourite ornaments: large china dogs. Quiet and respectable appearances of factory women. August 27. Visited spinning and weaving mills. Were taken over works by head manager. He preferred women to men for all work except overlooking engineers. Said they were easier to manage and cleverer with fingers. Said that present strike in cotton trade might lead to employing women to mind self acting mules. Present objection to their doing so is the amount of exercise required equal to walking 20 or 30 miles. Probably machine can be modified. He said it was common for mothers of young children to work. Said the women grew very fond of the work. Not uncommon for a family to make £4 a week. Noticed high ratio of women to men in Preston especially when over 15 years. Many Irish ....

> [September 21st. Sheffield] .... In afternoon saw Hutton's electroplate establishment. Were struck by inferiority of machinery. Women employed at scrubbery, electroplating, burnishing and packing. The scrubbing was very dirty and disagreeable work ....

The next day the Marshalls inspected a file making works 'and we saw all the process'. Advantages of the file cutting by machine were demonstrated by the fact that hand cutting required no less than a seven-year apprenticeship while after only three hours a girl with a machine 'could cut files fairly well. Guide said that the handcutters were gradually put to machine and there earned higher wages'. In 1888, a trip which included Leicester brought the following observation from a factory making boots and shoes:

Machinery, very complex and interesting. One machine had a metre to record stitches and 5d. per 1000 had to be paid to owner of the patent, an agent coming round to inspect metre from time to time. Machines for bending the 'uppers' for button holes, for putting in eyes. The work requiring most attention was clicking, or cutting out the uppers from the hides. The manager spoke very highly of the women; they were employed in such work as putting eyes in, button holing and stitching, for which last work some earned £1 a week. He said the women were quick and clever and could become checkers – only the men would object – only he confessed that marriage would interfere with the training to such work, and he objected to employing married women unless in exceptional cases. The women employed were very high class looking, and looked very healthy and cheerful. He said that they used their money better than the young men; they earned a good deal. He said that boys often earned high wages and spent them badly. One lad of 14 earned 16/– a week; 6/– he gave to his parents for board and 10[/–] would be wasted in theatre, gambling, etc. That men often only gave their wives half their wages and wasted the rest.

Evidence gathered by the Marshalls on the value of women as workers because of their special advantages and skills, had already been noted by Mill (1865, p. 179). It was, however, ignored by Marshall in the *Principles*, who likewise omitted any reference to hostile male reactions to such female workers' qualities in his account of labour and production.   This reveals that Marshall was prone to a certain selectiveness in his use of evidence, and a tendency to reject factual material not congenial to him.

Given his first-hand experience with women's work in factories and the dangers to which this occasionally exposed them, it is not surprising that Marshall used such information to argue for confining women's employment to more genteel occupations. Nursing, teaching and social work, all derivative from and associated with what he saw as women's main function in life in domestic household duties of serving the family, were the type of work, preferably on a voluntary basis, in which he liked to see women involved. Marshall expressed this strong belief in the necessity of such a sexual division of labour on many occasions, particularly in the context of intellectual pursuits and education. By way of example, a conversation on the subject with Beatrice Webb may be quoted first.

Interesting talk with Professor Marshall, first at dinner at the Creightons, and afterwards at lunch at his own house. It opened with chaff about men and women; he holding that woman was a subordinate being, and that, if she ceased to be subordinate, there would be no object for a man to marry. That marriage was a sacrifice of masculine freedom, and would only be tolerated by male creatures so long as it meant the devotion, body and soul, of the female to the male. Hence the woman must not develop her faculties in a way unpleasant to the man: that strength, courage, independence were not attractive in women; that rivalry in men's pursuits was positively unpleasant. Hence masculine strength and masculine ability in women must be firmly trampled on and boycotted by men. *Contrast* was the essence of the matrimonial relation: feminine weakness contrasted with masculine strength: masculine egotism with feminine self-devotion.

'If you compete with us we shan't marry you,' he summed up with a laugh. I maintained the opposite argument; that there was an ideal of character in which strength, courage, sympathy, self-devotion, persistent purpose were united to a clear and far-seeing intellect; that the ideal was common to the man and to the woman; that these qualities might manifest themselves in different ways in the man's and woman's life; that what you needed was not different qualities and different defects, but the same virtues working in different directions, and dedicated to the service of the community in different ways.

At lunch at his house our discussion was more practical. He said that he had heard that I was about to undertake a history of Co-operation.

'Do you think I am equal to it?' I asked.

'Now, Miss Potter, I am going to be perfectly frank: of course I think you are equal to a history of Co-operation: but it is not what you can do best. There is one thing that *you* and only you can do – an inquiry into the unknown field of female labour. You have, unlike most women, a fairly trained intellect, and the courage and capacity for original work; and you have a woman's insight into a woman's life. There is no man in England who could undertake with any prospect of success an enquiry into female labour. There are any number of men who could write a history of Co-operation, and would bring to this study of a purely economic question far greater strength and knowledge than you possess. For instance, your views on the relative amount of profit in the different trades, and the reason of the success of Co-operation in cotton and its failure in the woollen industry might interest me; but I should read what you said with grave doubt as to whether you had really probed the matter. On the other hand, if you describe the factors enabling combinations of women in one trade and destroying all chance of it in the other, I should take what you said as the opinion of the best authority on the subject. I should think to myself, well, if Miss Potter has not succeeded in sifting these facts no one else will do so, so I may as well take her conclusion as the final one. To sum up with perfect frankness: if you devote yourself to the study of your own sex as an industrial factor, your name will be a household word two hundred years hence: if you write a history of Co-operation it will be superseded and ignored in a year or two. In the one case you will be using unique qualities which no one else possesses, and in the other you will be using faculties which are common to most men, and given to a great many among them in a much higher degree. A book by you on the Cooperative Movement I may get my wife to read to me in the evening to while away the time, but I shan't pay any attention to it,' he added with shrill emphasis.

Of course I disputed the point, and tried to make him realise that I wanted this study in industrial administration as an education for economic science. The little professor, with bright eyes, shrugged his shoulders and became satirical on the subject of a woman dealing with scientific generalisation; not unkindly satirical, but chaffingly so. He stuck to his point and heaped on flattery to compensate for depreciation (Webb, 1938, pp. 398–9).[18]

Two fragments preserved in the Marshall Library, one dating from 1884 on technical education, and an undated one on the higher education of women, both filed with general notes on production and the division of labour, reiterate some of the views mentioned to Beatrice Webb and place them in a broader perspective. First the brief fragment on women and technical education, containing little more than a few sentences in note form.

What women can do.
Of course they may work as man in some cases this is no doubt right.
A washer woman ought certainly to have technical knowledge.
That the great point is that they are trained. If they will teach their children to do whatever they do with all their might, we all soon become a skilled nation.[19]

Second, a longer fragment headed 'The higher education of women'.[20]

This does not mean the opening to them new regions of thought. Their studies are, in name at least, ambitious as they are.
It means educating and applying firstly, the power of sustained close attention to one difficult point after another, and secondly, the power of consecutive thought in a large number of difficult points taken together so as to be able to realise the mutual relations of the various positions of one whole body of knowledge, thought or active feeling.

These powers do not constitute originality but they are absolutely indispensable conditions of it; provided the originality is to be of any service to the world. A one sided originality such as Rousseau's, great in its effects for good but often also great in its effects for evil, can be attained by long, continued brooding over one leading thought, emotion, desire, or artistic enthusiasm [Rousseau's life was one such long continued brooding] without systematic firm-willed thinking out of difficulties.

There is every reason to believe that the reason why women have held the first place in so very few departments even of literature and art is that they have not, save in exceptional cases, had such a training.

Whether five thousand years ago there was a distinction between the calibre of men's and women's minds, and whether there will be such a distinction five thousand years hence may be an open question. It is certain that such a distinction exists now: that women are quicker to perceive and more strengthful to feel than men; but that, on the average, they have less power of sustained concentration.

As Rita McWilliams-Tullberg (1991, p. 235) has shown, Marshall applied his doctrine of sexual division of labour also to economics studies. Fragments preserved in the Marshall Library indicate the nature of the division of labour he had in mind, partly generalized it seems from the advice he had given to Beatrice Webb some years before. Moreover, its specific implications for women's potential to contribute significantly to advanced work in economics was made quite explicit, a perception which explains Mary Paley's delight in 1933 when, on the publication of Joan Robinson's *The Economics of Imperfect Competition*, she told people she would now be able to inform her late husband that this event invalidated his thesis that women were incapable of developing economic theory and analysis (cited in Harcourt, 1982, p. 349). Marshall's musings on this aspect of female incapacity can be quoted in full: 'Economics is like a fine chest of tools, which will not turn out anything of value except in skilful hands. This indicates that economics is a subject generally unsuited for advance by women.' Women had comparative advantage in 'minor inquiries' enabling use of their specialized resource endowments of which the following were important examples:

a. abundance of leisure;
b. interest in the concrete;
c. interest in personal matters;
d. sympathies;
e. access to the Unimportant individually, but numerous and therefore important collectively;
f. power of pursuing certain delicate inquiries relating to women and children in which a man would be out of his element (cited in Rita McWilliams-Tullberg, 1991, p. 235).

of which the last could be called the Beatrice Webb case.

For Marshall therefore, his personal experience from observation and practice at the university had shown the need for a sexual division of labour from the 'self-evident' nature of things, at least in the foreseeable future.[21]   Women's 'natural' role in the family as child nurturers, mothers, comforters and guardians of a wholesome environment barred them from 'unwomanly' activities in factories and workshops. Their different mental capacities implied a distinct position for them from men with respect to the higher occupations of the professions and the arts. Ergo, their widely accepted status as home makers in the service of the family, combined with associated, if not derivative, occupations of nursing, teaching and organized charity or social work were the best possible outcome for the type of world and society which could be realistically envisaged. It also secured, as the scientific evidence showed to Marshall's satisfaction, the maximum benefit for the future of nation and race.

EVOLUTION, EUGENICS, CRANIOMETRY AND SEXUAL DIVISION OF LABOUR

The wider issues for the future which the perspectives of women's social and economic role raised for Marshall reflect his strong interest in evolutionary theory, 'social Darwinism', and its implications for heredity and eugenics. Although Marshall like most of his intellectual contemporaries had studied Darwin's *Origin of Species* during the 1860s and appreciated the importance of the ideas on social and biological evolution as developed by Herbert Spencer for the greater part of his life (Whitaker, 1977, especially pp. 459, 470–72, 477–8), such evolutionary views were not really interwoven with the fabric of his mature economic thought until he started writing the *Principles* from the early 1880s (Becattini, 1975, p. xix). Its motto from the title page, *natura non facit saltum*, combined with the *Principles'* underlying theme of demonstrating the principle of continuity in economic and social life in its various manifestations, emphasized the importance of these evolutionary aspects to Marshall's foundations for the science of man in the ordinary business of life. His perspectives on the importance and role of the family in social progress are a striking, and not too well known, illustration of this tendency in the *Principles*. A particularly fine example in this context is the opening chapter on industrial organization of the *Principles*, where this theme recurs again and again, and whose concluding section can be quoted to illustrate the features of his work to which this section draws attention:

Herbert Spencer has insisted with much force on the rule that, if any physical or mental exercise gives pleasure and is therefore frequent, those physical or mental organs which are used in it are likely to grow rapidly. Among the lower animals indeed the action of this rule is so intimately interwoven with that of the survival of the fittest, that the distinction between the two need not often be emphasised. For as it might be guessed *a priori*, and as seems to be proved by observation, the struggle for survival tends to prevent animals from taking much pleasure in the exercise of functions which do not contribute to their well-being.

But man, with his strong individuality, has greater freedom. He delights in the use of his faculties for their own sake; sometimes using them nobly, whether with the abandon of the great Greek burst of life, or under the control of a deliberate and steadfast striving towards important ends; sometimes ignobly, as in the case of a morbid development of the taste for drink. The religious, the moral, the intellectual and the artistic faculties on which the progress of industry depends, are not acquired solely for the sake of the things that may be got by them; but are developed by exercise for the sake of the pleasure and the happiness which they themselves bring: and, in the same way, that greater factor of economic prosperity, the organisation of a well-ordered state, in the product of an infinite variety of motives; many of which have no direct connection with the pursuit of national wealth.

No doubt it is true that physical peculiarities acquired by the parents during their life-time are seldom if ever transmitted to their offspring. But no conclusive case seems to have been made out for the assertion that the children of those who have led healthy lives, physically and morally, will not be born with a firmer fibre than they would have been had the same parents grown up under unwholesome influences which had enfeebled the fibre of their minds and their bodies. And it is certain that in the former case the children are likely after birth to be better nourished, and better trained; to acquire more wholesome instincts; and to have more of that regard for others and that self-respect, which are the mainsprings of human progress, than in the latter case.

It is needful then diligently to inquire whether the present industrial organisation might not with advantage be so modified as to increase the opportunities which the lower grades of industry have for using latent mental faculties, for deriving pleasure from their use, and for strengthening them by use; since the argument that if such a change had been beneficial, it would have been already brought about by the struggle for survival, must be rejected as invalid. Man's prerogative extends to a limited but effective control over natural development by forecasting the future and preparing the way for the next step.

Thus progress may be hastened by thought and work; by the application of the principles of Eugenics to the replenishment of the race from its higher rather than its lower strains, and by the appropriate education of the faculties of either sex: but however hastened it must be gradual and relatively slow. It must be slow relatively to man's growing command over technique and the forces of nature; a command which is making ever growing calls for courage and caution, for resource and steadfastness, for penetrating insight and for breadth of view. And it must be very much too slow to keep pace with the rapid inflow of proposals for the prompt reorganisation of society on a new basis. In fact our new command over nature, while opening the door to much larger schemes for industrial organisation than were physically possible even a short time ago, places greater responsibilities on those who would advocate new developments of social and industrial structure. For though, institutions may be changed rapidly; yet if they are to endure they must be appropriate to man: they cannot retain their stability if they change very much faster than he does. Thus progress itself increases the urgency of the warning that in the economic world, *Natura non facit saltum*.

Progress must be slow; but even from the merely material point of view it is to be remembered that changes, which add only a little to the immediate efficiency of production, may be worth having if they make mankind ready and fit for an organisation, which will be more effective in the production of wealth and more equal in its distribution;   and that every system, which allows for the higher faculties of the lower grades of industry to go to waste, is open to grave suspicion (Marshall, 1920, pp. 242–9).[22]

Marshall's fairly optimistic picture on the potential of mankind to control its destiny followed a more pessimistic prognosis on the future of the race. This was based on the weakening of natural, evolutionary forces as the means of preserving the 'vigour' of the population through a variety of causes. These included medical success in eliminating some infectious diseases and the growing tendency of the better classes of society to limit the size of their families, often for selfish economic reasons. Once again, these remarks highlight responsibility and duty of the family unit for Marshall, focusing particularly on the importance of the mother in ensuring the future quality of the population. Achieving this aim, in addition, required a steady rise in the standard of life ensured through the combination of increased wealth, the wisdom of government and the growth of knowledge:

Thus there are increasing reasons for fearing, that while the progress of medical science and sanitation is saving from death a continually increasing number of the children of those who are feeble physically and mentally; many of those who are most thoughtful and best endowed with energy, enterprise and self-control are tending to defer their marriages and in other ways to limit the number of children whom they leave behind them. The motive is sometimes selfish, and perhaps it is best that hard and frivolous people should leave but few descendants of their own type. But more often it is a desire to secure a good social position for their children. This desire contains many elements that fall short of the highest ideals of human aims, and in some cases, a few that are distinctly base; but after all it has been one of the chief factors of progress, and those who are affected by it include many of those whose children would probably be among the best and strongest of the race.

It must be remembered that the members of a large family educate one another, they are usually more genial and bright, often more vigorous in every way than the members of a small family. Partly, no doubt, this is because their parents were of unusual vigour; and for a like reason they in their turn are likely to have large and vigorous families. The progress of the race is due to a much greater extent than appears at first sight to the descendants of a few exceptionally large and vigorous families.

But on the other hand there is no doubt that the parents can often do better in many ways for a small family than a large one. Other things being equal, an increase in the number of children who are born causes an increase of infantile mortality; and that is an unmixed evil. The birth of children who die early from want of care and adequate means is a useless strain to the mother and an injury to the rest of the family. It seems *prima facie* advisable that people should not bring children into the world till they can see their way to giving them at least as good an education both physical and mental as they themselves had; and that it is best to marry moderately early provided there is sufficient self-control to keep the family within the requisite bounds without transgressing moral laws. The general adoption of these principles of action, combined with an adequate provision of fresh air and of healthy play for our town populations, could hardly fail to cause the strength and vigour of the race to improve. And we shall presently find reasons for believing that if the strength and vigour of the race improves, the increase of numbers will not for a long time to come cause a diminution of the average real income of the people.

Thus then the progress of knowledge, and in particular of medical science, the ever-growing activity and wisdom of Government in all matters relating to health, and the increase of material wealth, all tend to lessen mortality and to increase health and strength, and to lengthen life. On the other hand, vitality is lowered and the death-rate raised by the rapid increase of town life, and by the tendency of the higher strains of the population to marry later and to have fewer children then the lower. If the former set of causes were alone in action, but so regulated as to avoid the danger of over population, it is probable that man would quickly rise to a physical and mental excellence superior to any that the world has yet known; while if the latter set acted unchecked, he would speedily degenerate.

As it is, the two sets hold one another very nearly in balance, the former slightly preponderating. While the population of England is growing nearly as fast as ever, those who are out of health in body or mind are certainly not an increasing part of the whole: the rest are much better fed and clothed, and except in over-crowded industrial districts, are generally growing in strength. The average duration of life both for men and women has been increasing steadily for many years (Marshall, 1920, pp. 201–3).[23]

The changes in detail in these lengthy passages as compared with earlier editions[24] reveal several interesting features about Marshall's thinking on these matters. They show that from 1890 to 1920 Marshall was not just a passive, academic observer, writing on the subject of race improvement only as an adjunct to questions of the theory of production, industrial organization and quality of population in connection with labour supply. For Marshall, such discussion also involved the ends of economics, that is, the progressive improvement of all of mankind over time through raising the standard of life in the special sense in which he used that term (Marshall, 1920, pp. 689–90). Revisions in the detail recorded over these three decades reflect the passionate interest with which he followed advances in the 'science' of heredity and eugenics. Marshall's beliefs on these subjects cannot be discussed in detail, but his substantial involvement in eugenics and heredity needs to be emphasized to assist explaining some of his opinions on women.[25]

In the first place, Marshall became a foundation life member of the Cambridge Eugenics Society on its establishment, immediately sending a life membership subscription to its newly elected secretary, John Maynard Keynes.[26] Marshall also attended occasional lectures on heredity and eugenics at Cambridge University, an interest which sometimes led to correspondence with the lecturer to answer queries.[27] Marshall widely, and critically, followed the burgeoning literature on heredity, particularly books which placed the topic in its wider social context and likewise discussed aspects of their contents in correspondence with their authors.[28] In the summer of 1910, ably assisted by John Maynard Keynes, the topic induced him to enter public controversy with Karl Pearson on the issue of alcoholism in parents and heredity. This was a subject of long-standing interest to Marshall as indirectly shown, for example, in the passages from the *Principles* quoted at the start of this section.[29] Marshall's published views tended to follow changes in scientific knowledge on heredity rather closely, and his desire to present, as far as possible, up-to-date opinions, induced the frequent changes in detail which can be noted on this subject in the successive editions of the *Principles*.[30]

The fears and anxieties about the prospects for the British race expressed by Marshall in this material also reflected the times. Although never xenophobic,[31] Marshall was always the Englishman proud of his nation's achievements. His pride in being British made him all the more fearful about signs of its economic decline. Such decline he realistically saw as fairly imminent, and attributed to many factors.[32] A more skilled and vigorous labour force was clearly one way of counteracting British decline. Such considerations undoubtedly provide one of the reasons for Marshall's stress on heredity, eugenics and the standard of life in the context of production, and more specifically, that of the quality of future labour supply. The theory of heredity, as it was then understood, was a major input for his views on these matters, enabling linkages to the role of the family, and to the specific responsibilities of the parents therein.[33]

Marshall firmly believed that the evidence supported the view that the children of those who led a healthy life would themselves be healthy in the full sense of the word. He likewise believed on the basis of evidence he had gathered that such a healthy family environment was not easily provided in households where women worked in unhealthy surroundings of factories and in 'sweated trades'. Both mother and sisters of a family were essential to the necessary quality of the family environment which secured the health of its present and future members. Race progress and national survival in this sense depended on the role Marshall assigned to the family, and the necessary role of women in the family environment For him, this chain of reasoning did not rest on prejudice but on the empirical and scientific evidence gathered patiently by himself from the 'science' of heredity. The subjection of women to the needs of the family and the limitation on their freedom which that implied arose from his social Darwinist vision of race survival, race preservation and race progress. In that sense, as in others, Marshall reflected the spirit and the knowledge of his time (cf. Whitaker, 1977, p. 480; Richards, 1983, especially pp. 97–100).

Marshall gained more from evolutionary theory on the women's question. He gained the belief in the relative mental inferiority of women from the pioneers of evolutionary theory themselves, that is, from work by Darwin and Herbert Spencer. Both Darwin's *Descent of Man* (Darwin, 1871) and Spencer's *First Principles* (Spencer, 1862), the first largely basing himself on Galton's research on hereditary genius, explicitly argued women's mental inferiority to men as a justification for a sexual division of labour which, in particular, had important implications for policies on women's education. (For example, Darwin, 1871, pp. 888, 960–61, 923–6, 944–6; Spencer, 1862, pp. 136–7 and n. and for a detailed discussion of this subject, Richards, 1983.) For

Marshall, such evolutionary 'evidence'[34] would have strengthened his willingness to accept the views of other social scientists whom he admired. An example is Le Play's basic 'law of inequality governing all the interesting issues concerning the two sexes' with its application to education reaching the conclusion that 'the truest form of education for girls was found at the domestic fireside' (Le Play, 1887, Vol. 2, pp. 397–400, my translation).

Such 'truths' from the findings of social scientists supplemented Marshall's uncritical embrace of the crude applications made by eugenists of the lessons to be learned from what is now appropriately described as 'the mismeasurement of man' (Gould, 1981). Marshall, the youthful collector of pictures of the famous in the hope they would lead to conclusions which, according to his wife (Mary Paley Marshall, 1947, pp. 15–16), they never did, would have placed considerable credence on contemporary finding in craniometry when applied to higher education for women:

> A desire to give them [women] the same education, and as a consequence, to propose the same goals for them, is a dangerous chimera.... The day when, misunderstanding the interior occupations which nature has given her, women leave the home and take part in our battles, on this day a social revolution will begin, and everything that maintains the sacred ties of the family will disappear (Le Bon, 1870, cited in Gould, 1981, p. 105).

The science of evolution was crucial to the manner in which Marshall developed his views on women in the *Principles of Economics*, in which he assigned them the nurturing role to enhance the quality of future labour supply rather than a direct role in production for the market.

CONCLUSION

The picture of Marshall's treatment of the women's issue presented here enables a different explanation of his views than if that presentation had concentrated on his involvement in the women's degree issue at Cambridge or on the saga of his repudiation of the *Economics of Industry* when his own primer based on the *Principles* was ready to replace it (McWilliams-Tullberg, 1975, 1992). His attitudes to women in the labour force, outmoded as they are in terms of current thinking and practice, can be defended partly on grounds of both the lofty motives in the context of which they were presented and the contemporary scientific and empirical backing on which that presentation appeared to rely. Such a viewpoint can be briefly elaborated.

The logic of Marshall's argument has considerable consistency, given what he took as his factual premises about the importance of the appropriate family atmosphere for securing a progressive improvement in the 'race'.[35] Substantial evidence was available on the importance of female and family influence on the rearing of children while the general improvement of the genetic stock promulgated by a widespread rise in nurturing standards, education and quality of family life followed for him from Galton's theory of natural inheritance (Galton, 1889, especially Chapter 7). Marshall also assiduously collected evidence on the detrimental influence of women's factory work on households and children, both from his work on the Labour Commission, and earlier from his own factory inspections during the 1880s. As Edgeworth recalled after Marshall's death, the existing family structure was a crucial factor in Marshall's analysis of human progress to an eventual ideal state, since not only quality of labour supply but rises in the standard of life largely depended on it. Hence his hostility to the notion of 'modern women', which threatened established monogamous institutions of marriage on which the institution of the family rested; a hostility able to rise to ridiculous proportions when, as reported in J.N. Keynes's diaries,[36] Marshall 'refuses to meet Miss Clough because she is in favour of woman suffrage', despite the fact that as an employee at Newnham College, she was also his wife's close associate and friend.

On aspects of the woman's question, Marshall can therefore be described as 'the scientist observing his contemporaries' behaviour and attitudes' (Whitaker, 1977, p. 480), applying the latest lessons from published science to his findings. However, this unduly neglects his role as dogmatist and preacher in his stance on the subject, out of step with his scientific detachment. The rising relative wages of women and young persons, discussed briefly in the *Principles* and elsewhere in terms of technical and social progress, are in one of Marshall's more 'chivalrous' moments ascribed solely to the altruism of man (Marshall, 1907b, p. 327). More importantly, the question of the rights of married women to choose whether they work or not, reflecting the opinion of some women as noted in the *Final Report* of the Labour Commission that housework was a monotonous drudgery to be escaped, never found a place in later editions of his *Principles*. Such choices were detrimental to his views on household work as part of the necessities required to obtain efficiency from the agricultural labourer or unskilled working man. Moreover, the Commission's recognition that legislative reform and its enforcement could remove the worst effects on women from factory work was a lesson Marshall chose not to share with his readers. Nor was he willing to remove a necessity for married women to work by advocating a legal minimum wage designed to ensure adequate provision for the breadwinner's dependents.

Furthermore, much of Marshall's opinion on the economic and social role of woman was dictated by what he described as woman's natural mental abilities, which differed substantially from those of most men, and which prevented the vast majority of them from doing constructive theoretical work. Such ideas had been imbibed from his immersion in evolutionary thinking. When that picture started to crumble with the substantial academic successes women obtained at his own beloved Cambridge, and even in his more beloved Economics and Politics Tripos (cf. Macgregor, 1942, pp. 313–14), that picture of woman's mental ability was never revised in the light of the new evidence. In short, there was much unscientific prejudice, and perhaps even something 'selfish', in Marshall's support for the sexual division of labour and the arguments on which that rested.

The interesting point is, however, that Marshall raised these types of issue and did not, as a latter-day Robbinsian, cast them out as non-economic. Progress is more than maximizing utilities. Efficiency goes beyond the minimization of excess burdens. Marshall's discussion of the humble housewife allocating her scanty budget, or exploring the choice of technique in knitting a vest, and his perspectives on 'domestic economy' which place it within both the theory of production and consumption (Marshall, 1920, pp. 118–19 and 357, n.1), betray a definition of scope which takes economic behaviour well beyond the market. Even though the answers Marshall gave to the questions he posed in the context of women's issues are wrong and based on prejudice rather than scientific evidence, the questions he asked need asking and the social and dynamic dimension he introduced with them is worth emulating when framing questions today. Marshall clearly internalized the role of women in his *Principles of Economics*, to a far greater extent than Sidgwick, Fawcett or even Mill had done, even though this discussion gave as little space to women's paid work as did his contemporaries. It nevertheless gave women as nurturers an explicitly crucial role in economic development, fundamental to the future quality of the labour force, the preservation of the family and the race. However, it thereby also restricted their freedom to choose, a form of restriction he less easily condoned in other spheres of economic life.

NOTES

*   This paper is part of the research undertaken for my forthcoming biography of Alfred Marshall. Support for this project from the Australian Research Council is gratefully acknowledged.   The paper has benefited from comments given during the Centre's Workshop, in particular those by Flora Gill, and subsequently from those by Rita McWilliams-Tullberg and Michael White, without implicating them in the final product.

1. *Reynolds Magazine*, 30 July 1890 (cutting in Marshall's scrap-book, Marshall Archive, University of Cambridge).

2. Mary Paley, one of his students who sat for the Moral Sciences Tripos in 1874, and to whom he was married in 1877, continued her work as lecturer in Political Economy (begun at Newnham College in 1875) as a married woman while they lived in Bristol from 1878, in Oxford from 1883 to 1884 and in Cambridge from 1885 to 1909. They published the *Economics of Industry* jointly in 1879, the extensive paragraphs of which on women's wages quoted below. During the 1880s, Marshall's papers 'Theories and Facts about Wages' (*Cooperative Wholesale Annual*, 1885, pp. 379–88) and his 1887 'A Fair Rate of Wages' failed to mention women's issues in wage determination.

3. Marshall therefore gave little recognition to Mill's position on female comparative advantage in skill. See Mill (1865), p. 179.

4. This passage dates from Marshall, 1910, p. 694.

5. This passage dates from the fifth edition (Marshall, 1907a, p. 715, n.1).

6. This passage closely resembles the discussion presented by Mill (1865), pp. 242–3. In his second *Beehive* article, Marshall had drawn attention to closed shop practices in medicine applied particularly to women (Marshall, 1874, pp. 429–30) to which Marshall and Marshall (1879, p. 176) refers more obliquely.

7. The reference is probably to Francis Galton (1892, p. 319), which reprints the text of the 1869 first edition. Marshall's paraphrase of Galton's opinion is not completely correct, since Galton's remark on the mothers of great men in fact states, 'There is a common opinion that great men have remarkable mothers. No doubt they are largely indebted to maternal influences, but the popular belief ascribes an undue and incredible share to them. I account for the belief, by the fact that great men have usually high moral natures, and are affectionate and reverential, inasmuch as mere brain without heart is insufficient to achieve eminence. Such men are naturally disposed to show extreme filial regard, and to publish the good quality of their mothers, with exaggerated praise.' But cf. Galton (1892), pp. 189, 266–72, on the parental, especially maternal influence on men of science and on divines.

8. This passage dates from Marshall, 1895, p. 594.

9. Cf. Marshall, 1920, pp. 718–20, especially 720 for comments on the general role of women in the improvement of human nature; amending the slightly different, and shorter, version of this passage in the first edition (Marshall, 1890, pp. 730–31).

10. Alfred Marshall, evidence to the Committee on Higher Education in Wales and Monmouthshire, Cmnd 3047–1, Parliamentary Papers, Vol. XXXIII, 1881, pp. 767–79, answer to Question 18,276, p. 775, Question 18,304, p. 776.

11. Ibid., answers to Questions 18,305–6, p. 776.

12. In her notes for Walter Scott, to assist his preparation of an obituary of Alfred Marshall for the British Academy, Mary Paley recorded that his greatest love was reserved for his mother, his Aunt Louisa and his sister Mabel Louisa; sister Agnes died in India while looking after the family of her older brother Charles William. (Preserved in Marshall Archive, Large Brown Box item 24.)

13. Labour Commission, Minutes of Evidence, cited in T.G. Spyers, *The Labour Question, an epitome of the evidence and report of the Royal Commission on Labour*, London, Swan Sonnenscheinn and Company, 1894, p. 113, and see below, Chapter 5, pp. 115–16.

14. The greater part of this and the following paragraph are based on this reference.

15. There is little useful secondary evidence on this subject which would have been available to Marshall. Wood (1903), pp. 283–4, supports Marshall's contention that generally speaking since the 1860s women's wages rose relatively faster than wages as a whole. The subsequent study by Dorothea M. Barton (1919, pp. 508–44), provides no data on women's wage growth relative to that of men, while in addition, much of her data is coloured by the abnormal influences of the First World War on women's relative pay (above, pp. 9–11).

16. Royal Commission on Labour, *Fifth and Final Report*, Cmnd 7421, June 1894, pp. 93–4, 107–9. A further discussion of the Royal Commission findings is given in Chapter 5 below. Some of them were criticized by Clara Collet, 1898b, and see below Chapter 6.

17. This, and the following three paragraphs devoted to factory visits, draw on Mary Paley Marshall's notes, 'Travels in England', preserved in the Marshall Library, Red Box 1(5).

18. Beatrice Webb's efforts on analysing women's work with her husband in later life are discussed in Chapter 5 below.

19. Alfred Marshall, 1884 (?) fragment, 'Women and Technical Education', Marshall Library, Box 8 (1).

20. Alfred Marshall, 'The Higher Education of Women', Marshall Library, Box 8(2). An exceptional woman in literature in Marshall's scheme of things would have been George Eliot, who was one of Marshall's favourite novelists on the later recollections of Mary Paley Marshall (1947, p. 20).

21. As Edgeworth's reminiscences cited earlier suggest in the analogy he drew between Marshall's views on women's degrees and on socialism, the foreseeable future was very long, perhaps the five thousand years Marshall suggested in the last quoted fragment. Perhaps this is why a fragment (dated 23 February 1923) preserved among his papers devoted to 'Progress and Ideals' and proposing 'A Constitution of Public Well-Being', indicates both men and women drawn from medicine and business as the most desirable membership to constitute its governing body. Because these notes preserve Marshall's reflections on 'utopias', frequently from old age, they illustrate Edgeworth's analogy to perfection.

22. This material had been much changed with respect to its detail but not to its thrust. Cf. Marshall, 1890, pp. 307–9, Marshall, 1898, pp. 326–8.

23. The passage quoted changed substantially in detail but not in its thrust. Cf. Marshall, 1890, pp. 256–9; Marshall, 1898, pp. 280–83.

24. See notes 22 and 23 above, and more generally, Marshall, 1961, Volume II, pp. 303–5, 326–7.

25. Details are included in my forthcoming biography of Alfred Marshall.

26. Marshall to Keynes, 18 May 1911, in Keynes Papers File L/M/41, King's College Archives, Cambridge.

27. Marshall to Bateson, 24 and 26 October 1908 (Marshall Archive 1/272–3). On 20 October 1908, Bateson had started a series of advanced lectures for the Natural Sciences Tripos on the subject of genetics (*Cambridge University Reporter*, 10 October 1908, p. 98) and from the contents of the letters it appears that Marshall, then fresh in retirement, may have attended some of them. Bateson also gave occasional lectures to the Cambridge University community on what he called, 'Practical Evolution'. Bateson is thanked in the preface of the third edition of the *Principles*, presumably for correcting some of Marshall's more extravagant remarks on evolution in the previous two editions.

28. There were a large number of such works in Marshall's library, including Galton's major works, often referred to in the *Principles*; Benjamin Kidd's *Social Evolution* and his *Principles of Civilisation* on both of which Marshall corresponded with the author (Marshall to Kidd, 6 June 1894, 15 May 1895, 14 February 1898, 11 February and 27 May 1902, Cambridge University Library, Add 8089/M251–6) and which he also quoted in the *Principles*; J.B. Haycraft, *Darwinism and Race Progress*, London, Swan Sonnenscheinn, 1895 (heavily annotated by Marshall and cited in the *Principles*); Simon N. Patten, *Heredity and Social Progress*, London, Macmillan, 1903; while his correspondence with Kidd refers to technical aspects of the theories on heredity of the German geneticist, August Weismann. In addition, his interest in the subject is highlighted by the fact he was willing to give Bateson, a specialist, his personal copy of Richard Louis Dugdale's '*The Jukes', A Study in Crime, Pauperism, Disease and Heredity*, a case study of the influence of family on heredity which made a big impact on Marshall's thinking. See Marshall to Bateson, 24 October 1908 (Marshall Archive 1/272) where he described the book 'as holding as unique a position among family trees in relation to character as that which you showed us yesterday does in regard to height and blindness'.

29. See Marshall to the *Times*, 7 July, 4 and 19 August, 1910; the episode is described in some detail by R. Skidelsky (1983), pp. 223–7, and Moggridge (1992), pp. 205–7.

30. Noted above, especially notes 22–24, 27.

31. Marshall's half-dozen letters to the *Times* during the First World War invariably urged moderation of national hatred for Germany. The unpatriotic reputation this gained Marshall with the 'average' Englishman is strikingly illustrated by a letter Bertrand Russell received from a 'John Bull', on 20 September 1915 (Russell, 1978, p. 272).

32. These included the deleterious influence of some trade unions on work practice, productivity and hence British competitiveness; the rise of Germany and the United States and other countries in industrial strength, ineffective business education and so on. Marshall discussed these issues in correspondence (Pigou, 1925, pp. 398–902) and in *Industry and Trade* (Marshall, 1919).

33. See J.B. Haycraft (1895), Chapter VIII, 'Obligation in Parenthood' and cf. Marshall to Benjamin Kidd, 14 February 1898 (Cambridge University Library, Add 8069/M154) in which, in the context of the future progress for society, he expressed the view that 'if the present drift to new Womanhood should go far, I think stable monogamy may be endangered, but I don't expect it will go far'.

34. Darwin (1871, pp. 944–6) admitted these theories wanted 'scientific precision', a qualification his followers were less careful to recognize.

35. Cf. Galton (1892), p. 348, where the restoration of high honour to marriage is regarded as one of the essential features of a civilization designed for 'the improvement of the race'. And cf. Matthews (1990), p. 29.

36. John Neville Keynes, *Diaries*, entry for 8 April 1890. Keynes heard the story from Henry Sidgwick, who had heard it from Mrs. Frances Darwin, a very close friend and confidante

of Mrs. Mary Marshall, thereby indicating it was probably a source of discord at Balliol Croft, the Marshalls' residence (Cambridge University Library, Add. MSS 7827–7867).

5. The Webbs and the Rights of Women

Chris Nyland and Gaby Ramia

Beatrice and Sidney Webb's contribution to the economics of gender centred primarily on the right of women to enjoy at least a minimal standard of economic comfort and security. Throughout their lives these two scholars struggled to ensure that those women most vulnerable to economic exploitation were provided with a means for staving off those wishing to take advantage of their vulnerability. They were ardent advocates of the unionization of women workers and the enactment of legislation that was designed both to ensure all people were provided with at least the minimum requirements of a civilized life and which compelled employers to provide minimum standards of employment. That women should be denied their right to protection from excessive demands on the part of those who would exploit their vulnerability, simply because males were not equally protected, was a claim the Webbs considered outrageous. The latter conviction led them to engage in a prolonged debate with both theorists and activists who insisted that governments must always adopt gender-neutral labour market policies. This chapter examines the contribution made by the Webbs to these issues and outlines how their ideas were transformed through the period from 1887 to 1920.

The Webbs' initial contribution to the economics of gender was provided by Beatrice (1888a, 1888b, 1890, 1898, 1902a, 1902b, 1902c). Through the years 1887–92 she published a series of papers on sweated labour in East London. By sweated labour the Webbs meant:

> no particular method of remuneration, no peculiar form of industrial organisation, but certain conditions of employment – viz. *unusually low rates of wages, excessive hours of labour, and insanitary workplaces*. When we get any one of

these conditions in an extreme and exaggerated form – for instance, when we find a woman sewing neckties in her home, straining every nerve to earn only a halfpenny an hour – still more, when we see all these conditions combined ... then we say that the labour is sweated, and that the unfortunates are working under the sweating system (B. Webb, 1898, pp. 139–40).

In her articles and in the evidence she gave to the 1888 Committee of the House of Lords on the Sweating System, Beatrice strove to reveal the disastrous effect unbridled competition had on the lives of unskilled workers and especially on women. Her personal experience of East London caused her to break forever with the free market liberalism which her middle-class background had earlier led her to embrace:

[M]y investigations into the sweated industries of East London ... convinced me that if the capitalist system was not to lead to 'earnings barely sufficient to sustain existence; hours of labour such as to make the lives of the workers periods of almost ceaseless toil, hard and unlovely to the last degree; sanitary conditions injurious to the health of the persons employed and dangerous to the public' ... capitalist enterprise had to be controlled, not exceptionally or spasmodically, but universally, so as to secure to every worker prescribed minimum conditions of employment (B. Webb, 1948, p. 19).

Henceforth, Beatrice insisted that the 'evil spirit' that was the 'soul' of the sweating system she so deplored was 'unrestrained competition' (B. Webb, 1902b, p. 66).[1] As a consequence she urged the need for society to strengthen and extend both trade unionism and the Factory Acts and was highly critical of social analysts who celebrated the benefits of a free labour market. Her strongest criticism was reserved for those who lauded the market when their praise was based only on abstract reasoning. Thus she was scathing in her criticism of the 'Individualists' and that 'batch of excellent ladies ... eager for the Rights of Woman to work at all hours of day and night with the minimum of space and sanitation' who opposed the notion that employers should be responsible for the conditions under which outworkers were employed (B. Webb, 1890, p. 899).

Beatrice was convinced that social policy must be based on systematic empirical investigation. Like Charles Booth with whom she worked in East London she insisted that investigators must not start with *a priori* assumptions about economic laws. Rather, they must discover, as far as possible without bias, what were the facts of the phenomenon they were seeking to explain. In presenting her evidence to the

Committee on Sweating she stressed the fact that her knowledge of the conditions she described were the result of direct investigation and not simply of abstract theorizing. When researching the garment trade, for example, she reported that in order to gather information she had amassed data on 1300 sweat shops, classified these enterprises into five basic categories of work and then disguised herself as a seamstress and obtained employment in four out of the five categories. Further, she had followed up this exercise by having her secretary undertake interviews with the employers of the establishments in which she had worked (B. Webb, 1888a, p. 321).

Beatrice's stress on the factual nature of her evidence and her aversion to argument based solely on abstract reasoning was replicated by Sidney when in 1891 he was asked by the Economics Section of the British Association to prepare a paper 'upon the alleged differences in the wages paid to men and to women for similar work' (S. Webb, 1891, p. 635). Sidney reports that initially he was reluctant to take on this task, because he had no definite ideas as to why it was that women earned less than men and because the subject had seldom been discussed with any reference to the facts of modern industry. However, he decided that he would at least attempt to collect the available data. In so doing he made the point that he considered his efforts as merely an attempt to provide a preliminary survey which might generate some indications of the directions in which further study might usefully proceed.

In presenting the results of his investigation Sidney divided women's work into what he believed were four non-competing groups; manual, routine mental, artistic and intellectual. In his exposition of the data, he began by providing statistics on the time wages paid to male and female manual workers in the manufacturing industries of the United States and Britain. This evidence suggested that women manufacturing employees earned from one-third to two-thirds the amount paid to men. He next presented data on piece wages in order to determine if, in comparing occupational classifications, he was in fact equating like with like. The critical difficulty in fulfilling this latter task, he reported, was discovering any significant number of instances of men and women undertaking identical work in identical conditions. He found few instances of this situation because of the sharpness of the sexual division of labour and hence found few cases of men and women competing for the same type of employment.

Sidney next turned to 'routine mental work' a sphere in which, he reported, it was more common for men and women to undertake tasks of the same kind and yet receive different levels of remuneration. However, he advised that care needed to be taken in determining the prevalence of this phenomena because of the difficulty of ensuring the work undertaken was equal in terms of quantity and quality. Moreover, the situation was complicated by the fact that women tended to have higher levels of absenteeism due to illness, generally had lower qualifications and had a lower level of labour attachment. Having presented the statistical data relating to routine mental employment, Sidney reported that he had been unable to find any substantive factual information as regards the wages of female artistic and intellectual workers. He therefore sought to determine if it was possible to extract any general conclusions from the data he had managed to accumulate. He concluded tentatively that there seemed to be four primary factors which together explained women's inferior wages. The first was custom and public opinion. This was the most potent of the four and though it was founded on the other three it was greater than the sum of their parts. The three other influences were the lower standard of life maintained by women, their lower productivity (a function of their lesser strength, labour attachment and limited opportunities for training and promotion) and their lack of protective power. To counter these adverse influences, Webb advised there was need to undertake a campaign of public education to disabuse the community of the many invalid assumptions regarding women's supposed 'feminine disabilities'. Women must also be provided with the skills they needed to enhance their productivity, be permitted greater access to positions of public influence, be allowed greater freedom and independence and be encouraged to demand a higher standard of living.

> Summarizing roughly these suggestions, it may be said that women's inferiority of remuneration for equivalent work is, where it exists, the direct or indirect result, to a very large extent, of their past subjection; and that, dependent as it now mainly is upon the influence of custom and public opinion, it might be largely removed by education and combination among women themselves. I am inclined to hope most from a gradual spread of trade unions among women workers; and that even more in the direction of an increase in the efficiency of labour which trade unionism so often promotes, than in the improvement in its remuneration arising merely from collective bargaining (S. Webb, 1891, pp. 661–2).[2]

It is well known that the Webbs believed social analysis needed to be founded on a substantive factual foundation. They were very wary of making generalizations purely on the basis of deduction. This did not mean they were vulgar empiricists but rather that they believed effective investigation requires both facts and principles. Their commitment to a methodology which emphasized both these elements was made especially clear when, shortly after their marriage in 1892, Sidney gave evidence to the Royal Commission on Labour. When providing his testimony Sidney observed repeatedly that if the Commissioners were to obtain the knowledge they sought it was imperative that they undertake empirical and statistical studies and not confine their analysis to the use of logic, deduction and the cross-examination of witnesses. In short, they should abjure excessive reliance on abstract principles and realize that analysts must give consideration to both principles and facts (Royal Commission, 1893b, p. 266).

In his evidence to the Royal Commission Sidney also made a number of observations specific to the issue of women's position within the labour market. He repeated Beatrice's assessment that the Factory Act needed to be strengthened and extended. He also observed that ideally he would prefer to see a 'condition of society in which the mother of a family did not work for her living at all' though he insisted he was opposed to the state prohibiting their employment (Royal Commission, 1893b, pp. 259, 299–300). Sidney's assertion regarding the working mother is a reflection of the significance the Webbs placed on 'married women's work' within the home. The importance they attached to this form of labour had been revealed earlier by Beatrice when discussing the living conditions of dock workers.

> In common with all other working men with a moderate but regular income, the permanent dock labourer is made by his wife. If she be a tidy woman and a good manager, decently versed in the rare arts of cooking and sewing, the family life is independent, even comfortable, and the children may follow in the father's footsteps or rise to better things. If she be a gossip and a bungler – worse still, a drunkard – the family sink to the low level of the East London street; and the children are probably added to the number of those who gain their livelihood by irregular work and by irregular means (B. Webb, 1902a, p. 25).[3]

After the Royal Commission presented its final report Beatrice published a scathing review of its findings. In this commentary she castigated the Commissioners for their failure to undertake substantive empirical studies of the issues they had been asked to investigate. The Commission, she asserted, had failed. Indeed, it had proved to be a 'lamentable fiasco', because the overwhelming majority of the Commissioners had been content to settle for 'abstract considerations' rather than systematic investigation. She acknowledged that in some instances impressive investigative work had been undertaken which had produced important factual information. This included a study of women's employment. But these were rare exceptions and in the case of the investigation into women's labour the success achieved was due only to the fact that the investigators had largely ignored their terms of reference.

Beatrice also castigated the Commission for the 'timid acquiescence' manifest in its recommendations.[4] She excluded from this last criticism the Minority Report submitted by the four 'working-men' Commissioners. The series of recommendations advanced by these men, she observed, were useful, practical and most importantly were 'put forward avowedly as parts of a systematic industrial and political policy' (B. Webb, 1984, p. 8). That Beatrice approved of the Minority Report is not surprising given that it was in fact written for the trade unionists by Sidney Webb.

As regards women, the Minority Report observed that there appeared little hope that trade unionism alone could free the many thousands of workers in the sweated trades from the long hours and insanitary conditions they were forced to endure. Therefore, it was recommended that the Factory Act be extended in a manner which would deal effectively with these evils. It was observed that this did not require the enactment of 'special legislation for women'. The needed reforms, it was advised, should be designed to protect both male and female workers equally. The single exception the authors of the Minority Report made to this general rule was in the lead industry where it was concluded:

> [T]hough we are loath to recommend the closing of any career to women, we are driven, by the medical evidence of their greater susceptibility to lead poisoning, to the conclusion that their employment should be absolutely prohibited (Labour Commission, 1894, p. 138).

THE CASE FOR THE FACTORY ACTS

Through 1895 Beatrice delivered a series of lectures to women's groups on the need for labour market reform and in support of legislation that would extent the coverage of the Factory Act. Such a Bill was introduced in 1895 and immediately generated an intense and heated discussion. The proposed reforms gained the endorsement of the trade unions, the associations of working women, the labour feminists and the female factory inspectors, amongst others. As usual, most employers objected, though even amongst the capitalists there was no unanimity. However, the employers who did come out in opposition found that they were not alone. They received the active support of the 'equal rights' feminists, those whom Beatrice described as the 'able and devoted ladies who have usually led the cause of women's enfranchisement' (B. Webb, 1896, p. 3).

The equal rights feminists, as Hutchins (1915, p. 121) has observed, constituted the 'Right wing of the Women's Movement'. The faction was characterized by a tendency to place its primary emphasis on the need for women to attain the vote, by a hostility to men and by a commitment to classical liberal economics and ideology. Their involvement in the struggle for the rights of women was primarily an outcome of the discrimination experienced by the women from the middle class. The beliefs of these individuals reflected their origins in that they tended to emphasize the liberal freedoms and in particular the right of the individual to an equal chance to compete in the market place. Though aware that by the 1890s the most enthusiastic supporters of the Factory Acts were the women factory workers these individuals urged freedom of contract on their working-class sisters and bitterly opposed the imposition of legal restrictions on the capitalists' use of female labour.

By contrast, the labour feminists drew their support primarily from the working class and from those middle-class women who found it impossible to ignore the fact that the overwhelming majority of employed women appeared to support the extension of the Factory Acts. As with the equal rightists, the labour feminists opposed male domination and patriarchal social relations. However, they differed from the former in that they emphasized the need to give priority to improving the well-being of those women in greatest material need, urged solidarity between the sexes and tended towards a socialistic solution to women's oppression. Moreover, they believed the free market policies equal rightists were urging upon the women of the working class, were largely aimed to serve the interests of middle- and upper-class women. The latter individuals claimed to be fighting for the rights of all women just as the men of the bourgeoisie had claimed they fought for all men when they campaigned for the 'rights of man'. As far as the labour feminists were concerned, however, the rightists' claims were as fraudulent as had been the claims of the men of their class. They believed this was made clear above all by the fact that the rightists opposed regulation of the labour market despite the fact that the women of the working class wanted regulation and that the free market tended to have a disastrous effect on the lives of the women of the poorest section of society. In short, the labour feminists believed the rightists opposed regulation and ignored the interests of the women of the working class because the interests of the more privileged women in society who they represented were best served by an unregulated labour market. The difference between the two groups and the fact that their interests were not merely divergent but were diametrically opposed has been well captured by Hutchins:[5]

> The middle-class woman's agitation was inevitably influenced by the ideals of her class, a class largely engaged in competitive business of one kind or another. Equality of opportunity, permission to compete with men and try their luck in open market, was what the women of this type demanded, with considerable justification, and with admirable courage. The working woman, on the other hand, the victim of that very unrestricted competition which her better off sister was demanding, before all things needed improved wages and conditions of work, for which State protection and combination with men were essential (Hutchins, 1915, p. 196; see also Klein, 1971, p. 15, and Feuer, 1988).

The rightist feminists justified their alliance with the employers on the grounds that certain aspects of the Government's reform bill applied only to women. They insisted that this form of legislation was unacceptable as it limited women's ability to compete with men for employment. Women, they insisted, should be as free as were men to determine the conditions under which they sold their labour power and this was a principle which applied equally to the women of all classes (Hutchins and Harrison, 1966, pp. 173–99). In reply, though they preferred equal legal protection for both sexes, labour feminists argued that simply because male workers refused to accept state protection or could not convince the community that they should be protected was no reason for denying women protection from excessive demands on the part of their employers. Their general perspective as regard the principle of sex equality versus the principle of legislative regulation was encapsulated in Beatrice Webb's observation:

> [T]here seem to be two principles which, for the last century, have competed for public approval. There is the principle of sex equality; a principle which is good in itself and results, under certain circumstances, in bettering the conditions of a woman's life. But there is another principle: the principle of legislative regulation. Under the capitalist system we now perceive that it is imperative to regulate competitive wage-earning, and that without this regulation the physical and moral state of the workers suffers indefinite deterioration. Without this protection of the standard of life of the workers, no personal freedom or personal comfort is practicable. This principle of a legal minimum standard of life is of even greater value to women that [sic] it is to men because of their weaker bargaining power (B. Webb, 1978c, p. 387).

Considered in abstract, the Webbs were loath to assert which of the two principles they believed was the more significant. In the case of Britain, however, they believed that the needs of those least able to defend themselves were such that 'if regulation be impracticable with sex equality' they would 'prefer to get regulation and do without the sex equality' (B. Webb, 1978c, p. 388).

As far as the Webbs were concerned those individuals who refused to give due consideration to the facts relevant to the condition of working women and denied them the protection they needed, purely on the grounds of an abstract principle, were guilty of the same sin as had been the members of the Labour Commission. In short, the members of the women's rights faction were basing their arguments on abstract notions and were sacrificing the interests of the most vulnerable women in society because by so doing their own interests were advanced.

An example of the reasoning that the Webbs found so unacceptable was Millicent Fawcett's (1892) reply to Sidney's article on women's wages. Fawcett observed that she was in almost complete agreement with Sidney but felt that he had underestimated the importance of ensuring that the professions were opened up to women. Belittling the importance of trade unionism she argued that activists and theoreticians needed to emphasize the extent to which the market would induce a trickle-down effect were women able to obtain a larger share of the highest-paying occupations. The unacceptability of Fawcett's paper to the Webbs was increased because no substantive evidence was provided to support the claims advanced and because she disparaged the value of labour market regulation.

The paper was also unsatisfactory to them because it supported the right of women to act as blacklegs. Fawcett argued that she had always regarded it as an error, both in principle and in tactics, to advise women that they must demand the same wages when undertaking the same work as men. Given that in many occupations the oversupply of women was greater than that of men, she asserted it was acceptable for employers to pay their female employees less than they paid the males they hired. Moreover, it was acceptable for women to accede to these conditions even if this meant their male colleagues would be excluded and the standard wage rate for the industry subverted (Fawcett, 1892, p. 176).

The alliance of capital and right-wing feminism that opposed the Government's 1895 amendments to the Factory Act proved of great effect. It provided the employers with allies whose arguments undermined the support of those individuals who would normally have endorsed the moral right of employees to safe working conditions. As a consequence many important clauses in the Government's Bill were defeated. The proposal relating to the working day of women laundry workers, for example, was amended in a manner which meant that the only limit placed on the employers was that they could not compel their employees to labour more than fourteen hours per day. Likewise, the provision forbidding women and young persons from cleaning machinery while it was in motion suffered the deletion of the word 'woman'.

Outraged at this development, Beatrice replied by issuing a pamphlet in 1896 which was highly critical of both the actions and arguments of her rightist opponents. The tract began with her observation that it was important that nothing be done to impair the growing sense of personal responsibility in women. Indeed, reformers must seek in every way to increase women's freedom. But the question at issue was how best to attain this objective.

When we are concerned with the propertied classes – when, for instance, it is sought to open up to women higher education or the learned professions – it is easy to see that freedom is secured by abolishing restrictions. But when we come to the relations between capital and labor an entirely new set of considerations come into play. In the life of the wage-earning class, absence of regulation does not mean personal freedom. Fifty years' experience shows that Factory legislation, far from diminishing individual liberty, greatly increases the personal freedom of the workers who are subject to it. Everyone knows that the Lancashire woman weaver, whose hours of labor and conditions of work are rigidly fixed by law, enjoys, for this very reason, more personal liberty than the unregulated laundry-woman in Notting Hill. She is not only a more efficient producer, and more capable of associating with her fellows in Trade Unions, Friendly Societies, and Co-operative Stores, but an enormously more independent and self-reliant citizen. It is the law, in fact, which is the mother of freedom (B. Webb, 1896, p. 5).

The rightists' claim that they had only opposed the Government's reforms because the legislation was not gender neutral was challenged by Beatrice. She observed that if this was true it was curious that these individuals had seldom been active in support of protective legislation which pertained equally to both sexes. Nearly all of the clauses of the 1895 Bill, she noted, applied to both men and women yet the anti-protectionists had given no aid to ensure that at least the sex-neutral parts of the Bill were passed. This is an accusation that has been supported by Feuer's (1988) study of the two factions. She observes that the rightist feminists invariably advised that the way to attain equality between the sexes was to abolish protection for women rather than extend the laws to men. For Beatrice the implication was obvious:

> It is clear that there lurks behind the objection of inequality an inveterate scepticism as to the positive advantages of Factory legislation. Indeed, the most energetic and prominent opponents of women's Factory Acts openly avow as much. Mrs. Henry Fawcett and Miss Ada Heather-Bigg, for instance, usually speak of legal regulation as something which, whether for men or for women, decreases personal freedom, diminishes productive capacity, and handicaps the worker in the struggle for existence (B. Webb, 1896, p. 4).

The enthusiasm with which many of the opponents of regulation clung to the belief that a free labour market was in the interests of all women convinced Beatrice that before examining the issue of sex-specific labour legislation she needed to deal briefly with the question of protective labour law in general. To understand the need for this form of legislation, she observed, it was necessary to realize that these laws were based on a 'fundamental economic fact'. This fact was 'the essential and permanent inequality between the individual wage-earner and the capitalist employer' (B. Webb, 1896, p. 5). Citing Marshall in support, she argued that unfettered individual bargaining between capitalist and worker inevitably tends to result, not in the highest wage and the best working conditions that industry can afford, but in the lowest standard on which the worker and the worker's family can survive. Because of the existence of this imbalance in the bargaining power of employers and employees, workers generally accepted that a common rule fixing the minimum conditions of employment in an occupation was not necessarily an infringement on their liberty. Within the working class, Beatrice observed, the only issue that tended to be disputed in regard to regulation was whether the best means of introducing and enforcing the common rule was trade unionism or legislation. She also observed that workers' preferred method of regulation was normally determined purely on utilitarian grounds, that is they preferred that method which was most effective.

Having made clear her support for minimum standards which employers were compelled to heed, Beatrice turned to the question of women's labour. She began by castigating those individuals who had called upon the unskilled workers who would have been assisted by the Government's Bill to abjure state protection and rely solely on collective bargaining. She believed this call had been issued merely in order that the anti-protectionists might avoid the accusation that their policies left the unskilled women workers at the mercy of their employers. It was a 'cruel mockery', she insisted, to preach to these workers that they should rely solely on their ability to organize given the paucity of the emotional, temporal and economic resources they enjoyed. The Government's Bill, she observed, would have provided the women of the sweated trades with at least some of the resources they needed in order to organize. Hence, to deny them legal protection from their employers was to deny them any protection at all. As for the claim that sex-specific legislation would disadvantage women workers because it would lead them to be displaced by men she disdainfully observed that the threat of displacement had invariably been advanced by employers and their ideologists whenever any group of workers had sought to gain legislative protection. To her mind the opponents of the Government's Bill were merely voicing the tired and discredited arguments of their class. The only difference this time was that it was the 'capitalists' wives and daughters' who were the most vocal in denying women workers protection from the demands of their husbands and fathers.

Beatrice's recognition that many of the rightist feminists who had joined with the employers in opposing the Government's Bill were hostile to all forms of protective labour law did not prevent her recognizing that some of these women adhered to collectivist principles. She believed that unfortunately, these latter individuals had allowed their democratic sympathies to be overborne by a fear of handicapping women in their struggle for employment. Being sympathetic with these women's fears she sought to disabuse them of their concerns by explaining in some detail why she supported the Bill even though some of its provisions were sex specific. She began by observing that she was heartily in favour of regulating, by law, the working conditions of both sexes. However, as there existed a great prejudice within the community against the regulation of men's working conditions it was highly unlikely that in the near future men would be able to gain the level of protection that the women in the textile industry had enjoyed for nearly forty years. Consequently, if the women in the sweated trades were to gain any protection from their employers it was unfortunately necessary that the law apply only to females.

Drawing on the empirical evidence amassed by Sidney, women members of the Fabian Society and the female factory inspectors, Beatrice also observed that many of the arguments of her opponents were founded on abstract principles and assumptions which were not supported by the facts.[6] To begin with, it was simply not true that women and men within the manual trades competed actively for the same types of employment. She acknowledged there were cases where this did occur but, given the sharpness of the sexual division of labour, these instances were rare and it was important that they be viewed in their proper proportion to the whole field of industry:

> It would clearly be a calamity to the cause of women's advancement if we were to sacrifice the personal liberty and economic independence of three or four millions of wage-earning women in order to enable a few hundreds or a few thousands to supplant men in certain minor spheres of industry (B. Webb, 1896, p. 12).

The second assumption Beatrice Webb denied was the claim that placing legal restrictions on the employers' utilization of women's labour was a pure loss to women and a total gain to men. This assumption, she insisted, was simply a delusion. Experience suggested that the workers excluded from employment by the enactment of factory legislation were not the women who competed with men. Rather, they were the female casual 'amateurs' who laboured part-time and undertook factory work while being partly supported by their husbands. Because these amateurs did not have to survive solely on their wages they were able to undercut the rates and conditions of women who sought to earn their living as full-time employees. This was a claim which had been well documented by the Labour Commission, which had acknowledged it was a cause of much resentment amongst unmarried women workers. It was these amateurs, Beatrice insisted, who were excluded by the enactment of legal minimum employment standards but it was not to the benefit of men but to the benefit of the woman 'professional'.

In conclusion, Beatrice observed the claim that the sex-specific clauses in the Factory Act which restricted the employment opportunities of women, rested on a misunderstanding of the effect of this legislation on the structure of industry. Drawing on empirical research undertaken by Clara Collet she argued that the facts showed that the growth of the factory system was increasing the demand for female labour. Further, that this system of production had been shown to expand in the most dramatic manner precisely in those industries where state regulation of employment had undermined the economic viability of the sweaters' den and especially in those areas where men had worked at home with their wives and daughters as unpaid assistants. It was, she insisted, an

> arithmetical fact that it is the factory system which provides the great market for women's labor. Those well-meaning ladies who, by resisting the extension of Factory legislation, are keeping alive the domestic workshop and the sweaters' den, are thus positively curtailing the sphere of women's employment. The 'freedom' of the poor widow to work, in her own bedroom, 'all the hours that God made'; and the wife's privilege to supplement a drunken husband's wages by doing work at her own fireside, are, in sober truth, being purchased at the price of the exclusion from regular factory employment of thousands of 'independent women' (B. Webb, 1896, p. 14).

In the years through to the end of the century Beatrice remained active in the campaign labour feminists waged to improve the situation of women in industry. Much of her effort in this regard was put into the Labour Law Association a society formed to promote 'the dissemination of knowledge of what the Factory Acts were, how they came about, and what had been their effects, especially upon working women' (Ward, 1901, p. viii). In 1899 she attended the International Congress of Women where she defended wage regulation and argued that reliance on collective bargaining alone would induce a deterioration in women's wages. These claims elicited an angry response from her opponents who accused her of acting as a front for the interests of men (Feuer, 1988, p. 258; Collette, 1989, p. 17).

In response to these attacks, in 1901 Beatrice edited a book for the Labour Law Association which she titled *The Case for the Factory Acts*. Her chapter in this work was a feminized version of the defence of wage regulation she and Sidney had developed in their 1897 volume *Industrial Democracy*. Beatrice's objective in preparing this work and her understanding of the character of her opponents she detailed in her diary at the time:

> [The work] is to be a counterblast to the persistent opposition to factory legislation on the part of the 'women's rights' movement reinforced by the employers' wives. This opposition has for the last ten years blocked all progress in the effective application of the Factory Acts to other industries. It is led by a few blatant agitators, who would not count for much if they were not backed up by many 'society' women who belong to the governing clique, and by a solid opposition to further reform from vested interests (B. Webb, 1948, p. 205).

In her 1901 book Beatrice again observed that the individuals who were the greatest opponents of the Factory Acts were often in ignorance of the facts associated with this form of legislation and were merely arguing on the basis of abstract principles. She sought afresh, therefore, to explain why workers and indeed the wider society could not afford to allow conditions of employment to be determined solely by the market. She also explained the manner and extent to which the costs of sweated labour were forced on to the whole community and sought to clarify the practical lessons for women that were to be learned from studying the experience of factory legislation. For Beatrice and the labour feminists this experience showed conclusively working women's need for a comprehensive labour code which would prescribe the 'minimum conditions of wages, leisure, education and health, for each class of operatives, below which the community will not allow its industry to be carried on' (B. Webb, 1901, p. 74).

THE EXCLUSION OF WOMEN

In 1889 Beatrice's animosity to the rightist faction of the women's movement had led her to sign an article opposing the extension of the suffrage to women. This was an act she subsequently very much regretted and retracted publicly.[7] Her signing of the anti-suffrage document, nevertheless, has induced a number of commentators to brand her as an 'anti-feminist'. Caine (1982, p. 23), for example, has argued that not only was Beatrice not a feminist she was not even 'particularly active' in the late nineteenth- and early twentieth-century 'campaigns which were waged specifically to improve the situation of women'. Likewise, Pujol (1992, p. 84) asserts that Beatrice was 'outside the ranks' of the women's movement. These assessments, however, are difficult to sustain given Beatrice's fifty years of active involvement in the struggle to improve the lives of working-class women. They are only comprehensible if one equates the term 'women' merely with the female membership of the professional and upper classes though Caine and Pujol are not totally clear if this is their understanding.[8]

A more valid assessment of Beatrice's feminism and contribution to the struggle to improve the situation of women has been provided by Nolan and deserves citation in full:

> [D]espite having been branded 'anti–feminist' as a result of this single incident in her career, Beatrice Webb was, throughout her life, acutely aware of the inequities suffered by the women of her time, and of the need for discussion and organized action in their behalf. She frequently made clear to her male visitors her feelings on the equality of women. Upon hearing a friend's obviously biased remarks on the unattractiveness of virtues like courage, strength, and independence in women, and on the value of the subordination of women, she reports in her Diary:
>
> > I maintained the opposite argument (from Professor Marshall), that there was an ideal of character in which strength, courage ... persistent purpose were united to a clear and far seeing intellect; that the ideal was common to the man and to the woman....
>
> Like her predecessor, J.S. Mill, who stood in the forefront of those attempting to secure equal rights for women of nineteenth-century England, Webb's efforts on behalf of her sex took the form, not only of debate, but also of action. During a heated discussion on women with the wife of Samuel Barnett ... Webb told her 'that the only way in which we can convince the world of our power is to <u>show</u> it.' And she did just that, spending the next several decades of her life engaged in works designed to up-grade the status of women in England (Nolan, 1988, pp. 212–14).

In her analysis of Beatrice's relationship with the women's movement

Caine has also asserted that Beatrice failed to recognize the extent to which male trade unionists opposed the market interests of women because of their desire to keep them in the home:

> She was unable or unwilling to recognise the degree of male hostility to women within these movements and, when she did acknowledge it, regarded it as a sign of residual prejudice which would decline as soon as women displayed their competence and their solidarity with male workers (Caine, 1982, p. 39).

Caine's assertion suggests that she is unaware of the Webbs' discussion of what Beatrice termed the 'bad side of Trade Unionism' (B. Webb, 1901, p. 71) that appears in *Industrial Democracy*. Among the activities the Webbs included under this categorization was the male unionists' attempts to exclude women from certain trades merely because they were women. The Webbs believed the extent of this exclusion was overrated by the rightist feminists. They noted that because of the physical demands of manual occupations the question of women's exclusion simply never arose as an issue in many industries. Nevertheless, they accepted that such practices did occur and that often the male unionists' exclusion of women was purely a product of prejudice being based only on: 'a deeply-rooted conviction in the minds of the most conservative of classes, that, to use the words of a representative compositor, "the proper place for females is their home"' (Webb and Webb, 1897, p. 496).

The Webbs deplored these patriarchal attitudes and were pleased that by the turn of the century they could discern a growing feeling in favour of the equality of the sexes within organized labour. This development they put down to the fact, not that women had convinced the unionists of their competence and their solidarity, but rather to the growing dissemination of socialist principles and more importantly the fact that the men had become increasingly aware of the futility of the policy of exclusion. Where employers were determined to introduce women into a trade, the men had found, the exclusion strategy simply was not an effective means of defending male interests. Accordingly, organized labour was gradually abandoning the strategy of exclusion and was moving towards a policy which accepted women into all trades so long as they did not act as blacklegs, that is so long as they did not undermine the existing standard rate by offering to work for less than the terms normally demanded by men.

The Webbs sought to encourage trade unionists to accept women as members of their craft and union by highlighting the fact that where equal pay did exist, as in the weaving trade, there tended to exist a 'real, though unobtrusive, segregation'. Equality of rates, they observed, invariably reinforced the tendency for workers to divide by sex along fairly clear lines.

> In every mill we see both men and women at work, often at identical tasks. But, taking the ... trade as a whole, the great majority of the women will be found engaged on the comparatively light work paid for at the lower rates. On the other hand, a majority of the men will be found practically monopolising the heavy trade, priced at higher rates per yard, and resulting in larger weekly earnings. But there is no sex competition (Webb and Webb, 1897, p. 501).

This segregation was commonly a function of the natural or acquired attributes of the sexes. In the case of the weavers it was based primarily on physical strength. A woman weaver of 'exceptional strength' who was capable of undertaking the heavier tasks was free to do so. What she was not permitted was the right to 'offer her services at a lower rate than has been fixed for the men. She is not, as a woman, excluded from what is generally the men's work, but she must win her way by capacity, not by underbidding' (Webb and Webb, 1897, p. 501). In other words the notion of equality between the sexes was applied both in terms of what the woman could rightfully demand and what could be rightfully demanded of her.

The Webbs believed the form of sex segregation that tended to be associated with equal pay for the same work was unsatisfactory. However, in *Industrial Democracy* they argued that it was a compromise which had distinct advantages. Its primary benefit was that it decreased the ability of the employer to use women to undermine the standard rate in a trade while at the same time it enhanced the ability of women to establish and enforce their own standards. The Webbs observed of the notion of different pay standards for the work normally done by men and women that 'each party is bound up with the maintenance of the other's Standard Rate.' Women stood to gain by ensuring that men's rates remained high because it meant employers would not be inclined to substitute men for women. On the other hand, men stood to gain by ensuring women's rates were maintained at the highest level compatible with their productivity for by doing so it decreased the likelihood that women would be used as blacklegs by the employers. It did do so by both reducing the pressure on women to feel they had no choice but to act as scabs and by undermining their attractiveness as substitutes for men, as the employer was compelled to pay a wage commensurate with their productivity. The essential point was that underbidding was contained and a disastrous downward spiral in wages avoided. The need to be clear on the Webbs' position in this regard justifies the following extensive citation:

> [W]orkers at each operation should establish and enforce definite Common Rules, binding on all who work at their operation, whether they be men or women. The occupations which demanded the strength, skill, and endurance of a trained man would ... be carried on with a relatively high Standard Rate. On the other hand, the operatives in those processes which were within the capacity of the average woman would aim at such Common Rules as to wages, hours, and other conditions of labor, as corresponded to their position, efforts, and needs. The experience of the Lancashire Cotton-weavers indicates that such a differentiation of earnings is not necessarily incompatible with the thorough maintenance of a Standard Rate, and also that it results in an almost complete industrial segregation of the sexes. Women are not engaged at the men's jobs, because the employers, having to pay them at the same high rate as the men, find the men's labor more profitable. On the other hand, the ordinary man does not offer himself for the woman's job, as it is paid for at a rate below that which he can earn elsewhere, and upon which, indeed, he could not permanently maintain himself. But there need be no rigid exclusion of exceptional individuals. If a woman proves herself capable of working as well and as profitably to the employer as a man, and is engaged at the man's Standard Rate, there is no Trade Union objection to her being admitted to membership ... on the same terms as a man. If, on the other hand, a man is so weak that he can do nothing but the light work of the women, these may well admit him, as do the Lancashire Weavers, at what is virtually the women's rate. The key to this as to so many other positions is, in fact, a thorough application of the principle of the Standard Rate (Webb and Webb, 1897, pp. 506–7).

THE FABIAN WOMEN'S GROUP

In 1906 Beatrice decided the time had come for her to take an active part in the struggle for women's right to vote. She consequently wrote a letter to Millicent Fawcett publicly endorsing the women's suffrage movement. She also began taking a more active part in the Fabian Society. The Society had always given nominal support to the notion of political equality between the sexes but had treated the suffrage issue as a topic of secondary importance. Beatrice determined this was a situation which needed to be redressed. Accordingly, in January 1907 she seconded a motion by Mrs. Pember Reeves to have the political equality of the sexes made part of the basis of the Society (Pease, 1963, pp. 175–6). She followed up this act in 1908 by assisting in the establishment of the Fabian Women's Group. The members of this body became highly active in the struggle for the suffrage but were distinguished by the fact that they refused to accept the sufficiency of the demand for the vote. They believed that too great an emphasis on the franchise would result in women attaining no more than had the men of the working class who had campaigned for the Reform Bill. Of the latter Wingfield-Stratford has observed: 'They had roared for the Bill, the whole Bill and nothing but the Bill, and it took them a little time to discover that what they had got was nothing but the Bill' (cited in Klein, 1971, p. 24). The Fabian Women's wider focus and purpose was encapsulated in the statement as to why the group had been established:

> The Fabian Women's Group was formed in order to study and to strengthen the economic position of women and to bring them into line with men in the advance towards paid work for all, for the equal advantage of all. It asks for equality of opportunity for women as for men: it asserts that if half the community is to remain in a weak economic position, progress for the other half must, in the nature of things, be retarded (Fabian Women's Group, 1915, p. xvi).

Beatrice explained her 'change of attitude' towards the issue of female suffrage as a product of her conviction that the state was failing to give women adequate support in those areas she considered the particular province of her sex – 'The rearing of children, the advancement of learning, and the promotion of spiritual life' (B. Webb, 1978b, p. 242). The adverse consequences of this failure were so great, Beatrice had become convinced, that there was an obligation on women to claim a share in the conduct of political affairs. In 1905 she had been appointed to the Royal Commission on the Poor Laws and the Relief of Distress. As a result of this experience and of the research she and Sidney had been undertaking into local government the Webbs had developed a much deeper understanding of the extent of destitution in Britain. They had also became aware that destitution was an especially acute problem for women.

> That poverty had a female face was evident from the tragic evidence collected by Mrs Harlow [for the Royal Commission on Poverty]. Ninety-five per cent of

Outdoor Relief was given to 'able-bodied' women, sixty thousand in all, who had young dependent children and yet were forced to work . ... The most pitiful tales of human suffering were of those families refused relief because of 'bad character': the single mother visited in January living in one room with five children, her one-month-old baby wasting away, dependent on her neighbours for a half-pennyworth of cow's milk or the occasional tin of condensed milk; by March the baby was dead, the mother evicted; or the old lady whom the Charity Organisation Society called 'a vile woman – too vile to be called a woman at all', because she was alcoholic (Seymour-Jones, 1992, p. 275).

By 1906 the Webbs had become convinced that the elimination of destitution required social policies which would ensure that all members of the community were able to enjoy at least a minimal standard of civilized life. In other words the demand that there must exist minimum standards had to be extended beyond the employment relationship. It had to become a demand which would 'cleanse the base of society', eradicate destitution and guarantee all members of the community the right to at least a minimal standard of decency. In short, they insisted the community must establish the welfare state.

In order to induce the Liberal Ministry that was swept to office in the general election of 1906 to introduce the reforms they believed were so desperately required, the Webbs determined that it was necessary to 'make an atmosphere'. This must be of a character such that the nation's leaders would feel compelled to enact the appropriate legislation. The letter to Fawcett was almost certainly part of their attempt to create this milieu. In her letter Beatrice stated that she had never believed in 'abstract rights' but rather regarded 'life as a series of obligations – obligations of the individual to the community and of the community to the individual' (B. Webb, 1978b, p. 241). Considered in the abstract, she believed women had no particular obligation to engage in parliamentary politics. However, a different situation existed if their failure or inability to undertake this activity resulted in the community failing its obligations to the individual and made it impossible for women to fulfil their particular obligations. In such a situation women must demand that they be given a say in directing the life of the community. They must have the vote.

Through the years 1906 to 1912 the Webbs campaigned in favour of a comprehensive system of social welfare designed to eradicate destitution. In 1909 Beatrice submitted a Minority Report to the Royal Commission on Poverty, which she wrote together with Sidney. When it became clear that the Government wished to avoid its obligations they turned to the public forming the National Committee for the Prevention of Destitution which at its height was to have some 16,000 active members campaigning for a legislative programme based on the Minority Report.

As part of this campaign Beatrice encouraged and actively participated in the production of a number of tracts of specific relevance to women. Caine (1982, p. 43) has suggested that Beatrice did not play an active role in the Fabian Women's Group. However, as Pugh (1984, p. 114), has observed, the reality was that:

> Until mid-1912 Beatrice Webb kept the [Fabian Women's] Group busy supplementing her work on trade unionism and industrial democracy by investigating women's place in the unions, the obstacles preventing their full contribution to the national economy and proposing remedial legislative measures.

In the years prior to 1914 several important publications emerged from these efforts. These included a book defending factory legislation, *Socialism and National Minimum,* which Beatrice published together with B.L. Hutchins, a pamphlet which documented the fact that paid employment was of vital necessity to a third of the female population, another which criticized the treatment of women by the philanthropic societies and two others which criticized Lloyd George's National Insurance Bill. Beatrice helped construct the last two tracts while at the same time preparing her own 'counter-blast', *The Prevention of Destitution,* which she and Sidney published in 1911.

THE NEW STATESMAN

The Webbs' campaign managed to win a number of significant reforms though these were far less than what they had hoped to achieve. By 1912 it was clear the steam had gone out of the campaign. However, they were far from finished with the struggle for women's rights. In 1912, Sidney edited a book, *Seasonal Trades,* which detailed the oppressive conditions of employment experienced by women in a number of occupations. The following year the Webbs founded *The New Statesman* as a socialist weekly and Beatrice immediately began utilizing the paper as a vehicle to improve the situation of women. In

November 1913 she edited and wrote an introduction to a special supplement of the paper, titled 'The Awakening of Women'. The contributors to the supplement included Charlotte Perkins Gilman, Christabel Pankhurst, Mrs. Pember Reeves and Millicent Fawcett. In her introduction Beatrice argued that to understand women's demand for 'a place in the sun' it was necessary to be aware that their awakening was not a manifestation of 'mere feminism'. Rather it was part of something bigger:

> It is one of three simultaneous world-movements towards a more equal partnership among human beings in human affairs ... paralleled, on the one hand, by the International Movement of Labour ... and, on the other, by the unrest among subject-peoples struggling for freedom to develop their own peculiar civilisations (B. Webb, 1913, p. iii).

These three great movements, Beatrice observed, did not always advance together. Indeed, they oft-times appeared in mutual opposition. Nevertheless, they moved in the same direction and that was towards greater equality within humanity. In the case of all three the oppressed were compelled to struggle against those who would arrest their development and who justified their oppression on the grounds that the dominated were inferior beings. In the case of women, millions of females had been forced to become wage earners but had been denied the potential for liberation inherent in this development on the ground that they were mentally and physically inadequate:

> The tragedy of the situation is that, whilst we have forced these millions of women to walk along the wage-earning road, we have not unbound their feet! By continuing to brand the woman as the social inferior of the man, unworthy of any share in the direction of the country, upon the economic development of which we have made her directly dependent; by providing for her much less technical training and higher education than for the boy; by telling her that she has slighter faculties and smaller needs, and that nothing but toil of routine character is expected from her; by barring her out ... from the more remunerative occupations ... man has made woman not merely into a wage earner, but, taken as a whole, in the world of labour, unfortunately, also into a 'blackleg,' insidiously undermining the wages of man himself (B. Webb, 1913, p. iv).

Both the claim that the women's movement was part of a greater crusade and that women continued to suffer oppression despite the advances they had made were key themes in Fawcett's contribution to the supplement. The latter observed that one might be inclined to say that women's awakening was the biggest event in the history of the world but for the fact 'that it certainly forms a part of a still bigger thing – the rise and progress of democracy' (Fawcett, 1913, p. viii). There remained many, she observed, who continued to deny women their humanity but increasingly these reactionaries were becoming a conservative rump. They were being driven back by women who were demanding their share of political power and responsibility, their chance in education and the right to employment within all occupations. In a reversal of her earlier commitment to the free market and to unrestrained individualism Fawcett denied employers the right to employ women for less than men and observed that in industry the cause of women was being advanced by the rise of trade unionism and by the work of the factory inspectors.

Fawcett's rapprochement with the Webbs has been missed by those analysts, such as Caine (1992), who have examined their relationship. How such a transformation could have occurred Beatrice explained in the paper, 'Voteless Women and Social Revolution' that she published in *The New Statesman* in February 1914. Beatrice observed that despite the breadth and intensity with which the women's movement was advancing the demand for female suffrage it was plain to all that there was no hope that Parliament would accede the demand in the immediate future. While this fact was to be lamented she noted it also had 'some counterbalancing advantages' for those who were intent on the reconstruction of society. For what the intransigence of the anti-suffrage forces was inducing was a radicalization of the women's movement.

> British womanhood, taken as a whole, is being transformed, under our eyes, from a passively conservative into an actively revolutionary force. In the early days of the suffrage agitation social reformers felt, with some pain, that, except on the one question of votes for women (usually for propertied women only), the 'Women's Rights Movement' spelt social reaction. The eminent group of women who first claimed the vote belonged exclusively to the propertied class. They had been brought up, for the most part, in the strictest sect of Philosophic Radicalism. They were opposed to factory legislation, to the 'tyranny of trade unions,' to any increase in the taxation of the rich, and to any development of Municipal Socialism. They reflected, in short, the vested interests and the personal prejudices of the existing order. No one in those days doubted that if votes were given to women on the same terms as to men the Crown, the Church and the peerage, as well as the landlords and the capitalists, would thereby strengthen their hold on the British Constitution and on public administration (B. Webb, 1914a, p. 585)

Had nineteenth-century women attained the right to vote with ease, Beatrice further noted, they would almost certainly have accorded this freedom little esteem. As it was, the fact that the two major political parties had opposed female suffrage had made its attainment a burning issue to millions of women. Moreover, the fact that only the socialists had consistently, even if somewhat mechanically, supported the demand for universal suffrage had not been lost on these millions. As a consequence, almost unintentionally, the women's movement was coming to embrace the Labour Party and socialist politics. And it was doing so to an extent where the most 'Right-Wing' section of the women's movement, Millicent Fawcett's National Union of Women's Suffrage Societies, had formally allied itself with the party of the left. Prophetically, Beatrice observed that were women to be granted the vote by Parliament there would be a 'stampede' of these activists back into the ranks of the right. But the longer this was delayed, she observed, the less would be the 'reversion to the creed of laissez-faire in social and economic questions.'

> But this is not all. Among the four millions of salaried and wage-earning women – the teachers, the clerks, the factory hands – the growing intensity of sex consciousness is being fused, by close comradeship with Socialists, into the 'class consciousness' of the proletariat eager not merely for political but for economic 'enfranchisement.' I wonder whether Liberal Ministers quite realise how the contemptuous refusal of the suffrage by a party that claims to be democratic strikes the average woman in Lancashire cotton mills or Leicester shoe shops? The insincerities, prevarications and tyrannies of the male Cabinet Minister, the male judge and male party journalist are becoming identified in the working woman's mind with a growing revolt against the low wages and the degrading conditions of employment which seem part and parcel of an essentially masculine capitalism. The votelessness of women [sic] is, at the present moment, tantamount to a rapidly spreading Socialism from one end of Great Britain to the other (B. Webb, 1914a, p. 586).

The following week Beatrice continued her promotion of the cause of women by writing the introduction to the second special supplement on women to be published in *The New Statesman*. This publication focused on women in industry. It was prepared by the Fabian Women's Group and dealt with women's wages, trade unionism, the minimum wage and the need for childcare. In her introduction Beatrice castigated those individuals who continued to insist that 'woman's place is the home' observing that an ever increasing proportion of the female population simply had no choice but to sell their labour power in the market. She also challenged the notion that female wage-earners have fewer needs of body and mind, criticized the fact that women were expected to undertake the labour of the home even when they worked as full-time employees and denounced the fact that the woman worker had no say as regards the taxes she paid and the laws under which she was employed (B. Webb, 1914b, pp. 1–2).

Reflecting the fact that the Webbs were by now concerned with wider issues than those relating only to the workplace and to the industrial working class Beatrice followed up this contribution in July and August of 1914 by publishing a series of five papers which she collected under the general title, 'Personal Rights and the Woman's Movement'. These papers dealt with the relationship between individuals and between the individual and the community, the birth-rate, women's right to maternity, the right of women to free entry into all occupations and their right to equal remuneration with men (B. Webb, 1914c). She also published a paper on motherhood in 1914 in yet a third special supplement of *The New Statesman* that was directly related to improving the situation of women and produced a major report for the Fabian Research Department. This latter report examined the problems of developing trade union organization amongst school teachers, an occupation which she stressed was predominantly female (B. Webb, 1915).

THE WAR CABINET COMMITTEE ON WOMEN IN INDUSTRY

In September 1918 Beatrice was appointed to the War Cabinet Committee on Women in Industry.[9] This body was created to 'investigate and report upon the relation which should be maintained between the wages of women and men, having regard to the interests of both, as well as to the value of their work' (War Cabinet Committee, 1919, p. ii). The Committee was subsequently also asked to consider the nature of a 1915 agreement that had been forged between the trade union movement and the Government. The unions believed that the essence of this agreement was that pre-war employment conditions would be maintained and that 'all women who should be put to do the work hitherto done by men should receive the same pay as the men whose work they undertook' (B. Webb, 1919a, p. 3). The Government denied the agreement had contained any such pledge and the War Cabinet Committee was asked to comment on the validity of the two interpretations.

Beatrice did not enjoy her membership on the Committee. She and the other members considered their efforts to be largely a waste of time given it was certain their report would be ignored:

> [W]e all feel that the Committee's Report will be still-born: the War Pledges are ancient history and any conclusions we come to about the future relation between men's and women's wages will have little or no effect on what actually happens. Alterations of the wage system will depend on the relative political and industrial forces and neither the Government nor the Trade Unions, certainly not the employers, will proceed on the lines of ideal principle (B. Webb, 1978d, p. 3652).

This suspicion was validated even before the Committee had completed its work when the Government appointed a more representative body charged with examining the whole industrial situation (B. Webb, 1978d, p. 3671). Nevertheless, in characteristic fashion Beatrice not only produced a Minority Report she also had her contribution reproduced by the Fabian Society and published as a tract titled, *The Wages of Men and Women: Should they Be Equal?*

Beatrice's answer to this question was a resounding yes as was her conclusion that the Government had pledged to pay women the wage rate formerly paid to men and that it had reneged on its promise. Her disagreement with those who signed the Majority Report centred on the fact that they had only considered the conditions under which women attain employment and had refused to acknowledge publicly that the Government was actively attempting to use the women who had entered industry during the war as blacklegs in order to undermine pre-war wage rates. She objected to the Majority's decision to focus on women's problems because she believed that to do so was to assume industry is normally a male domain. If the purpose of the investigation was to advise on the relationship which should be maintained between the wages of women and men, she insisted there should be an equal focus on both sexes. Thus, in her Report she assumed that her task was to examine the principles upon which wages and conditions had traditionally been determined. She also assumed that the purpose of this examination was to decide whether these principles affected men and women differently, whether any such difference was justified given the interests of both sexes and the needs of industry and whether any new principle was needed upon which to base the relationship between the wages of men and women (B. Webb, 1919a, p. 7).

In her Report Beatrice argued that the existing wage structure was detrimental to the personal character and professional efficiency of both sexes. It was also inimical to the economic well-being of the nation. The exclusion of women from the better-paid occupations crowded them into the lower grades. Here, they were compelled to accept even less than the inadequate wages paid to men on the pretence that women have no family obligations and have less needs, less capacity and a lower level of intelligence. She denied that women constituted a separate class who could justifiably be treated differently from men and insisted the time had:

> come for the removal of all sex exclusions; for the opening of all posts and vocations to any individuals who are qualified for the work, irrespective of sex, creed or race; and for the insistence, as minima, of the same qualifications, the same conditions of employment, and the same occupational rates, for all those accepted by the private or public employers as fit to be engaged in any particular pursuit (B. Webb, 1919a, pp. 71–2).

The attainment of these objectives, Beatrice insisted, could not be founded on the popular formula of 'Equal Pay for Equal Work'. While expressing the correct ideal, this notion was so ambiguous and open to manipulation it did not constitute any principle by which the relation between the wages of men and women could be safely determined. Evidence provided to the Committee had shown that employers were utilizing the fact that it was often difficult to assess what constituted equal work as a device by which they could substitute women for men within industry – when doing so paying them at a markedly lower rate than that formerly received by the men. To overcome this difficulty Beatrice advised that the principle which should govern all systems of remuneration must be clearly defined 'Occupational and Standard Rates' to be prescribed for all members of the same industrial grade irrespective of sex. These rates must be set by collective bargaining between the trade unions and the employers' organizations and enforced as minima on the whole industry. Moreover, there must exist a legal National Minimum as regards rest-time, education, sanitation and subsistence which must apply equally to both sexes.

Pujol (1992, p. 86) has asserted that Beatrice's Minority Report essentially restates the position developed in *Industrial Democracy*. This assessment, however, misses two critical developments. First, Beatrice no longer accepted there was any case for a protective labour law that was sex specific. The male-dominated unions now believed that these laws should apply equally to both sexes. Consequently, Beatrice observed it was appropriate that all special provisions applying to only one sex should be amended in a manner which would ensure that men and women were protected equally.

Beatrice's attitude towards different pay rates for men and women also diverged from the position adopted in *Industrial Democracy*. In the latter work the Webbs had argued that men and women should be paid the same rate where they did the same job but had accepted that women's lesser strength and skill commonly justified the notion of male and female occupations which were paid at different rates. In her 1919 Report, on the other hand, Beatrice rejected this notion. She argued that the existence of a male and female rate served only the 'vested interest of the male'. The notion of a dual standard was utilized through all the professions and crafts as a device to exclude women from the higher-paying forms of employment. In the case of the crafts, much of this exclusion was a result of the fact that workers were compelled constantly to defend the standard rates of the occupation from the attempts by employers to use women as blacklegs. However, where Beatrice had previously approved of segregation as a means of combating these attacks she now observed that this form of isolation was unacceptable because it was invariably used by men as a means of ensuring they monopolized the better-paying jobs. Further, it had given rise to the notion that whatever was women's work could be paid for at a lower rate irrespective of the skill and effort required. Accordingly, Beatrice argued that within every occupation there should exist only one rate and that this must be paid to both sexes. In reply to the employers' claim that women were not as efficient as men Beatrice replied that this generalization was unacceptable as a basis for setting standard rates as it discriminated against those women who did have the required level of efficiency. It was imperative, therefore, that the notion of a male and a female rate be expunged from all forms of employment:

There is no ground whatever for any deliberately imposed exclusion or inclusion with regard to any occupation whatever of a whole class, whether marked out by sex, height, weight, colour, race or creed. Any such artificial eligibility or ineligibility by class necessarily involves unfairness to individuals. There can plainly be no warrant for any other ground of selection or exclusion, whether in manual working occupations or in the brain-working professions, in capital enterprise or in the public service, than the aptitude and fitness of each individual (B. Webb, 1919a, pp. 44–5).

Turning to the suggestion that the effect of abandoning the notion of a female rate would be a collapse in the demand for women's labour Beatrice observed that taking all occupations together she could see no reason why more women than men would be adversely affected by gender-neutral standard rates. She admitted it was difficult to forecast the effect of introducing this standard on each occupational grade because of the existing ignorance as to the influence of sex characteristics on the efficiency of the worker. However, she did not consider this an insurmountable difficulty. If it happened to be the case that in an occupation the attributes of either sex were such that they gave one or the other a significant comparative advantage it was to be expected that the advantaged sex would come to numerically dominate the trade. This was not a matter of concern so long as the efficient individual was not precluded, indeed, it was in the interests of the community as a whole as it would help to ensure an efficient allocation of the nation's labour resources.

Overall, in her 1919 Report, Beatrice adopted a much less compromising stance than she had in *Industrial Democracy*. The tone and language adopted in the Report suggests that part of the reason she did so was because she had become aware of the extent to which men were continuing to exclude women from the skilled occupations. However, this is certainly only part of the explanation. To understand the other critical factor it is necessary to be aware of the debate regarding the employment of women that had been undertaken through the war years. In 1914 Beatrice had observed that a paradox existed at the threshold of the debate regarding equal remuneration for men and women. Feminists who insisted on women's right to equal pay found that within the trade union movement their strongest allies were in the most anti-feminist male organizations. The members of these latter bodies endorsed the demand that women should have free entry into their craft and union. However, they also insisted that women must be paid at least the same rate as men. Beatrice reported that the men's reason for insisting on the last proviso was because they were aware that in many trades the demand that all rates be gender neutral was a very effective means of inducing employers to exclude women. In short, they realized that where employers were compelled to pay men and women the same rate they commonly adopted a policy of only employing men.

The great attraction that women had in the struggle for jobs, as far as employers were concerned, was the fact that they could be hired for less than men. It was for this reason that many nineteenth-century free market feminists had insisted that women had the right to take work at any price and under any conditions they chose. Beatrice, of course, found this suggestion totally objectionable because of the deleterious effect unrestrained competition had on the lives of the men and women concerned and indeed on the life of the whole community. She observed that women had no more right to take employment for less than the standard rate than they had to drive on the wrong side of the road. At the same time she was aware that to assert as an absolute principle that women must always be paid the same rate as men was to fall into the trap of the male exclusionists. Accordingly, while she believed that 'paying women low wages, just because they are women, is a scandal that amounts to a crime' (B. Webb, 1914c, p. 526) as late as 1914 she continued to accept that in many trades it was still necessary to maintain a separate female and male standard rate.

Two years later, in September 1916, Sidney again discussed the conflict between the principle that women had a right both to work and that which decreed they should receive equal pay in a tract he published with Freeman titled, *When Peace Comes – The Way of Industrial Reconstruction*. Sidney argued that the period of demobilization that would follow the declaration of peace was likely to be characterized by mass discontent. Indeed, there was the gravest danger that with the end of the war on the battlefield there would erupt 'spasmodic and possibly widespread industrial war' (S. Webb and Freeman, 1916, p. 12). Employers were counting on being able to secure a heavy fall in wages, when several millions of men and women were simultaneously compelled to seek employment as the army and the war industries demobilized. The coming class conflict, Sidney added, would revolve around wages, speed-up and the fact that the employers were certain to oppose the reintroduction of those craft occupations that had been diluted, supposedly for the duration of the war, so that the work of the craftsmen could be undertaken by partly trained women and male labourers. He reported that the Government's pledge that they would protect the rights of the skilled workers to their former jobs and that they would protect pre-war employment conditions was being mocked by the employers who were stating openly that after the war there would be no return to the former industrial situation, that the employers would be the masters.

For Sidney, the key to minimizing the intensity of the coming conflict was the creation of sufficient work to ensure that the craftsmen were not terrified by the fear of unemployment. This development was critical for if the skilled workers came to believe their families faced destitution as a consequence of others taking their jobs, men or women, they would feel compelled to fight. Indeed, against 'being thrown into a sea of unemployment all the trades will fight like tigers' (S. Webb and Freeman, 1916, p. 17).

If there was mass unemployment after the war, Sidney forecast, the unemployed men will demand that the Government maintain its promise that their jobs and conditions would be saved and insist that the women and the newly introduced male labourers be removed. If, however, there was abundant employment the skilled workers might be concerned that these newcomers could be used to undermine the standard rate but they were much less likely to insist on their removal. Assuming the Government adopted policies which ensured there was abundant employment, Sidney added, this left the question of how could the standard rate be maintained and the women and male labourers kept in work. To insist that these individuals be paid the same rate as the craftsmen would almost certainly lead to their exclusion given that employers had generally found they were not as productive as the men they had replaced. As this was the case it was not reasonable to expect that the women and the labourers would agree to insist on the established standard. It was necessary. therefore, that there be established a separate standard which would reflect the difference in the productivity of the two forms of labour:

> What is required is ... 'the fixing of a rate for men and women which shall be in equitable proportion to any less degree of physical endurance, skill, or responsibility exacted from the women, or to any additional strain thrown on the men, and which shall neither exclude women on the one side, nor blackleg men on

the other.' It is this delicate adjustment that the Government will have to make, perhaps by one of the devices suggested below (*prescribing minima only*, and securing by law the rigid enforcement of the minimum rates thus fixed). Only at this price can very serious trouble be averted (S. Webb and Freeman, 1916, pp. 19–20).

Awareness that there were bound to be difficulties in reabsorbing men into those sections of industry which had been feminized during the war was of course shared by others. Edith Rathbone (1917), for example, agreed that many women would be ousted from paid employment after the demobilization if they were to demand equal pay as the unions insisted. She also agreed that the employers would invariably seek to use the women they had hired as blacklegs during the war in a campaign designed to break the standard rates paid in many occupations. Like the Webbs she suggested the solution to this dilemma was a legally enforceable wage that accepted the principle of equal pay but also accepted that where women's biology or social position gave them a disadvantage they should be able to accept lower rates. The level of women's pay, Rathbone advised, should be 'sufficiently lower than men's rates to balance, but not more than balance, the inherent disadvantages of female labour' (Rathbone, 1917, p. 64).

Fawcett, on the other hand, argued that it was imperative that women be paid the same rate as men in all occupations. She applauded the fact that the men's trade unions had accepted the need for equal pay and lambasted the men of her own class for failing to do likewise. In developing her argument Fawcett (1917) used much of the research undertaken by the Webbs and the Fabian Women's Group. She disagreed with their perspective, however, in that she believed that paying women a substantially lower rate than was paid to men was against the interests of both sexes as it induced 'a downward pull' on the wages of all workers.

Fawcett believed that those who advocated the payment of a woman's rate had overstated the extent to which a productivity gap actually existed between the sexes and underestimated the debilitating influence trade union exclusionism and society's belief in women's incapacity to undertake skilled work had exerted prior to the war. Both these influences had diminished through the war years, she asserted, and to argue for separate rates for the sexes was to assist in the revitalization of these ideas. Given free entry into the trades and the support of the trade unions and the state she could not see any reason why the principle of equal pay for equal work would not find an almost universal acceptance (Fawcett, 1917, p. 4). Indeed, she concluded, if this principle was not accepted there was no possibility that male workers would accept women into the skilled trades:

> The one chance of women being received into industry by the men already employed as comrades and fellow-workers, not as enemies and blacklegs, is in their standing for the principle, equal pay for equal work, or, as it is sometimes expressed, equal pay for equal results. ... I am convinced that the best chance of women preserving, after peace returns, the industrial freedom which the war has brought them lies in the earnestness and sincerity with which industrial women maintain the principle 'equal pay for equal work' (Fawcett, 1917, pp. 4–5).

An examination of Beatrice's diary shows that she believed herself to be the only representative of 'advanced thought' on the 1919 War Cabinet Committee. By this term she appears to have meant she was the only individual who sought to preserve the interests of labour. She accepted that the three legal members of the Committee represented the interests of the Government and the Chairman-Judge she considered a 'reactionary about wages', a man whose decisions were influenced by his 'class prejudice'. The two non-lawyers she believed were conservatives who wanted 'a philanthropic settlement of women's wages, based largely on the function of motherhood but preserving the woman the right to undercut the man' (B. Webb, 1978d, pp. 3652, 3670–72). As has been shown, for the Webbs no such right existed. It appears to have been this fact, together with the clear evidence that the Government was setting an example to the employers of how to use women to cut standard rates, that induced them to abandon the compromise regarding the need to ensure equal pay, preserve standard occupational rates and save women's jobs they had supported since 1897. In short, in 1919 the Webbs saw correctly that the employers were intending to use women as blacklegs to break the existing standard rates and that the Government had no intention of preventing this happening. Caine (1982, pp. 40–41) has criticized Beatrice for refusing to accept women's right to act as blacklegs in this situation. But for the Webbs there was no real choice if compelled to choose between the right of women to work at a lower rate than men, in order to enhance their ability to take the jobs of others, and the need to preserve the ability of the working class to exert some degree of control over the wage determination process. In this situation Beatrice remained true to her belief that 'if regulation be impracticable with sex equality, I prefer to get regulation and do without sex equality.' Hence, she accepted Fawcett's demand that equal pay for the sexes be treated as an absolute principle and did so irrespective of the likely effect this would have on job segregation and the demand for female labour.

EPILOGUE

In 1918 the women of Britain won the right to vote. Subsequently, the Webbs again focused their attention on the issue of the welfare state and Beatrice appears to have ceased her concern with 'mere feminism'. Likewise, when they turned to examining the Soviet Union the lot of women was accorded little specific attention in their writing it being clear that as far as the Webbs were concerned it was the interests of all human beings that was essential. Immediately following the winning of female suffrage Beatrice gave clear indication of where her priorities lay in the preface she wrote to a book advising women on the nature of the British electoral system and in a chapter she contributed to a book on the relationship between women and the Labour Party (B. Webb, 1918, 1919b). In both publications the key theme was that it was imperative that the struggle not now be abandoned, that winning the vote must be seen as merely a step on the path to women's emancipation. Moreover, Beatrice clearly believed that it was imperative that women remain aware that their struggle was part of something greater. While fully cognisant that many within the women's movement who had been radicalized by the fight to win the suffrage would all too soon 'stampede' back to the right, she urged women to remember those others in the great struggle for democracy when they came to use their vote.

NOTES

1. Beatrice's abandonment of support for such notions as freedom of contract and an unregulated labour market, as a consequence of her experience in East London, was replicated by many other feminists through the last two decades of the nineteenth century. As Feuer has observed in her excellent article:

   [T]he effect of practical experience caused many activists to reexamine their position. Actual contact with working women and experience with attempts to help improve their working conditions often challenged the old ideological braces for feminists' position on protective legislation. ... Activists were brought face to face with women's problems in the workplace, which led them to reexamine positions regarding state interference, the labor market, and the possibility of women's self-help (Feuer, 1988, p. 249).

2. As the quote makes clear this was Sidney's summation of his position regarding women's wages. As a concluding summation it was meant to be his definitive statement on this question. In her discussion of Sidney's paper, Pujol (1992, p. 54), has ignored this summary and has asserted that Sidney believed that women's lesser pay was simply a consequence of their relative productivity. For Pujol the advantage of ignoring the summary statement is that it enables her to maintain her assertion that Sidney was a purveyor of a patriarchal economics. This is an argument that is difficult to sustain if one acknowledges that he concluded that women's lesser pay is a consequence of their past subjection and the influence of patriarchal ideas and customs and that he suggested that wage inequality might be most effectively overcome by encouraging women to become organized.

3. The Webbs were very much aware that many working-class families could not survive in a world in which mothers concentrated solely on the care of their families. For this reason by the early 1890s they were urging the need for the 'endowment of motherhood', that is the community payment of a wage for housework (B. Webb, 1983, pp. 53–4).

4. Margaret Cole (1945, p. 73) subsequently described the product of the Labour Commission as 'a mountainous *Report* running to seventeen volumes and containing practically no conclusions which were of any value to anyone.' Beatrice believed that the poor outcome of the Commission was not a product of chance but rather was a consequence of the fact that the majority of Commissioners had actively striven to transform the Commission from an instrument of inquiry into a 'State trial of the leaders of trade-union opinion' (B. Webb, 1894, p. 18). This was a transformation in which the 'professional brainworkers' on the Commission, amongst whom she included Alfred Marshall, had actively striven to bring about.

5. Hutchins's assertion that the different perspective adopted by the two factions reflected the class interests of each is similar to the argument developed by M.A. (1914, pp. 14–16) in her pamphlet *The Economic Foundations of the Women's Movement* and a more recent assessment in the same vein has been advanced by Feuer:

   To labor women [the avocation of free market economics] ... seemed to deny the historical position of women in the labor market. While unregulated access to employment meant greater freedom to middle–class women, it condemned working women to intolerable conditions. ... They could point to the many prosecutions of women dress-shop owners who violated the factory acts as evidence that women's interests often diverged. ... The challenge from ... feminist opponents of protective legislation was derided and dismissed by female labor activists as the rantings of upper- and middle-class women who denied the reality of working women's conditions (Feuer, 1988, pp. 258–9).

   The rightists' disdain for the opinions of working-class women, moreover, is indicated by their opposition to the regulation of the hours of laundresses. Despite the fact that there were virtually no men in the industry and a survey of 67,000 laundresses found 65,939 in support of regulatory legislation, the *Englishwoman's Review* opposed regulation and reported that it was 'incredible' that women such as Beatrice Webb would endorse a law of this nature (cited in Feuer, 1988, pp. 252, 256).

6. That the Fabian Society's support for protection for women was a fallback position is attested to by the fact that in 1895 a conference of Fabian women had called on the Government to ensure that its proposed reform of the Factory Act should apply to both sexes. This demand was subsequently supported by the Fabian Executive.

7. Beatrice regretted this step almost immediately. Her first published self-criticism in this regard occurred not in 1906 as is commonly asserted but in 1894 in her denunciation of the Labour Commission and she voiced regret at signing the document in her diary in 1889.

8. Modern rightist feminists have experienced great difficulty comprehending Beatrice's hostility to their equivalents of the late nineteenth and early twentieth century. A recent member of this school who has sought to explain Beatrice's animosity is Greenberg (1987, pp. 313–14). The latter has advanced the notion that Beatrice's antagonism was probably a manifestation of penis envy!

9. Following the outbreak of the First World War Sidney produced a Fabian tract, *The War and the Workers* which was a handbook of some of the immediate measures the Webbs believed needed to be undertaken to prevent unemployment and distress. As far as women were concerned he argued that special action needed to be taken to ensure there was adequate work available for those women discharged from their pre-war employment and that training schemes be established to prepare women for new forms of employment. He also argued that it was vital that steps be taken to ensure there was adequate maternity and infancy care available both for those women who were employed and for those who were not. He followed up this contribution in 1915 by assisting the Fabian Women's Group to produce a further tract, *The War; Women; and Unemployment* which also dealt with the widespread distress amongst women workers caused by lack of employment, training and adequate welfare.

6. A Neglected Daughter of Adam Smith: Clara Elizabeth Collet (1860–1948)*

Peter Groenewegen

In a pioneering study of women political economists, Thomson (1973) used the term, 'daughters of Adam Smith', to describe the six subjects of her book: Jane Marcet, Harriet Martineau, Millicent Fawcett, Rosa Luxembourg, Beatrice Webb (Potter) and Joan Robinson. In introducing her study, Thomson (1973, p.3) noted that some of these writers, especially the first two, 'are derided ... , ignored, or their existence barely acknowledged by the profession'. Nevertheless, these first three were pioneers in the writing of elementary textbooks, no more dogmatic in their stance than the products from their economist-brothers used in principles courses in late twentieth-century tertiary institutions. The fifth was a noted social researcher contributing to specific economic issues at various stages of her long career, while the other two were prominent economic theorists, one in the male-dominated circles of Marxist social democracy in Germany, the other in equally male-dominated Cambridge from the 1930s. All six of course have this in common, they share the characteristic of having contributed to the science which Adam Smith made famous at the end of the eighteenth century and did so in a manner recognized by both their contemporaries and later generations. In addition, they were all recognized in *The New Palgrave Dictionary of Economics* (Eatwell et al. (eds), 1987) in separate articles on their own, an honour they share with only 23 other women. One of these women, Clara Collet, is the subject of this chapter.

In some ways, the omission of Clara Collet from Thomson's (1973) study is not surprising, given the relative fame achieved by the six persons she actually included in her study of female economists. Her omission from other studies devoted to the history of economics on the women's question (for example, Madden, 1972; Pujol, 1992) is more difficult to explain, though she is included in a forthcoming study of women economists (Dimand et al., forthcoming). At the turn of the century, Clara Collet was a well-known and respected author on women's labour issues, which she herself preferred to describe, in the manner of Beatrice Webb, as studies of 'social conditions' (Bowley, 1950, p. 408). She had published a collection of articles on educated working women (Collet, 1902), had assisted in the production of a major report on women's work and wages as a specially appointed lady assistant commissioner on the Royal Commission on Labour (1891–94) and later wrote several reports on women's labour issues for the Board of Trade's newly created Labour Department (Collet, 1898a). Like Beatrice Webb, Clara Collet had assisted Charles Booth's study of *Life and Work in London* (Collet, 1889). In addition, she published important statistical studies of women's issues in prestigious journals like the *Journal of the Royal Statistical Society* (Collet, 1898b) and the *Economic Journal* (Collet, 1891a and b; 1898c, 1901, 1915), for the second journal gaining the distinction of being the only person who had contributed both to its first and fiftieth, jubilee, volume (Bowley, 1950, p. 408). She also wrote two entries for the original *Palgrave Dictionary of Political Economy* (Collet 1896a and b) dealing with female labour and the earnings of women and children. She therefore seems to have become a neglected daughter of Adam Smith from ignorance and oversight.

In the period of her life as an active economist she was not ignored, nor was she forgotten at the time of death by the learned societies to which she had contributed so greatly when in her thirties. It may be noted she was a founding member of the British Economic Association, which some years later became the Royal Economic Society; and an active member of the Royal Statistical Society. In 1890, she had initiated a move to organize the Junior Economic Club in London, as an offshoot of the more celebrated London economic circle which met at Hampstead as a bridge between economic theory (Wicksteed, Edgeworth and Marshall), bimetallism (Foxwell and Beeton) and the Fabians (Bernard Shaw and Sidney Webb) and others involved in the formative years of the London School of Economics (Graham Wallas). She was a close friend of Henry Higgs and Foxwell, knew Wicksteed well and as a child attended Shakespeare readings at the Marx residence, 1 Maitland Park Road. She later (1914) befriended the Indian planner, Mahalanobis. She attended popular lectures on economics by Toynbee, Ruskin and Symes, followed British Economic Association meetings and was one of the first women to achieve high positions in the government service. She ought, therefore, to be a celebrated rather than a neglected daughter of Adam Smith.

The following intends to set the record straight on this important woman economist of the Victorian era, who studied women's issues with the tools and techniques of modern economic analysis. The chapter thereby supplements the brief entry by Black (1987) for the *New Palgrave*, and earlier mention of her work in chapters in this volume dealing with Jevons, Marshall and the Webbs. After a biographical sketch, successive sections of the chapter provide an evaluation of her research on educated working women, general women labour market conditions, statistics on wages and statistical method, to conclude more generally on her importance as a female Victorian economist anxious to resolve the problems facing women's labour at that time. Her work is as noted a political economy contribution to issues of Victorian feminism as that of her more celebrated colleagues and contemporaries who featured in the previous four chapters.

A RICH AND INTERESTING LIFE

Clara Collet was born in 1860 into an ancient and gifted family, whose ancestry could be traced back to Rouen traders of that name who came to England not long after the Norman Conquest. Her male ancestry continued to be drawn predominantly from the merchant class, including a great-great-great uncle, Joseph Collet, an official of the East India Company but also a Governor of Madras in 1717, whose papers she later edited (Collet, 1933). Her older brother, Sir Wilfred Collet, continued this public administration tradition by becoming Governor first of British Guiana, then of British Honduras.

Her father, Collet Dobson Collet, was a noted radical reformer, rationalist and student of the law, and during his life wrote a great many books. One of his close friends, the secularist and social reformer, George Jacob Holyoake, wrote in the introduction to Collet's *History of*

Taxes on Knowledge (Collet, 1933) that its author was 'an unusual man, ... incessant in promoting public causes ... with absolute disinterestedness'. Collet was also an acquaintance of Marx and Engels. Clara Collet's diary mentions visits with her father to the Marxes for readings of *The Merchant of Venice* and *Richard III* in November 1877 and February 1878, and in June remarks that 'the Marxes and the Oswalds are the only people I care for now' (Collet, 1876–1914, pp. 12, 13, 15). Apart from information contained in her diary, very little is known of her childhood and early education. The last involved voracious reading (Darwin, Mill, Goethe) as well as early contacts with social reformers and radicals (Toynbee, Symes, Wicksteed) drawn from secular as well as clerical and unitarian circles.

An article written late in life (Collet, 1945) records that she was introduced to Political Economy because it was a compulsory course for the degree of MA at University College, London. Her political economy essays, as her diary records, were corrected by Ashley and Symes; the lectures were given by Foxwell, who became a lifelong friend (Collet, 1936). As part of the required political economy studies, she read Adam Smith, John Stuart Mill's *Principles of Political Economy* and Ruskin's *Unto this Last*. Although in 1876 she had complained that reading Mill was dull (Collet, 1876–1914, p. 17), her reading of Ruskin made her very 'indignant at Ruskin's gross misinterpretations of Smith and Mill'. This critical flair she never lost. However, Ruskin's social conscience was more to her liking and in her diary she expressed the wish for a society which would examine the logical consequences of taking Ruskin's basic axioms and postulates as the starting point for political economy. Ministers of religion reinforced this interest in social questions, and attracted her particularly to the increasingly important problem during the mid-1880s of the unemployed (C[atherine] T[horburn], 1948, p. 652). It was presumably this type of interest that brought her into contact with Charles Booth, for whose initial survey she contributed a number of chapters on women's labour; experience which undoubtedly qualified her for the position of Assistant Commissioner for the Royal Commission on Labour to investigate aspects of women's work. From then on, she became one 'of those who wove the women's movement concern with work into progressive philosophy' (Collette, 1989, p. 13), an interconnection which her experience with Booth, the Labour Commission, as well as her studies of political economy taught her, required the tools of economic and statistical analysis.

Although she completed her MA with honours, and later became the first woman Fellow at University College, London, her thirst for economic knowledge was such that she wished to continue her study of political economy by the device of a regular study group. Her friendship with Henry Higgs and Foxwell, combined with her zeal for serious discussion of social questions, enabled her to form such a group of progressive economists from among University College students as the London Junior Economic Club. Although Higgs advised her that the junior club should await the formation of the senior 'club' or Economic Association, 'with the usual impulsiveness of women she convened a meeting of students for next Friday [27 June 1890], which drew a number of interested people'. 'There were present Miss Heather Bigg, Miss Collet, Miss Foley, Aves, C.S. Loch, Llewellyn-Smith, Robinson, Hensman (a pupil of Edgeworth) and Henry Higgs'. Foxwell not long thereafter gave an inaugural address to the new club. This was followed by a contribution from Marshall which criticized aspects of his own *Principles of Economics* partly in the light of Edgeworth's earlier criticism (Collet, 1940, citing the Foxwell-Higgs correspondence and her own diary). The club thrived until well into the new century, drawing speakers from Cambridge, Oxford and the growing economic membership of the public service. One benefit it provided for Collet's later work was its interest in workers' budgets, based on the methods of Le Play, in whose work Higgs was interested to the extent of applying it to the contemporary British situation, an example Collet followed by investigating the expenditure patterns of British working women (Higgs, 1890).

When the British Economic Association was founded in November 1890, Clara Collet was one of the half dozen women recorded as present at the inaugural meeting. She subsequently served on the Council of the Royal Economic Society from 1920 to 1941, regularly attending its meetings and contributing to its work. In 1894 she was elected Fellow of the Royal Statistical Society in recognition of her statistical work on women's labour, and she served on its Council from 1919 to 1935. Activities in the professional associations coincided with advancement in the public service, where she became the first woman trained economist on the staff of the Board of Trade. She became its labour correspondent from 1893 to 1903 as a consequence of recommendations from the Labour Commission she had served, a senior investigator from 1903 to 1917 and transferred to the newly created Ministry of Labour in the same capacity (1917–20). Her public career ended as a member of the Trade Boards (1921–32). In line with her later views on broadening opportunities for the employment of women, she abandoned at an early age her position as an assistant school mistress in Leicester, with which she started (1878–85) her career, for first, that of private social investigation, followed by extensive public service.

Clara Collet's spasmodic diary over the following decade contains snippets of her professional activities at this time, and the economists she was meeting. A detailed account of her attendance at the 1904 Cambridge meeting of the British Economic Association is of particular interest. During a reception at Trinity Hall (Fawcett's old College) she met and talked with William Smart, a fellow worker for women's rights in the labour market (Jones, 1916, pp. xxiv–xxv), Gonner, Dr. Pierson (the Dutch economist and former Prime Minister of Holland), Macgregor and Mary Paley Marshall. The next day she recorded the debate over free trade and protection. This was introduced by speeches from Guyot, Lotz and Dietzel on protection in France and Germany, followed by Price's attack on the English Professors' manifesto in favour of free trade, for which he received a dressing down from a hyper-serious Alfred Marshall in a speech Collet described as showing his 'usual want of balance'. A subsequent gathering at Girton College found her in the company of Emily Davies, Professor Lotz and once again, Mary Paley Marshall by herself (Collet, 1876–1914, pp. 68–9). Some years later, the diary records meetings at the Board of Trade in the company of its new Minister, Winston Churchill, and William Beveridge (Collet, 1876–1914, pp. 129–30).

Of particular interest for the context of this paper is an entry for 2 June 1910. This indicates her intention to resign from the Labour Department in order to be able 'to speak more freely about the way in which the women's side of the Labour Exchanges is being organised, capable women being subordinated to men who know nothing and care nothing about women's interests' (Collet, 1876–1914, p. 137). In the end, she was persuaded not to resign but the entry indicates her passionate interest in securing women's rights in the labour market at all levels, the topic she had made her applied domain for research and policy advice.

Her later close friend, the Indian physicist, statistician and economic planner, P.C. Mahalanobis, left a striking account of her qualities stressing that independence of mind and life which Clara Collet herself always highlighted as an essential feature of a truly liberated woman:

> She had gathered round her a circle of friends with broad intellectual interests, who used to meet in the evening in a small flat in Holborn, where she was then living. I and other Indian students would sometimes join this group. Miss Collet would pour out coffee and would constantly make penetrating observations and witty remarks with a twinkle in her eyes. She was keenly interested in statistics. Through her I came to realize, for the first time, the importance of statistics, with which I had no direct concern at that time, as I was studying mathematics and physics. She had an extremely critical mind. Speaking of a recently published book on human heredity, she remarked, with a dry smile, that the author had taken great pains to collect a large mass of evidence in favour of his own theory. She had a keen sense of humour, and made many witty remarks on the controversy about the relative importance of nature and nurture in which Karl Pearson was engaged at that time. I did not meet Karl Pearson in my student days, but learned a good deal of his work indirectly through Miss Collet. ... She had a brilliant mind, and a charming personality; and always looked on the brighter side of things. I consider myself fortunate in having come into close contact with her when I was young, and I recognize her formative influence on my life in many ways. It is my great regret that, although I was in England several times during the last two years, I was unable to meet her once more before her death (Mahalanobis, 1948, p. 254).

Her eventual retirement from public service did not mean inactivity. She edited family papers, and on the basis of her rich collection of family letters was going to edit for publication a collection of letters by women indicating the social questions of the day combined with perspectives on the mental and moral qualities of the writers. At one time (see below, p. 159) she entertained the idea for a statistical study of social issues from data to be extracted from novels. She was therefore not a narrow economist. Her reading covered literature, poetry, biblical studies, ancient Jewish history as well as Blue Books and economics texts. Her obituary writer in the *Journal of the Royal Statistical Society* paints a picture of the qualities, personality, independence and eccentricity of this fascinating woman economist who lived to the full her rich and interesting life until her death aged 88:

One would say that her outstanding qualities were vigour and alertness of mind and body, sincerity and directness, practical common-sense, independence of judgement, and the courage of her opinions. These latter traits were probably not entirely ingratiating to her immediate official superiors, but her colleagues and subordinates found her 'very pleasant to work with' and she was noted among her friends for her readiness to listen and to give weight to the opinions of others. She was indeed kindly; but she refused to be fettered by convention, custom, or anything that stood in the way of what she thought should be done – a characteristic gesture was her arrival at the Ministry, during the General Strike, in a hearse, which had offered the simplest way of getting there. She was, in fact, thoroughly practical and applied economic principles in her daily life – by which parsimony is by no means to be understood. On the contrary; Miss Collet was exceedingly generous, and moreover, at a meeting of the Society's Council firmly denied that you should cut your coat according to your cloth. But she had no time to spend on trimmings which would have got in the way of things that really mattered. The garden of the little house she had for a time at Highgate was a riot of anything that liked to grow there – mostly St. John's wort, as it happened – and the result seemed to her just as it should be. Her practical sense also insisted on the removal, in 1936, of herself, her bachelor brother and two sisters (at ages averaging not far short of 80) from a tall house in London to a bungalow on top of the cliff at Sidmouth; and a judicious economy of time and trouble was shown in all her domestic arrangements. These, like everyone's, became more difficult as time went on. In 1947, Miss Collet, the last survivor of the family, was left alone and with very little domestic help; but nothing discouraged her; in January, 1948, she wrote 'this year of complete solitude has done me no harm; and it has ... made me aware of how easily I can look after my merely personal wants.' Nor did her interest diminish in all that was happening. Her library list covered many subjects, from theology to novels; she read *The Times* thoroughly every day and solved the crossword, with particular relish for its more subtle ingenuities. Except for a liability to acute neuralgia, which kept her almost entirely indoors the last two years or so, she remained active in body, moving about the house with light quick steps, until a few months before her death. Even a couple of months before the end, her mind was busy with arrangements for her publications and she remained full of interest in the doings of her young relations, of whom she was very fond and proud. Few of her own contemporaries survive, but she remains alive in the minds of all who knew her (C[atherine] T[horburn], 1948, p. 253).

THE ECONOMICS OF EDUCATED WORKING WOMEN

As an educated working woman herself, Clara Collet was very conscious of the problems such women faced in the 1890s, particularly those of persons who, like her, were unable or unwilling to marry and therefore had to provide for themselves. The six essays she wrote and published during the final decade of the nineteenth century cover most of the major economic issues faced by such women and moreover provide an interesting example of the manner in which Clara Collet used economic and statistical techniques to shed light on social issues related to women of her own class. The places where these papers were originally published indicate the varied avenues open to late-Victorian women to air their views on women's issues.

The first of these papers was read to the Ethical Society in 1890, that secular haven for social reformers and moralists during the 1890s (Budd, 1977). It evaluates the overall economic situation of working women at the start of the new decade, as compared to the situation reflected in the 'advice offered by Mrs. Elizabeth Browning' more than thirty years previously at the mid-point of the century. At that stage, women were actively discouraged from using their minds, particularly on 'male' subjects such as mathematics and logical reasoning, because 'reasoning power was considered undesirable in women and like to hinder their chances of marriage' (Collet, 1902, pp. 2–3). By the 1870s these attitudes began slowly to change through women's successful struggle to gain admission to the universities, so that by 1890 London and Cambridge enabled women to sit their examinations on equal terms with men, though at Cambridge without granting them the degree which gave them full membership of the university (McWilliams-Tullberg, 1975). Many of the newer University Colleges, such as that at Bristol, started on a policy of admitting women to their classes on equal terms with men (Collet, 1902, pp. 5–6). This led her to conclude,

So far so good. But there are not yet 800 women graduates of London and Cambridge. Of these the majority are assistant mistresses in public or private schools, visiting teachers, lecturers, or head mistresses. There were in 1881, according to the Census of that year, 123,000 women teachers, and over 4,000,000 girls between the ages of five years and twenty; and yet already this little handful of graduates is told that it is in excess of the demand and that it must lower salaries accordingly (Collet, 1902, pp. 6–7).

This brief quotation shows Clara Collet's method of analysis at its simplest. Some easily grasped facts, drawn from unassailable data like the census, are followed by a simple inference to ridicule the conclusions others were trumpeting as correct without ever having examined the facts. A few further comments follow her conclusion. First, women graduates should not agree to working at rates of remuneration below an agreed minimum, so as not to undercut the already under-paid non-graduate teachers.   Secondly, standards in women's education should be raised by raising the demand for graduate teachers through raising parental (that is, fathers') demand for quality education for their daughters.   The last Collet diagnosed as a major hurdle, despite the fact that many women needed to be educated because they had to be capable of earning their own living.   However, a broadening of the opportunities for work for women was almost equally important.   Women could be usefully trained for such activities as business and farming, and in particular should be considered suitable for factory management jobs ranging from foreign correspondence clerks (because of their undoubted aptitude for modern language studies) to chemist or artistic designer.

Extension of women employment opportunities had a double consequence.   In the first place, it enabled young women to do more easily what they wished to work at, thereby extending to them a greater freedom of choice.   More importantly, it enabled better determination of the economic worth of women by assessment of their efficiency. 'Teachers are paid out of fixed income, and their salaries are almost entirely determined by standard of living' (Collet, 1902, p. 21). If this method of wage determination was abandoned and replaced by payment according to the value of their work, more young women would seek paid employment and desire superior education opportunities to improve their skills.

Two additional conclusions mark this introductory essay on educated working women. 'Women who give their service for nothing are rarely told the truth; it will be a good thing for them when they receive instead of flattery and thanks, criticism and payment' (Collet, 1902, p. 23). Secondly, there should be no presumption that women have to marry young or have to marry at all in order to be 'happy and fulfilled'. Hannah More, Jane Austen, Maria Edgeworth, Joanna Baillie, Caroline Herschell, Harriet Martineau, 'all women of brilliant intellect, have left their mark on history as good and happy women. ... Likewise unmarried women of our own acquaintance who have found their vocation, can have bright and contented lives' (Collet, 1902, p. 25). This freedom from obligation to marry has liberating consequences for both men[1] and women, Collet argued, but by the beginning of 1890 had not yet achieved the acceptance it deserved, so that the rights of educated working women were still only secured in a very imperfect way.

An essay originally published in the *Nineteenth Century* in 1892 analysed the limited prospects of marriage for middle-class women on the basis of demographic data. This indicated that the general belief that 'every woman can get married if she will only make herself agreeable, and not be too particular' (Collet, 1902, p. 28) was a false one. Age differences at marriage between husbands and wives was a major explanation of this; locational inequalities in the number of the sexes of marriageable age was another. This paper likewise reveals Collet's statistical common-sense and her feel for asking the appropriate statistical questions. Analysing the available demographic data showed that 'the proportion of women who may be expected to remain unmarried [in all England and Wales] is, roughly speaking, one in six; in London, it is one in five' (Collet, 1902, p. 34). Hence, 'a considerable number of women *must* remain unmarried' (Collet, 1902, p. 38, my emphasis) and therefore, generally speaking, need to enter the labour market. An analysis of the 1881 census data showed 593,326 women in employment subdivided as follows by occupation. Forty per cent were indoor domestic servants, twelve per cent were in cleaning, laundry and associated work including that in public institutions such as hospitals and workhouses, while sixteen per cent worked in the clothing and textile industry. Of the remaining ten per cent most were employed in what Collet described as 'purely women's trades' within general industry.[2] Two factors kept the rate of wages for these working women low and well below that of men. Many women workers accepted low wages because they expected help from their friends or relatives; secondly, parents were reluctant to educate their daughters because they considered the cost to be wasted when these daughters married. A strong conclusion followed. Not only is it not necessarily true, Collet argued, that

Man's love is of man's life a thing apart;
'tis women's whole existence

but 'that marriage has naturally very much less attraction for women than for men' (Collet, 1902, p. 65).

An essay in the *Economic Journal* in 1898 analysed expenditure patterns of middle-class working women to implicitly illustrate the proposition that cost of living kept women's salaries low. Actual expenditure tended to suggest, relative to income from work received, that such workers had to rely on some form of assistance and support from parents, relatives or friends, particularly during the extensive periods of school holidays if they were teachers. The underlying premiss of the article is the Marshallian proposition that workers cannot become highly efficient in their work if their salaries are inadequate. (Collet, 1902, p. 70; Marshall, 1890, pp. 245–53). The data presented in the paper was a purely 'inductive' exercise on the Le Play method. It consisted of eight budgets relative to salary drawn from four actual teachers, two clerks, one headmistress and one from a young woman living at home meeting personal expenditure from a parental allowance. None of these budgets, Collet admitted, 'could be regarded as typical', they were simply samples of the kind of material that needed to be collected to enable the establishment of typical occupational expenditure patterns in order to derive conclusions on the necessary efficiency wages for certain classes of female labour (Collet, 1902, p. 89).

The age limit placed conventionally on women seeking work was investigated in a paper published in the *Contemporary Review* for 1899. Examination of job advertisements suggested to Collet that 'women are [considered to be] unfit to undertake serious responsibility after the age of thirty-five' (Collet, 1902, p. 91), a *de facto* limitation on women's right to employment the validity of which needed challenge. Drawing on eighteenth-century literature, Collet inferred that 'the age of childish responsibility' had been raised from six to about twelve years over the past hundred years (Collet, 1902, p. 111) while the age at which 'invalid mothers' could retire to the sofa by expecting their daughters to take over household duties had greatly risen from the standard set by the eighteenth century at eighteen years. Hence 'failure of power after thirty-five years of age has become absurd' by the start of the twentieth century even though such anecdotal (literary) evidence she used to reach this conclusion could not be adapted to determine the age at which 'the value of a woman's increased experience is counter-balanced by diminished physical power' (Collet, 1902, p. 113).

A book review on Mrs. Stetson's book, *Women and Economics* (originally published in the *Charity Organisation Review*), shows that Collet could apply her critical faculties to authors of both sexes. In particular, the review casts doubt on the benefits of externalizing housework such as cooking, cleaning and even nurturing, and it questioned some of the broad generalizations the author had made about the historical duration of women's servitude to men. Collet's concluding sentence tells much of her personality: 'What the author says, even when not absolutely absurd, may be of little importance; but her feeling is so genuine and strong as to merit respect and attention' (Collet, 1902, p. 133). The final essay reintroduced the use of literary sources as tools of social investigation in order to test the degree of economic progress women had achieved over the second half of the nineteenth century. It especially cast doubts on over-optimistic forecasts about what economic liberation can achieve for women and warned of the dangers for young women of too hastily associating a glamorous existence with economic independence. The conclusion to the article and the book reflects the general tone of caution in Collet's work. Great strides, she observed, had been made in the right direction, but there was still an enormous amount to do, particularly to make the less gifted women competent to reach fruitful employment (Collet, 1902, pp. 142–3). Sad to say, this conclusion remains as apt in the 1990s as it was the century before.

In her review of Collet's book in which these essays were collected, Mary Paley Marshall (1902) made a number of very pertinent points about both its author and its contents. First, Collet's qualifications for writing these essays in her view arose not only from her valuable experience as co-worker on Charles Booth's survey of the London poor and, subsequently, Assistant Labour Commissioner, it owed much to her talent to combine 'trained economic thought' with the data gathered from her wide experience of life. Clear economic thinking enabled her to write so well on these issues. Second, unlike some feminists, Collet openly rejoiced in the differences between men and women (Mary Paley Marshall, 1902, p. 252), thereby avoiding the search for spurious equalities. Two of Collet's conclusions are also emphasized to indicate the relationship between Collet's use of the economic tool box and Mary Marshall's husband's aims and objectives in economics. The capacity for economic independence is an essential part of individual self-respect and hence of character. Second, rising standards of life in nutrition, exercise, recreation and physical environment have greatly extended women's 'period of efficient life'. Although work for married women with young children may have problematical consequences,[3] overall the widening of employment opportunities for women raised the level of society's welfare and constituted genuine progress (Mary Paley Marshall, 1902, pp. 256–7).

The war produced Clara Collet's final journal contribution on middle-class women's work opportunities in the professions. The new labour market situation created by general mobilization of men for the front provided unique demands for women's labour which Collet (1915) argued were likely to make for splendid opportunities for placing the principles of determining women's remuneration on a sound foundation. The first of these principles reiterated the view put in her volume of essays that the notion of efficiency wages implied adequate salaries for women's professional work and not rates of pay which contained an implicit cost of living subsidy from friends or family. Secondly, given the positive association between productivity and levels of pay, highly paid women's labour in professional activities often was more economically employed than cheaper, and by implication, less-skilled labour. This also applied in hiring practices for less-skilled clerical positions, where employing untrained juvenile female labour at low rates invariably proved to be less economical in the long run.

The job opportunities opened up by the war were classified into three categories by Collet:

(1) Neutral work, in which it is a matter of indifference whether it is done by men or by women if they can do it equally well. Most of the work of the Post Office is of this character.

(2) Women's work, supplementary to what is mainly men's work. A good deal of controversy would arise in determining what work should come under this heading, but very little as to what does come under it, e.g., nursing under the War Office, prison inspection under the Home Office, inspection of work-houses under the Local Government Board.

(3) Women's work, frequently controlled by men from financial reasons, but almost invariably superintended by women (Collet, 1915, p. 629).

Collet described married women as generally much more skilled in tasks coming under category (3) of women's work because of the additional proficiency gained in this area from their experience in the home. Moreover, part-time employment opportunities should be provided for this class of women workers. In occupations such as maternity services and more general health visiting, part-time employment of married, rather than unmarried, women raised efficiency. This came from the former's greater experience and at relatively little cost in terms of disruptions to the home from the more limited absence at work part-time work entailed. Collet was, therefore, fully aware that the war was producing changes in the labour market beneficial for accelerating the changes in women job opportunities which peace would only have been able to achieve more gradually.

A WOMEN'S STATISTICAL AND ECONOMIC PERSPECTIVE ON WOMEN'S PLACE IN THE LABOUR MARKET

Neglecting her contribution to the Charles Booth project of *Life and Work in London*, Collet's first published piece on women's employment in factories was included in the first volume of the *Economic Journal*. It investigated women's work and wages in Leeds, largely in its textile industry, as a general contribution to the analysis of women's labour. Sources for Collet's data were census returns, reports from government factory inspectors, surveys of women employees,[4] and other field work which gained her broad impressions of the atmosphere in the workplace with female labour, as well as information on wages and general hiring practices from specific factory owners.

The article opened by relating the growth of women's employment in the cloth industry to the introduction of the power loom. This enabled cloth manufacturers to substitute women for men as part of the deskilling process which replaced handwork by machines. However, cloth making in Leeds itself as a major form of women's employment was replaced by the ready-made clothing industry, again through the introduction of machinery (for cutting, button holing and sewing), thereby making the introduction of a factory system in place of domestic workshops inevitable. Here, and attributed by Collet to the good work environment produced in the households of highly skilled male labourers in Leeds, girls and women factory hands tended to be more skilled, particularly when compared to the clothing industry of East London investigated by Beatrice Webb (Potter) (1888a and b). Women could therefore obtain higher wages, and were generally employed on equal terms as the men. The eventual outcome predicted by Collet was that men will inevitably be substituted for women, because her earlier findings of such sexual substitution in the cloth industry suggested that 'women were employed because wages were low, and not *vice versa*' (Collet, 1891b, p. 462).

The type of investigation she had conducted in Leeds undoubtedly assisted Collet's appointment, and subsequently, the quality of her work as Assistant Lady Commissioner to the Labour Commission. Their report discussed average rates of remuneration for women by particular industries, the issue of competition between men and women for scarce jobs in times of unemployment, women's wages in so far as they were ascertainable in the domestic and sweated industries, grievances connected with net wage determination with special reference to the practice of fines for misbehaviour in the workplace, hours of labour, problems with excessive overtime, the consequences of employing married women especially on health and quality of their offspring, working conditions with respect to sanitation and hygiene in the workplace and associated facilities, and the remedy for such problems from legislative regulation enforced by government inspection. The last topic included consideration of restricting the employment of married women in certain industries, anomalies in factory legislation for women, adequacy of the present system of factory inspection including the desirability of appointing women factory inspectors and investigations of hiring practices, morality in the factories and the contribution thereto of the behaviour of foremen and general overseers of women's labour. Last, but not least, the report from the Lady Commissioners considered the need for women labour organizations, largely drawn from examination of the consequences of those existing on wages and working conditions. The mass of information contained in this report awaits the labour historian of late Victorian England interested in studying women's work for the market at the end of the nineteenth century (Dilke, 1891; Bulley, 1894).

The dilemma from the terms of reference the male commissioners imposed on these pioneering Lady Assistant Commissioners, created difficulties for the conduct of their investigations. This is well illustrated in the following:

> The terms of reference also posed a problem for the investigators in that they implied bias against women's work. Inevitably during their investigations, horrifically bad conditions of work were exposed in many trades and the difficulties of combining dangerous work and domestic chores and the adverse effects of heavy

work on pregnancy, childbirth and child care were revealed; the women Commissioners wanted improvements in all these areas. On the other hand, they were reluctant to 'prove' that women's work in any specific trade was a social danger and to jeopardise the independence of women wage-earners. The women interviewed seem themselves to have recognised the dilemma, denying obvious grievances and refusing to complain about the most harsh and demanding labour.

Whether from resentment of their inferior status or in order not to deny women's right to work, the investigative women Commissioners decided not to include any specific recommendations, but to let the facts speak. They divided trades and regions between them and surveyed hours, health and safety, the availability of rest and refreshment, sleeping accommodation, sanitary arrangements, trade union activity and wage rates. The volume of work and their commitment to it was tremendous. For instance, as she was responsible for investigating shops, Margaret Irwin had often to call after 10.00 p.m. at night to interview shop assistants in private and to find if they had been released from work (shop hours were meant to be no longer than 8.30 a.m. to 9.30 p.m.). Apart from making available a mass of evidence to the women's movement and the trade unions, one positive result of the Labour Commission was the founding of the first women's factory inspectorate (Collette, 1989, pp. 14–15).

Inferences from the Lady Assistant Commissioners' work drawn by others were discussed previously (Chapters 3–5), and Clara Collet undoubtedly gained enormously from her experience with the Commission in a variety of ways. Her immersion in the reality of women's work enabled her to effectively demolish long-standing prejudices in this controversial area when the consequences of the emergence of 'modern women' were placed under particularly careful scrutiny by generally male social scientists. This required skill, balance and diplomacy in order to satisfactorily trade-off the various interests involved. A striking example is her careful evaluation of the statistical evidence on the consequences of married women's work on infant mortality (Collet, 1898b) as a result of which she successfully combated the biased views peddled on this emotive subject on the basis of what generally proved to be the most slender evidence. This was discussed above in the context of Jevons's crusade on the issue published in the *Contemporary Review*; other, more low-keyed factual demonstrations of wrong preconceptions were mentioned in the previous section on the excess supply of skilled women workers and the ability of every woman to marry who wished to do so. Defence against her potent criticism was often by way of character assassination. She was 'branded a failure because not supported by a man', and her eccentricities, such as wearing 'short (ankle-length) skirts ... for comfort at work' drew unfavourable comment (Collette, 1989, p. 13).

Her articles for the *Palgrave Dictionary* (1896) indicated a number of questions which the history of women's employment should explain, on only one of which, she argued, adequate data were available from reports prepared in conjunction with the Factory Acts. Apart from the issue of women competing with men for employment, the other burning issues on women's work included:

> (2) the effect of such competition on the wages of men in the same trade; (3) the effect of the economic independence of women on the rate of wages of men in the same class, and hence on the income of the family; (4) the effect of the employment of married women in factories on the well-being of the family (Collet, 1896a, p. 49).

More generally, Collet concluded that the effect of women's labour on men's wages and employment was difficult to ascertain and that, broadly speaking, women's remuneration was well below that obtained by men, particularly in employment requiring training and education. This had not always been the case, she claimed, and was therefore not inevitable. Research on the fifteenth-century labour market by Thorold Rogers showed that then unskilled female labour at least 'was equally well paid with that of men' (Collet, 1896a, p. 50). She likewise argued that there was 'insufficient evidence to form any judgment as to the effects of married women's labour on the wage of the husband' (Collet, 1896, p. 50). She reiterated the lack of satisfactory contemporary data on wages, partly from the nature of female employment and its concentration in domestic service, an area of employment where such comparable data were almost impossible to obtain.

A report prepared for the Labour Department of the Board of Trade (Collet, 1898a) investigated the four fundamental issues mentioned in *Palgrave* for major industrial centres. It started by noting that data on women's employment were invariably collected as 'incidental to some earlier inquiry into men's labour', except in the well-known cases generated by influential protest against the employment of children in factories (Collet, 1898a, p. 4). This inquiry, to the contrary, was particularly designed to obtain information on the effects on home life from the industrial occupation of women, so that it contained a special emphasis on the 'industrial employment of married women'. This was also a controversial question, as the deliberations of the Labour Commission at the start of the decade had shown.[5]

The industrial centres covered in the study were the cotton and linen manufactures of Dundee, Ulster (especially Belfast) and Leeds and the West Riding. Data were drawn from the hand-loom inquiries of the 1830s and compared with the more contemporary data coming from censuses and factory returns for the 1880s and 1890s. The data permitted no simple conclusions in any of the four basic questions Collet had identified as fundamental in the context of understanding women's labour in her *Palgrave* contribution.

Conclusions were most complex with respect to wages. Under the old domestic system based on hand-loom technology, 'when both men and women worked the loom, there seems to have been no question of difference of payment for the same work. The women did a lighter work than 'able-bodied men', and were paid the same rate as the 'old men and boys' who did the same kind of work. ... Although, however, paid the same rates for the same work, women and girls were rarely owners of their looms, and their fathers and husbands usually drew their wages under the domestic system' (Collet, 1898a, p. 65). The advance of the power loom altered the situation drastically. Women's wages in the textile trades of Dundee and Belfast rose relatively much faster than men's wages, while within women's wages there was a shift from the high compression of rates for all women over thirteen years old to a much more extended range with respect to age, and, Collet presumed, skill levels (Collet, 1898a, pp. 17, 65). Other wage changes pointed to differences in experience between Dundee and Belfast. Although wages in both centres were at a maximum in 1873, fluctuations were more frequent in Dundee than in Belfast after that date. Given productivity growth, earnings had continued to grow after 1873, since most of the rates were piece rates. In general, wage growth was substantial over the whole of the period, most wages of women and children doubling over the sixty years in money terms (Collet, 1898a, pp. 65–6).

The study also confirmed Collet's earlier conclusion that the substitution of machinery under a factory system for manual skills practised at home in the weaving industry had greatly favoured female employment in weaving. However, the explanation for this shift arose from male dislike of the power loom, a task men tended to equate with 'women's work'. 'In the weaving factories from the very first the work has been done by women, and there has been no displacement of men within the factory. Some heavy power loom weaving is [only] done by men' (Collet, 1898a, p. 64).

Effects of women's work on the family wage were also discussed by Collet. The rise in the proportion of married women in work between the census years of 1881 and 1891 from 19.4 to 24.0 per cent of employed women, was implicitly explained by economic necessity; 'nearly all the occupied married women in Lochee [a sub-registration district of Dundee], with husbands at home, were married to men earning low wages' (Collet, 1898a, pp. 37, 39). A preference from some employers may indicate an additional reason why this growth in employment of married women had occurred: 'The work is less skilled; women may be taken on after marriage with very little previous experience, and their habits and circumstances in such cases are generally conducive to irregularity. ... One employer, however, states, in both [spinning and weaving] the married women are the best workers' (Collet, 1898a, p. 31 and n.2).

In the context of employment of married women, Collet also raised the issue of infant mortality, which earlier that year she had examined at length in the *Journal of the Royal Statistical Society* (Collet, 1898b). Her data provided no real evidence for any 'relation between the employment of married women and infant mortality'. The incidence of illegitimate children made this finding somewhat problematical because the 'percentage of illegitimate children who die of neglect is greater than that of legitimate children' though data were not at hand for investigating this subject more fully. In addition, the number of mothers with children under one year of age did not enable estimates of 'the number who had lost children while working at the mills', nor was 'there any means of establishing any connexion between infant mortality and the occupation of the mother, as the death certificate states the occupation of the *father* only. Until it is possible to obtain the insertion of the occupation of the mother, both before and after marriage, very little progress can be made towards estimating the effect of women's industrial life on infant health' (Collet, 1898a, p. 39).

Finally, the study permitted some general comparative conclusions about the situation of working women at Belfast and Dundee, though no explanations were offered for these largely statistical findings. Despite lower average earnings, 'the social condition of women in the industrial class in Belfast appears to be more satisfactory than in Dundee. The percentage of adult women occupied is much lower, and is not increasing; the disproportion between the sexes is not so great, and is diminishing; there is greater variety of employment for women, and there are more openings for skilled workmen (Collet, 1898a, pp. 66–7). In line with contemporary thinking, Collet praised the social implications of fewer adult women in the workforce, presumably because greater balance of the sexes permitted a higher incidence of marriage, perhaps likewise explaining the lower rate of infant mortality and level of illegitimate births in Belfast.

In 1891, Clara Collet had praised the Massachusetts Board of Statistics for preparing historical studies on women's labour and its consequences. Three items were singled out in this review, excepting her rather sceptical remarks on the reliability of some of the data supplied. The social and even intellectual life of some working women reported for Boston clothing factories seemed very praiseworthy, though admittedly it drew on somewhat anecdotal evidence. The lavish breakfasts enjoyed by women factory workers, despite their inevitable consequences for the onset of dyspepsia, was another major difference between women workers' life-styles across the Atlantic. Last but not least, the rapid rise in working women as a proportion of the workforce between the census years of 1875 and 1885 was very impressive, female employment relative to female population growth rising more than threefold as compared to that for male employment (Collet, 1891a, pp. 399–400, 401). A study of Wages Boards in Victoria (Collet, 1901) attempted to shed light on the effects of the minimum wage on wages and employment in industries not subject to this measure. Her reading of the evidence was that 'the natural flow of labour into channels in which wages are highest was checked and directed into those where they were lowest, by the regulations of the Special Boards'. Employment growth in wage-determined trades was slower than in unregulated activity; in addition, with respect to women employment in the textile trade, 'The rich [that is, the highly paid workers] may have been growing richer, but the proportion of the poor has been growing greater' (Collet, 1901, pp. 563–5). For Clara Collet, minimum wage legislation was clearly not an unmitigated success, and needed more careful study.

Clara Collet's statistical investigations of women's work, both official and privately published, examined the four crucial questions of concern in contemporary discussions over women in the workforce. She did so on a statistical basis, trying to find the facts of the matter before reaching conclusions. Such factual analysis was invariably conducted in a critical manner. She never drew conclusions for which the statistical basis was inadequate; on the other hand, she invariably drew the conclusions which the data warranted even if they were unpalatable to her own beliefs. In this way, she combated contemporary beliefs about the consequences for infant mortality from married women in the workforce, and about the displacement of men's employment opportunities by women paid lower wages. At the same time, she found it difficult to generalize about wage growth for women and, for that matter, on the effects of women's wages on family income.

A SIGNIFICANT DAUGHTER OF ADAM SMITH

Her work clearly makes Clara Collet a significant daughter of Adam Smith. Less outstanding than some of his female descendants in terms of the production of economic theory, or in gaining the wide-scale recognition or notoriety for her publication as Harriet Martineau had done, she nevertheless contributed important work. As a follower of Smith, she can be ranked on the level of Sir Frederick Morton Eden, that careful statistical investigator from the late eighteenth century on the plight of the poor and a source, though rarely celebrated in the histories of economic thought, who was highly valued by practitioners of economics over the subsequent decades and centuries. Collet's interest in household budgets of middle-class, single, working women, and in the overall social consequences of women's entry into the factory workforce is on a par with Eden's painstaking, specialist, factual inquiry at a period when society itself was subject to major change.

The richness of her work has made her an unduly neglected daughter of Adam Smith. She was an economist in whose writing women figure prominently, in their own right and with their own set of economic problems deserving exploration. This makes her an exception in the contemporary literature, as suggested by Pujol (1992, p. 1), and also an astonishing pioneer. Her research tried to integrate the subject of women's work into the general corpus of labour economics, looking at the consequences of that work in its manifold aspects. These covered the economic in the form of effects on wages for women, and for men in the same or associated industries, together with consequences for employment opportunities. They covered the social by attempting to analyse the consequences of the growth of women in the workforce for their families, for their unborn offspring, and more widely, for morality in general. Collet from the beginning of her investigations had a firm research agenda which she correctly argued had been unduly neglected by official concentration of research into men's labour problems. The result of this neglect was much misinformed prejudice, often not benign but maliciously used to serve ends against broadening the opportunities for women in work and life.

The method Collet employed in this research was also that of Smith in its widest sense. Her premisses were grounded in economic theory, whose findings with respect to labour she ruthlessly applied to the particular problems she was analysing. Marshall's views on efficiency wages, for example, which he applied in favour of men and as a rationale for confining married women to the home as a matter of national imperative, were used by Collet to argue against the systematic underpayment of women, especially in the teaching service where wages were kept to a minimum, by trading on the fact that the family background of most teachers would ensure assistance to them during extensive holiday periods especially over the summer. She was also well aware of the use of supply and demand in labour market analysis; analysing demand factors in terms of the commodity produced, and of the beneficent influence increased demand for quality and quantity of the output had on the extent and nature of the demand for the labour being considered. She was likewise fully cognizant of the influence of wages, training and education levels on the scope of employment opportunities and the productivity of the workers. The novelty of her contribution was that she applied these general principles to women's activities in the workforce, in part to facilitate giving women equal access to the consequences of their growing employment similar to men. As the previous sections have illustrated, the tool box of economics as it was shaped at this time was clearly of significance to her work.

Statistical analysis and in some respects, 'induction', was the major tool of her research. Much of her official work on women's employment in industry was of the essentially painstaking fact-gathering kind, trying to obtain comparable data from which to draw conclusions on the major questions raised about the impact and consequences of rising female participation in the workforce including that especially of married women. Her study of the textile industry in Dundee and Belfast is a perfect example of this type of 'induction', drawing comparative inferences from the data without attempting any broad explanations unless there are specific explanatory variables which suggest themselves unambiguously from within the facts. The reader is therefore not told why Belfast's social conditions for women's work are superior to Dundee's despite the latter's higher wage levels; however, data are presented for a variety of hypotheses on this matter, perhaps commencing with those on the greater equality in numbers of the sexes, including those of marriageable age in Belfast as compared with Dundee. Only in the case of the replacement of men's labour in weaving by that of women as a result of the introduction of the power loom, is an inference made about the nature of this complex substitution, which relied partly on the technical considerations of this change in the production process and partly on the traditional employment preferences of the hand-loom weavers.

In what for contemporary readers is probably a more acceptable manner of using facts, Collet also used them for falsification of wrong hypotheses or prejudiced statements. Her most potent use of the facts in this way is in the context of the suggestion that married working women increased infant mortality. Her careful sifting of the available data shows that the evidence in fact warranted no such general conclusion. This type of analysis shows her qualities as a careful researcher at its best. In the context of complex social phenomena, she is ever dubious of accepting simple causal relationships and mono-causal explanations from what are said to be the facts. Moreover, when discussing controversial issues, she took the evidence from the contradictory case particularly seriously; there can be no generalization where the associations are not unambiguously clear cut. Her care in interpreting the data, her precision in identifying both what they mean and cannot be taken to mean, and her inordinate sense of social responsibility which never allowed her to draw more from her data than these warranted, was undoubtedly one of the reasons why that great Indian statistician and economist, Mahalanobis, praised her contribution to his own (informal) statistical education. Here again, she was a praiseworthy daughter of Adam Smith who, like her master, was sceptical of the sometimes fantastical claims made on behalf of inferences drawn from rather inconclusive data.

Her stance on scientific detachment in drawing the findings of her research was matched by an open-mindedness in her opinions, which tended to avoid extreme positions. She never criticized women's willingness to marry and to become mothers and nurturers of their children; she simply pointed out the right of other women not to marry, and that the unmarried female state could be as great a source of happiness and fulfilment as any other. Such a position was facilitated by her demographic demonstration that in any case not all women could expect to marry, given the conventions about age differences between husband and wife marriage then entailed, and facilitating in turn a demand that society recognize this inability by paying adequate salaries to working women, especially to teachers. She likewise did not argue the equality of the sexes; she only desired equal treatment when appropriate and equal outcomes with respect to equal capacities and equal work. In this way, her views still merit considerable attention. They contain sensible perspectives on equal opportunity and the means by which unequal opportunities can be curtailed through changing the ingrained values and prejudices of the older generation (as in the case of some late Victorian fathers with respect to the education of their daughters).

These wider social perspectives and critical, common-sense thinking of Clara Collet are well illustrated in her perceptive and sympathetic review of Helen Bosanquet's *The Strength of the People* (Collet, 1903, pp. 81–4). This was a manual for social workers and charity organizers by a former student of Alfred Marshall at Cambridge,[6] and the wife of Bernard Bosanquet, student and colleague of T.H. Green at Oxford and prominent activist in the Charity Organisation Society (McBriar, 1987). It attempted to indicate the road to developing some 'theory of human nature and human life which will be a guide to us when applied to the actual problems which we have to face'. This was a laudable objective, particularly when part of Helen Bosanquet's aim was to provide economic awareness to the many charity workers, who all too often were 'adults of neglected economic education'. However, the 'practical critic' can have less patience with the book, Collet argued, because it reveals that despite the considerable experience of its author in charitable work, she does not fully realize the scope of her inquiry as disclosed by the facts of the case. This deficiency is briefly illustrated by Bosanquet's misleading treatment of early marriages, and illegitimate births, which indicates her misunderstanding of the full significance of their inter-connections and the ramifications of that relationship. Her sense of numbers is also inadequate, and Collet makes the plea that 'it is only through the smoked glass of the statistician that we can venture to estimate ... proportions of the problem at hand'. In addition, 'Mrs. Bosanquet would strengthen her argument and would win many more people to her cause if she could regard it as thinkable that the hostility of many to the teaching of the trained organisers of charity is due to a broader experience of life than many of the latter possess and not to a weaker intellect or lack of principle'. Knowledge and tolerance are essential parts of the armament of the social investigator and advocate of particular remedies.

'An authoritative figure in her field, and a good example of the educated woman of the period' (Rubinstein, 1988, p. 71) is the assessment of one historian of women's emancipation in the 1890s. 'Throughout her active life it was to her that one naturally turned for help, if one was concerned with any problem of women's work or wages' was the recognition bestowed on her skills by perhaps the major economic statistician in England of her generation (Bowley, 1950, pp. 409–10). The words which she applied to her superior in the public service, her friend, co-investigator and fellow political economy student at London University, George Armitage-Smith (Collet, 1923, p. 127) apply with equal force to herself. 'He had for many years attended to the business of the Royal Economics Society as a member of its Council. He figured in the *Economic Journal* both as reviewer and reviewed. He was among the founders of our society. ... His special interest was Political Economy'. Her own thirst for useful knowledge in economics of relevance to understanding and improving the employment situation of women made her a true daughter of Adam Smith, whose pioneering labours on the subject deserve fuller recognition than they have at present received.

NOTES

* This chapter was inspired by the Centre Workshop from which this book originates through a phone call by Michael White which his own contribution to the Workshop generated. It drew my attention to Clara Collet as an informant of Keynes on Jevons and Foxwell in his *Essays in Biography* and as supplementing the obituary of Higgs in the *Economic Journal* (Collet, 1940). Her quotations in that obituary from her diary and correspondence about Higgs's altercations with Marshall over procedures in setting up the Junior London Economic Club sparked further interest in Clara Collet on my part because of its relevance to my work on Marshall's biography (*A Soaring Eagle: Alfred Marshall 1842–1924*, Aldershot, Elgar, forthcoming) particularly when I realized she had also worked on the Labour Commission and that her one book had been reviewed by Mary Paley Marshall (1902). For my subsequent, successful search for the Clara Collet Diaries I acknowledge assistance from Bob Black, the (London) National Registrar of Archives and the Librarian of the Modern Records Centre at Warwick University. I am grateful for permission from Dr. Jane Miller to quote from the diary and from other Collet manuscript material. Research for this chapter has been assisted by financial support from the Australian Research Council and from research assistants Mark Donoghue, Sue King and Jack Towe who dug out relevant library material and researched background.

1. It allows men 'to escape the degradation' of being accepted in marriage by young women solely 'as a means of [their] livelihood and an escape from poverty' (Collet, 1902, pp. 25–6).
2. This can only be a regional sub-section of the aggregate 1881 census data. The 1881 census indicates 3,887 thousand women to be employed; 45 per cent in domestic service, 5.5 per cent in professional occupations; 36 per cent in clothing and textile. Using her earlier figure (above, p. 155) of 123,000 teachers, this constituted 60 per cent of 'professional occupations and their subordinate services', or 3.2 per cent of the total female labour force (Mitchell, 1962, p. 60).
3. In this context, Mary Paley Marshall (1902) praised Collet's work on infant mortality and married working mothers (Collet, 1898b), discussed in Chapter 3 above (pp. 64–5). Marshall, as shown in Chapter 4 above, applied these propositions only to general (that is, male) labour and not to female paid labour, which he opposed particularly for married women.
4. Collet (1891b, p. 471) noted the difficulties in obtaining information from social surveys, on the basis of circularizing questionnaires to women workers in Leeds. 'The willingness to satisfy abstract curiosity is not universal; nearly 800 cards were given back to me in sealed envelopes of which nearly 300 were blank; a few conveyed an intimation of the writer's opinion of the impertinence of the questions, and 479 answered carefully and accurately except on one point, [the pre-marital occupation of their mother]'.
5. Above, pp. 162–3 and Chapter 4, pp. 89–91.
6. Helen Bosanquet completed her examinations in the Moral Science Tripos with first class honours in 1889, taking Marshall's advanced class in political economy in the company of Flux and Chapman. See Groenewegen, 1990, p. 52. She sent Marshall a complimentary copy of the book mentioned in the text, on which correspondence ensued which is reprinted in the *Memorials* (Pigou, 1925, pp. 443–6) and in the preface to its second edition.

References

Albury, R. (1975), 'Darwinian Evolution and the Inferiority of Women', *GLP! A Journal of Sexual Politics*, 7, pp. 10–19.

Alexander, S. (1913), 'Introduction' to P. Reeves (ed.), *Round About a Pound a Week*, Virago, London.

Alexander, Sally (1983), *Women's Work in Nineteenth Century London: A Study of the Years 1820–1850*, Journeyman, London.

Anonymous (1871), 'Economic Fallacies and Labour Utopias', *Quarterly Review*, 131 (261), pp. 229–63.

Banks, Olive (1986), *Becoming a Feminist: the Social Origins of 'First Wave' Feminism*, Wheatsheaf, Brighton,

Barton, D.M. (1919), 'The Course of Women's Wages', *Journal of the Royal Statistical Society*, 82 (4), July, pp. 508–44.

Barton, D.M. (1921), 'Women's Minimum Wages', *Journal of the Royal Statistical Society*, 84 (4), July, pp. 538–75.

Baxendell, J. (1869), 'On Observations of Atmospheric Ozone', *Proceedings of the Literary and Philosophical Society of Manchester, Session 1868–69*, 8, pp. 21–33.

Baxendell, J. (1870a), 'On the Influences of Changes in the Character of the Seasons on the Rate of Mortality', *Proceedings of the Literary and Philosophical Society of Manchester, Session 1869–70*, 9, pp. 159–68.

Baxendell, J. (1870b), 'Infant Mortality in Manchester', *Proceedings of the Literary and Philosophical Society of Manchester, Session 1869–70*, 9, pp. 177–80.

Becattini, G. (1975), *Invito a una Rilettura di Marshall*, Isedi, Milan.

Behlmer, G.K. (1982), *Child Abuse and Moral Reform in England, 1870–1908*, Stanford University Press, Stanford.

Berg, Maxine (1988), *The Age of Manufactures 1700–1820*, Collins, London.

Best, G. (1979), *Mid-Victorian Britain 1851–75*, Fontana/Collins, London.

Black, R.D.C. (1973–81), *The Papers and Correspondence of William Stanley Jevons*, vols II–VII, Macmillan, for the Royal Economic Society, London.

Black, R.D.C. (1987), 'Clara E. Collet (1860–1948)', *The New Palgrave Dictionary of Economics*, vol. 1, Macmillan, London, pp. 481–2.

Bladen, Vincent (1974), *From Adam Smith to John Maynard Keynes*, Toronto University Press, Toronto.

Blagg, H. and C. Wilson (1912), *Women and Prisons*, Fabian Tract No. 163, Fabian Society, London.

Bowley, A.L. (1919), 'Comment on Dorothea Barton', *Journal of the Royal Statistical Society*, **82** (4), July, pp. 544–7.

Bowley, A.L. (1950), 'Obituary of Clara E. Collet', *Economic Journal*, **60** (238), June, pp. 408–10.

Bowman, R.S. (1989), 'Jevons' Economic Theory in Relation to Social Change and Public Policy', *Journal of Economic Issues*, **23** (4), pp. 1123–47.

Brassey, Thomas (1873), *Work and Wages*, Dell & Daldy, London.

British Library of Political and Economic Science (1973), *Publications of Sidney and Beatrice Webb: An Interim Check List*, British Library of Political and Economic Science, London.

Budd, Susan (1977), *Varieties of Unbelief*, Heinemann, London.

Bulley, A.A. (1894), 'The Employment of Women. The Lady Assistant Commissioner's Report', *Fortnightly Review*, January–June, pp. 39–48.

Bulley, A.A. and M. Whitley, (1894), *Women's Work*, Methuen & Co., London.

Caine, Barbara (1978), 'John Stuart Mill and the English Women Movement', *Historical Studies*, **18**, pp. 52–67.

Caine, Barbara (1982), 'Beatrice Webb and the Woman Question', *History Workshop*, **14**, Autumn.

Caine, Barbara (1992), *Victorian Feminists*, Oxford University Press, Oxford.

Carlyle, Thomas (1843), *Past and Present*, Chapman & Hill, 1893 edition, London.

Cole, M. (1945), *Beatrice Webb*, Longmans, London.

Cole, M. (ed.) (1949), *The Webbs and their Work*, Frederick Miller Ltd., London.

Collet, Clara (1876–1914) *Diary*, Warwick University, Modern Records Centre, MS 29.

Collet, Clara (1889), in Charles Booth (ed.), *Life and Labour of the People in London*, Macmillan, London.

Collet, Clara (1891a), 'Report of the Massachusetts Board of Statistics of Labour on Working Women 1870–1889', *Economic Journal*, 1 (2), June, pp. 398–405.

Collet, Clara (1891b), 'Women's Work in Leeds', *Economic Journal*, 1 (3), September, pp. 460–73.

Collet, Clara E. (1896a), 'Female Labour', *Palgrave Dictionary of Political Economy*, Macmillan, London, vol. 2, pp. 49–50.

Collet, Clara E. (1896b), 'Females and Children, Earnings of', *Palgrave Dictionary of Political Economy*, Macmillan, London, vol. 2, pp. 50–52.

Collet, Clara E. (1898a), *Changes in the Employment of Women and Girls in Industrial Centres*, HMSO, Cmnd 8794, London.

Collet, Clara E. (1898b), 'The Collection and Utilisation of Official Statistics Bearing on the Extent and Effects of the Industrial Employment of Women', *Journal of the Royal Statistical Society*, 62 (2), June, pp. 229–60.

Collet, Clara E. (1898c), 'The Expenditure of Middle Class Working Women', *Economic Journal*, 8 (32), December, pp. 543–53.

Collet, Clara E. (1901), 'Wages Boards in Victoria', *Economic Journal*, 11 (44), December, pp. 557–65.

Collet, Clara E. (1902), *Educated Working Women*, P.S. King & Sons, London.

Collet, Clara E. (1903), 'Review of *The Strength of the People*', *Economic Journal*, 13 (43), March, pp. 81–4.

Collet, Clara E. (1915), 'The Professional Employment of Women', *Economic Journal*, 25 (100), December, pp. 627–30.

Collet, Clara E. (1919), 'Comment on Dorothea Barton', *Journal of the Royal Statistical Society*, 82 (4), July, pp. 547–9.

Collet, Clara E. (1923), 'Obituary of George Armitage-Smith', *Economic Journal*, 33 (129), March, pp. 127–8.

Collet, Clara E. (1933), *Joseph Collet 1673–1725. The Irvine Letters. Books,* edited by H.H. Dodwell with an appendix by Clara Collet, Longmans, Green, London.

Collet, Clara E. (1936), 'Professor Foxwell and University College', *Economic Journal*, 46 (184), December, pp. 614–19.

Collet, Clara E. (1940), 'Obituary of Henry Higgs', *Economic Journal*, 50 (200), December, pp. 546–61.

Collet, Clara (1945), 'Charles Booth, the Denison Club and H. Llewellyn Smith', *Journal of the Royal Statistical Society*, CVIII, Parts I–II, pp. 482–5.

Collet, Collet Dobson (1933), *History of the Taxes on Knowledge*, Watts & Co., London.

Collette, Christine (1989), *For Labour and for Women. The Women's Labour League, 1906–1918*, Manchester University Press, Manchester.

Collini, Stefan, Donald Winch and John Burrow (1983), *That Noble Art of Politics*, Cambridge University Press, Cambridge.

Condorcet, M.J.A.N. Caritat de (1795), *Esquise d'un Tableau historique des progrès de l'esprit humain*, ouvrage posthume, Paris.

Cooke-Taylor, W.C. (1875), 'The Employment of Mothers in Factories', *The Fortnightly Review*, **17** (101), pp. 664–79.

Cooke-Taylor, W.C. (1882a), 'Married Women in Factories', *Pall Mall Gazette*, 10 February, p. 2.

Cooke-Taylor, W.C. (1882b), 'Married Women in Factories: A Reply', *The Contemporary Review*, **52**, September, pp. 428–41.

Darwin, Charles (1871), *The Descent of Man*, Murray, London, second edition, 1906 reprint.

Davidoff, Leonore and Catherine Hall (1987), *Family Fortunes: Men and Women in the English Middle Class 1780–1850*, Hutchinson, London.

Delmar, Rosalind (1986), 'What is Feminism', in J. Mitchell and A. Oakley (eds), *What is Feminism,* Blackwell, Oxford.

Dilke, Emilia F.S. (1891), 'Women and the Royal Commission', *Fortnightly Review*, July–December, pp. 535–8.

Dimand, Robert, Mary Ann Ormond and Evelyn Target (eds), *Women of Value, Essays on the History of Women in Economics*, Edward Elgar, Aldershot (forthcoming).

Dyhouse, C. (1978), 'Working Class Mothers and Infant Mortality in England 1895–1914', *Journal of Social History*, **12** (2), pp. 248–67.

Eatwell, John, Murray Milgate and Peter Neuman (eds) (1987), *The New Palgrave Dictionary of Economics*, Macmillan, London.

Edgeworth, F.Y. (1925), 'Reminiscences', in Pigou (1925), pp. 66–73.

Fabian Society (1895), *Sweating: its Cause and Remedy*, Fabian Tract No. 50, Fabian Society, London.

Fabian Women's Group (1915), *The War; Women; and Unemployment*, Fabian Tract No. 178, Fabian Society, London.

Fawcett, Henry (1863), *The Manual of Political Economy*, third edition, Macmillan, London.

Fawcett, Millicent Garrett (1888), 'The Women's Suffrage Movement', in T. Stanton (ed.), *The Woman Question in Europe*, Macmillan, London.

Fawcett, Millicent Garrett (1889), 'The Appeal Against Female Suffrage: A Reply', *The Nineteenth Century*, **26**, July.

Fawcett, Millicent Garrett (1892), 'Mr. Sidney Webb's Article on Women's Wages', *Economic Journal*, **2** (5), March.

Fawcett, Millicent Garrett (1904), 'Review of Women in the Printing Trades: A Sociological Study', *Economic Journal*, **14** (54), June.

Fawcett, Millicent Garrett (1913), 'The Remedy of Political Emancipation', in B. Webb (ed.), 'Special Supplement on the Awakening of Women', *The New Statesman*, **2**, November.

Fawcett, Millicent Garrett (1917), 'The Position of Women in Economic Life', in W.H. Dawson (ed.), *After-War Problems*, Allen & Unwin, London.

Feuer, R. (1988), 'The Meaning of Sisterhood', in 'The British Women's Movement and Protective Labour Legislation 1870–1900', *Victorian Studies*, **31** (2).

Folbre, Nancy (1992), 'The Improper Arts: Sex in Classical Political Economy', *Population and Development Review*, **18** (1), March, pp. 105–21.

Folbre, N. and H. Hartman, (1988), 'The Rhetoric of Self Interest: Ideology and Gender in Economic Theory', in A. Kramer, D. McCloskey and R. Solow (eds), *The Consequences of Economic Rhetoric*, Cambridge University Press, Cambridge.

Fourier, Charles (1901), *Design for Utopia. Selected Writings*, with an introduction by Charles Gide (1971), Schocken Books, New York.

Galton, Francis (1889), *Natural Inheritance*, Macmillan, London.

Galton, Francis (1892), *Hereditary Genius*, Macmillan, London.

Gould, Stephen Jay (1981), *The Mismeasurement of Man*, W.W. Norton, New York.

Green, M. (1992), 'Conflicting Principles of Completing Counterparts, J.S. Mill on Political Economy and the Equality of Women', paper presented to International Utilitarian Conference, University of Western Ontario, April.

Greenburg, R.P. (1987), *Fabian Couples. Feminist Issues*, Garland Publishing, Inc., New York.

Groenewegen, Peter, (1990), 'Teaching Economics at Cambridge', *Scottish Journal of Political Economy*, **37** (1) February, pp. 40–60.

Groenewegen, Peter (1994), 'Alfred Marshall and the Labour Commission', *European Journal of the History of Economic Thought*, 1 (2), Spring, pp. 273–96.

Habermas, Jurgen (1984), *The Structural Transformation of the Public Sphere*, Blackwell, Oxford.

Harcourt, G.C. (1982), 'Joan Robinson', in Prue Kerr (ed.), *The Social Science Imperialists. Selected Essays*, Routledge & Kegan Paul, London.

Haycraft, J.B. (1895), *Darwinism and Race Progress*, Swan Sonnenscheinn, London.

Heather-Bigg, A. (1894), 'The Wife's Contribution to Family Income', *Economic Journal*, 4 (13), March.

Hewitt, M. (1958), *Wives and Mothers in Victorian Industry*, Greenwood Press, Westport.

Hey, David and D.W. Winch (eds) (1990), *A Century of Economics. 100 Years of the Royal Economic Society and the Economic Journal*, Blackwell, Oxford.

Higgs, Henry (1890), 'Frederic Le Play', *Quarterly Journal of Economics*, 4, July, pp. 408–33, 467–77.

Higgs, Henry (ed.) (1925), *Palgrave Dictionary of Political Economy*, revised edition, Macmillan, London.

Hodgskin, Thomas (1827), *Popular Political Economy*, Charles Tait, London.

Holton, S.S. (1986), *Feminism and Democracy: Women's Suffrage and Reform Politics in Britain 1900–1918*, Cambridge University Press, Cambridge.

Hutchins, B.L. (1915), *Women in Modern Industry*, G. Bell, London.

Hutchins, B.L. and A. Harrison, (1966), *A History of Factory Legislation*, Frank Cass & Co., London.

Hutchison, T.W. (1982), 'The Politics and Philosophy of Jevons' Political Economy', *The Manchester School*, 50 (4), pp. 366–78.

Jevons, H.A. (ed.) (1886), *Letters and Journals of W. Stanley Jevons*, Macmillan, London.

Jevons, W.S. (1866), 'Brief Account of a General Mathematical Theory of Political Economy', *Journal of the Statistical Society*, 19, pp. 282–7.

Jevons, W.S. (1869), 'Remarks on Mr. Baxendell's Laws of Atmospheric Ozone', *Proceedings of the Literary and Philosophical Society of Manchester Session 1868–69*, 8, pp. 33–4.

Jevons, W.S. (1870), 'Opening Address of the President of Section F (Economic Science and Statistics), of the British Association for the Advancement of Science, 40th Meeting, Liverpool, September, *Journal of the Statistical Society*, **33** (3), pp. 309–26.

Jevons, W.S. (1871), *The Theory of Political Economy*, Macmillan, London.

Jevons, W.S. (1879), 'Discussion' of the Paper of E. Ravenstein, 'On the Celtic Language in the British Isles: A Statistical Survey', *Journal of the Statistical Society*, **42**, September, p. 640.

Jevons, W.S. (1882a), 'Married Women in Factories', *The Contemporary Review*, **41**, January, pp. 37–53.

Jevons, W.S. (1882b), 'Married Women in Factories', *Pall Mall Gazette*, 10 February, pp. 11–12.

Jevons, W.S. (1882c), *The State in Relation to Labour*, Macmillan, London.

Jevons, W.S. (1883), *Methods of Social Reform*, Macmillan, London.

Jevons, W.S. (1887), *The Principles of Science. A Treatise of Logic and Scientific Method*, second edition, Macmillan, London.

Jevons, W.S. (1890), *Pure Logic and Other Minor Works*, edited by R. Adamson and M.A. Jevons, Macmillan, London.

Jevons, W.S. (1910), *Theory of Political Economy*, second edition, reprinted in fourth, Macmillan, London.

Jones, Thomas (1916), 'Biographical Sketch of William Smart', in William Smart, *Second Thoughts of an Economist*, Macmillan, London, pp. ix–lxxix.

Kidd, A. (1985), 'Outcast Manchester, Voluntary Relief, Poor Relief, and the Casual Poor 1860–1905', in A.J. Kidd and K.W. Roberts, *City Class and Culture. Studies of Social Policy and Cultural Production in Victorian Manchester*, Manchester University Press, Manchester.

Klein, V. (1971), *The Feminine Character: History of an Ideology*, Routledge, London.

Le Bon, G. (1870), 'Recherches anatomiques et mathématiques sur les lois des variations du volume du cerveau et sur leur relations avec l'intelligence', *Revue d'Anthropologie*, vol. 2.

Le Play, M.F. (1887), *La Reforme Sociale en France*, seventh edition, Alfred Mamé, Tours.

Lewis, J. (1986), 'The Working Class Wife and Mother and State Intervention, 1870–1918', in J. Lewis (ed.), *Labour and Love. Women's Experience of Home and Family 1850–1940*, Basil Blackwell, Oxford.

Lewis, J. and C. Davies (1991), 'Protective Legislation in Britain 1870–1990, Equality, Difference and their Implications for Women', *Policy and Politics*, **19** (1).

Libby, Barbara (1984), 'Women in Economics Before 1940', *Essays in Economic and Business History*, **3**, pp. 173–90.

Libby, Barbara (1987), 'A Statistical Analysis of Women in the Economics Professions, 1900–1940', *Essays in Economic and Business History*, **V**, pp. 179–201.

Libby, Barbara (1989), 'A Further Analysis of Women in the Economics Profession', *Economic and Business History Studies*, Charleston.

Libby, Barbara (1990), 'Women in the Economics Profession, 1900–1940. Factors in their Declining Visibility', *Essays in Economic and Business History*, **VIII**, pp. 121–30.

M.A. (1914), *The Economic Foundations of the Women's Movement*, Fabian Tract No. 175, Fabian Society, London.

Macgregor, D.H. (1942), 'Marshall and his Book', *Economica*, N.S. **9**, pp. 313–24.

McBriar, A.M. (1962), *Fabian Socialism and English Politics 1889–1918*, Cambridge University Press, Cambridge.

McBriar, A.M. (1987), *An Edwardian Mixed Doubles: The Bosanquets versus the Webbs: a Study in British Social Policy 1890–1929*, Oxford University Press, New York.

McCulloch, J.R. (1854), *A Treatise of the Circumstances which Determine the Rate of Wages and the Conditions of the Labouring Classes*, Routledge, London.

McGregor, O.R. (1955), 'The Social Position of Women in England 1850–1914: A Bibliography', *The British Journal of Sociology*, **6**, March.

McWilliams-Tullberg, Rita (1975), *A Men's University – Though of a Mixed Type. Women at Cambridge*, Victor Gollancz, London.

McWilliams-Tullberg (1990), 'Alfred Marshall and the "Woman Question" at Cambridge', *Economie Appliquée*, **43** (1), pp. 209–30.

McWilliams-Tullberg, Rita (1991), 'Alfred Marshall and the Male Priesthood of Economics', *Quaderni di storia dell' economia politica*, **9** (2–3), pp. 235–68.

McWilliams-Tullberg, Rita (1992), 'Alfred Marshall's Attitude towards the Economics of Industry', *Journal of the History of Economic Thought*, **14** (2), pp. 257–70.

182   *References*

Madden, Janice F. (1972), 'The Development of Economic Thought on the "Women Problem" ', *Review of Radical Political Economics*, 4 (3), pp. 21–39.

Mahalanobis, P.C. (1948), 'Clara Elizabeth Collet', *Journal of the Royal Statistical Society*, Series A, 111 (3) p. 254.

Maloney, John (1990), 'Gentlemen versus Players, 1891–1914', in John D. Hey and Donald Winch (eds), *A Century of Economics 100 Years of the Royal Economic Society and the Economic Journal*, Basil Blackwell, Oxford.

Marcet, J. (1826), *Conversations on Political Economy*, fifth edition, Longman, Hunt, Rees, Brown & Green, London.

Marshall, Alfred (1873), 'The Future of the Working Classes', in Pigou (ed.) (1925), pp. 101–18.

Marshall, Alfred (1874), 'The Province of Political Economy', *Bee-Hive*, May, in R. Harrison, 'Two Early Articles by Alfred Marshall', *Economic Journal* (1963), June, pp. 422–30.

Marshall, Alfred (1890), *Principles of Economics*, first edition, Macmillan, London.

Marshall, Alfred (1895), *Principles of Economics*, third edition, Macmillan, London.

Marshall, Alfred (1898), *Principles of Economics*, fourth edition, Macmillan, London.

Marshall, Alfred (1907a), *Principles of Economics*, fifth edition, Macmillan, London.

Marshall, Alfred (1907b), 'Social Possibilities of Economic Chivalry', in Pigou (ed.) (1925), pp. 323–46.

Marshall, Alfred (1910), *Principles of Economics*, sixth edition, Macmillan, London.

Marshall, Alfred (1919), *Industry and Trade*, Macmillan, London.

Marshall, Alfred (1920), *Principles of Economics*, eighth edition, Macmillan, London.

Marshall, Alfred (1961), *Principles of Economics*, ninth variorum edition, edited by C.W. Guillebaud, Macmillan, London.

Marshall, Alfred and M.P. Marshall (1879), *The Economics of Industry*, second edition, 1881, Macmillan, London.

Marshall, Mary Paley (1902), Review of 'Educated Working Women' by Clara E. Collet, *Economic Journal*, 12 (46), June, pp. 252–7.

Marshall, Mary Paley (1947), *What I Remember*, Cambridge University Press, Cambridge.

Marx, Karl (1974), *Capital. A Critical Analysis of Capitalist Production*, vol. 1, Progress Publishers, Moscow.

Matthews, R.C.O. (1990), 'Marshall and the Labour Market', in J.K. Whitaker (ed.), *Centenary Essays on Alfred Marshall*, Cambridge University Press, Cambridge.

Metcalfe, A.E. (1919), *'At Last': Conclusion of 'Woman's Effort'*, B.H. Blackwell, Oxford.

Mill, John Stuart (1848), *Principles of Political Economy*, first edition, Longmans, London.

Mill, John Stuart (1865), *Principles of Political Economy*, Longmans Green & Company (people's edition), London.

Mill, John Stuart (1871), *Principles of Political Economy*, seventh edition, Longmans, London.

Mill, John Stuart (1971), *Autobiography*, edited by Jack Stillinger, Oxford University Press, Oxford.

Mill, John Stuart (1975), *Three Essays: On Liberty, Representative Government, the Subjection of Women*, Oxford University Press, Oxford.

Mill, John Stuart and Harriet Taylor (1970), *Essays on Sex Equality*, edited by Alice Rossi, Chicago University Press, Chicago.

Mitchell, B.R. (1962), *Abstract of British Historical Statistics*, with the collaboration of Phyllis Deane, Cambridge University Press, Cambridge.

Moggridge, Don (1992), *Maynard Keynes. An Economist's Biography*, Routledge, London.

Morris, J. (1986), *Women Workers in the Sweated Trades: The Origins of Minimum Wage Legislation*, Gower Publishing Co. Ltd., London.

Muggridge K. and R. Adam, (1967), *Beatrice Webb: A Life 1858–1943*, Secker & Warburg, London.

Nolan, B.E. (1988), *The Political Theory of Beatrice Webb*, AMS Press Inc., New York.

Nyland, C. (1987), 'Marx, Jevons and the Home', typescript, Flinders University of South Australia.

Nyland, C. and D. Kelly, (1992), 'Beatrice Webb and the National Standard for Manual Handling', *Journal of Industrial Relations*, **34**, June.

Owen, Robert (1816), 'A New View of Society', in *A New View of Society and Other Writings*, J.M. Dent, London.

Owen, Robert (1817a), 'Relief of the Poor', in *A New View of Society and Other Writings*, J.M. Dent, London.

Owen, Robert (1817b), 'Letters on Poor Relief', in *A New View of Society and Other Writings*, J.M. Dent, London.

Pateman, Carole (1989), *The Disorder of Women*, Oxford University Press, Oxford.

Peart, S.J. (1990a), 'The Population Mechanism in W.S. Jevons' Applied Economics', *The Manchester School*, **58** (1), pp. 32–53.

Peart, S.J. (1990b), 'Jevons's Application of Utilitarian Theory to Economic Policy', *Utilitas*, **2** (2), pp. 281–306.

Pease, E.R. (1963), *The History of the Fabian Society*, Frank Cass & Co. Ltd., London.

Pigou, A.C. (1925) (ed.), *Memorials of Alfred Marshall*, Macmillan, London.

[Price B.] (1871), 'Mr. Mill on Land', *Blackwood's Edinburgh Magazine*, **110**, (DCL XIX), pp. 30–45.

Privy Council (1864), *Sixth Report of the Medical Officer of the Privy Council with Appendix*, Parliamentary Papers, no. 3416, Vol. XXVIII, **1**, London.

Pugh, P. (1984), *Educate, Agitate, Organise: 100 Years of Fabian Socialism*, Methuen, London.

Pujol, Michèle A. (1984), 'Gender and Class in Marshall's Principles of Economics', *Cambridge Journal of Economics*, **8** (3), September, pp. 217–34.

Pujol, Michèle A. (1992), *Feminism and Anti-Feminism in Early Economic Thought*, Elgar, Aldershot.

Radice, L. (1984), *Beatrice and Sidney Webb: Fabian Socialists*, Macmillan, London.

Rathbone, E. (1917), 'The Remuneration of Women's Services', *Economic Journal*, **27**, March.

Reeves, M.P. (1912), *Family Life on a Pound a Week*, Fabian Tract No. 162, Fabian Society, London.

Reeves, M.P. (1913), *Round About a Pound a Week*, Virago, London.

Reiss, E. (1934), *Rights and Duties of English Women: a Study in Law and Public Opinion*, Shearatt & Hughes, Manchester.

Rendall, Jane (1988), 'Virtue and Commerce: Women in the Making of Smith's Political Economy', in Ellen Kennedy and Susan Mendus (eds), *Western Philosophy. Kant to Nietzsche*, Wheatsheaf, Brighton, pp. 44–73.

Richards, Evelleen (1983), 'Darwin and the Descent of Women', in David Oldroup and Ian Langham (eds), *The Wider Domain of Evolutionary Thought*, Reidel, Dordrecht, pp. 57–112.

Roberts, Elizabeth (1988), *Women's Work*, Macmillan Education, London.

Roberts, M.J.D. (1991), 'Reshaping the Gilt Relationship. The London Mendicity Society and the Repression of Begging in England 1818–1869', *International Review of Social History*, **36** (2), pp. 201–31.

Rose, L. (1986), *The Massacre of the Innocents, Infanticide in Britain 1800–1939*, Routledge & Kegan Paul, London.

Rose, S.O. (1991), 'From Behind Women's Petticoats, The English Factory Acts of 1874 as a Cultural Production', *Journal of Historical Sociology*, **4** (1), pp. 33–51.

Rover, C. (1967), *Women's Suffrage and Party Politics in Britain 1866–1914*, Routledge & Kegan Paul, London.

Royal Commission on Labour (1892), *Minutes of Evidence Group B*, vol. II, HMSO, Cmnd. 6703–V, London.

Royal Commission on Labour (1893a), *Minutes of Evidence Group B*, vol. III, HMSO, Cmnd. 6894–VIII, London.

Royal Commission on Labour (1893b), *Fourth Report*, HMSO, Cmnd. 7063, London.

Royal Commission on Labour (1894a), *Reports from Commissioners, Inspectors and Others*, HMSO, XXV, London.

Royal Commission on Labour (1894b), *Fifth and Final Report*, HMSO, Cmnd. 7421, London.

Rubinstein, David (1988), 'Victorian Feminists: Henry and Millicent Fawcett', in Lawrence Goldman (ed.), *The Blind Victorian: Essays on Henry Fawcett*, Cambridge University Press, Cambridge.

Ruskin, John (1862–63), *Munera Pulveris (Essays on Political Economy)*, Routledge, 1907 edition, London.

Ruskin, John (1865), *Sesame and Lilies*, J.M. Dent, edition, n.d., London.

Russell, Bertrand (1978), *Autobiography*, Allen & Unwin, London.

Say, J. -B. (1970), *A Treatise of Political Economy*, translated by C.R. Princep, 1880, Kelley, New York.

Seed, J. (1982), 'Unitarianism, Political Economy and the Antinomies of Liberal Culture in Manchester 1830–50', *Social History*, **7**, pp. 1–25.

Select Committee of the House of Lords on the Sweating System (1887–88), British Parliamentary Papers, Cmnd. 5913.

Seymour-Jones C. (1992), *Beatrice Webb: Woman of Conflict*, Allison & Busby, London.

Shanley, M.L. (1989), *Feminism, Marriage and the Law in Victorian England*, Princeton University Press, Princeton.

Sidgwick, Arthur and Eleanor Sidgwick (1906), *Henry Sidgwick: A Memoir*, Macmillan, London.

Sidgwick, Eleanor (1913), 'The Progress of the Women's Suffrage Movement', Conservative and Unionist Women's Frachise Association, Cambridge.

Sidgwick, Ethel (1938), *Mrs. Henry Sidgwick. A Memoir by her Niece*, Sidgwick & Jackson, London.

Sidgwick, Henry (1887), *Principles of Political Economy*, second edition, Macmillan, London.

Sidgwick, Henry (1891), *Elements of Politics*, first edition, Macmillan, London.

Skidelsky, Robert (1983), *John Maynard Keynes: Hopes Betrayed 1883–1920*, Macmillan, London.

Smart, W. (1895), *Studies in Economics*, Macmillan & Co., London.

Smiles, Samuel (1859), *Self Help, with Illustrations of Character and Conduct*, John Murray, London.

Smiles, Samuel (1875), *Thrift*, John Murray, London.

Smith, E. (1915), *Wage-Earning Women and their Dependants*, Fabian Society, London.

Smith, R. (1973), 'The Background of Physiological Psychology in Natural Philosophy', *History of Science*, 11 (2), pp. 75–123.

Spencer, Herbert (1862), *First Principles*, sixth edition (1919), Williams & Norgate, London.

Stigler, S. (1982), 'Jevons as Statistician', *The Manchester School*, 50 (4), pp. 384–65.

Strachey, Ray (1931), *Millicent Garrett Fawcett*, J. Murray, London.

Tawney, R.H. (n.d.), *Beatrice Webb 1858–1943*, Geoffrey Cumberlege, London.

Thane, P. (1978), 'Women and the Poor Law in Victorian and Edwardian England', *History Workshop* (6), Autumn, pp. 29–51.

Thomson, Dorothy Lampeen (1973), *Adam Smith's Daughters*, Exposition Press, New York.

T[horburn], C[atherine] (1948), 'Clara Elizabeth Collet', *Journal of the Royal Statistical Society*, Series A, 111 (3), pp. 252–3.

War Cabinet Committee (1919), 'Women in Industry', British Parliamentary Papers, Cmnd. 135.

Ward, Mrs. Humphrey (1901), Preface, in Beatrice Webb (ed.), *The Case for the Factory Acts*, Grant Richards, London.

Webb (Potter), B. (1888a), 'Pages from a Work-Girl's Diary', *The Nineteenth Century*, 24 (89).

Webb (Potter), B. (1888b), 'East London Labour', *The Nineteenth Century*, **24** (138).

Webb (Potter), B. (1890) 'The Lords and the Sweating System', *The Nineteenth Century*, **27** (90).

Webb (Potter), B. (1894), 'The Failure of the Labour Commission', *The Nineteenth Century*, **26**, July.

Webb (Potter), B. (1896), *Women and the Factory Acts*, Fabian Tract No. 67, Fabian Society, London.

Webb (Potter), B. (1898), 'How to do Away with the Sweating System', in S. and B. Webb (eds), *Problems of Modern Industry*, Longman's Green & Co., London.

Webb, (Potter), B. (ed.) (1901), *The Case for the Factory Acts*, Grant Richards, London.

Webb (Potter), B. (1902a), 'The Docks', in Charles Booth (ed.), *Life and Labour of the People in London*, Macmillan & Co., London.

Webb (Potter), B. (1902b), 'The Tailoring Trade', in Charles Booth (ed.), *Life and Labour of the People in London*, Macmillan & Co., London.

Webb (Potter), B. (1902c), 'The Jewish Community (East London)', in Charles Booth (ed.), *Life and Labour of the People in London*, Macmillan & Co., London.

Webb (Potter), B. (ed.) (1913), 'Special Supplement on the Awakening of Women', *The New Statesman*, **2**, November.

Webb (Potter), B. (1914a), 'Voteless Women and Social Revolution', *The New Statesman*, **2**, February.

Webb, (Potter), B. (ed.) (1914b), 'Special Supplement on Women in Industry', *The New Statesman*, **2**, February.

Webb (Potter), B. (1914c), 'Personal Rights and the Woman's Movement', *The New Statesman*, **3**, July.

Webb (Potter), B. (1914d), 'Motherhood and Citizenship', *The New Statesman*, **3** (58), pp. 10–11.

Webb (Potter), B. (1915), 'Special Supplement on English Teachers and their Professional Organisation', *The New Statesman*, **5** (129), September.

Webb (Potter), B. (1918), 'Preface', in A.E. Metcalf (ed.), *Woman: A Citizen*, Allen & Unwin, London.

Webb (Potter), B. (1919a), *The Wages of Men and Women: Should they be Equal?*, Fabian Society, London.

Webb (Potter), B. (1919b), 'The End of the Poor Law', in Various Women Writers (eds), *Women and the Labour Party*, Headley Bros. Ltd., London.

Webb (Potter), B. (1938), *My Apprenticeship*, Pelican, Harmondsworth.

Webb (Potter), B. (1948), *Our Partnership*, edited by B. Drake and M.I. Cole, Longmans, Green & Co., London.

Webb (Potter), B. (1978a), *The Letters of Sidney and Beatrice Webb, vol. 1 1873–1892*, edited by N. MacKenzie, Cambridge University Press, Cambridge.

Webb (Potter), B. (1978b), *The Letters of Sidney and Beatrice Webb, vol. II, 1892–1912*, edited by N. MacKenzie, Cambridge University Press, Cambridge.

Webb (Potter), B. (1978c), *The Letters of Sidney and Beatrice Webb, vol. III 1912–1947*, edited by N. MacKenzie, Cambridge University Press, Cambridge.

Webb (Potter), B. (1978d), *The Diary of Beatrice Webb (Microfiche), 1873–1943*, Chadwyck-Healey Ltd., Cambridge.

Webb (Potter), B. (1982), *The Diary of Beatrice Webb, vol. 1, 1873–1892*, edited by N. and J. MacKenzie, Virago, London.

Webb (Potter), B. (1983), *The Diary of Beatrice Webb, vol. 2, 1892–1905*, edited by N. and J. MacKenzie, Virago, London.

Webb (Potter), B. (1984), *The Diary of Beatrice Webb, vol. 3, 1905–1924*, edited by N. and J. MacKenzie, Virago, London.

Webb (Potter), B. (1985), *The Diary of Beatrice Webb, vol. 4, 1924–1943*, edited by N. and J. MacKenzie, Virago, London.

Webb (Potter), B., B.L. Hutchins and the Fabian Society (eds) (1909), *Socialism and the National Minimum*, Fabian Society, London.

Webb (Potter), B. and Mrs. H. Ward (eds) (1901), *The Case of the Factory Acts*, Grant Richards, London.

Webb, S. (1891), 'The Alleged Difference in the Wages Paid to Men and to Women for Similar Work', *Economic Journal*, **1**, December.

Webb, S. (1909), 'The Economic Aspects of Poor Law Reform', *English Review*, **3** (*).

Webb, S. (1912), 'The Economic Theory of a Legal Minimum Wage', *The Journal of Political Economy*, **20** (10), March.

Webb, S. (1914), *The War and the Workers*, Fabian Tract No. 176, Fabian Society, London.

Webb, S. and A. Freeman (1916), *When Peace Comes – The Way of Industrial Reconstruction*, Fabian Tract No. 181, Fabian Society, London.

Webb, S. and B. Webb (Potter) (1897), *Industrial Democracy*, Longmans, London.

Webb, S. and B. Webb (Potter) (1898), *Problems of Modern Industry*, Longmans, Green & Co., London.

Webb, S. and B. Webb (Potter) (1909), *The Break-Up of the Poor Law: Being Part One of the Poor Law Commission*, Longmans, Green & Co., London.

Webb, S. and B. Webb (Potter) (1911), *The History of Trade Unionism*, Longmans, Green & Co., London.

Webb, S. and B. Webb (Potter) (1919), *The State and the Doctor*, Longmans, Green & Co., London.

Webb, S. and B. Webb (Potter) (1923), *The Decay of Capitalist Civilisation*, Fabian Society, London.

Webb, S. and B. Webb (Potter) (1937), *Soviet Communism: A New Civilisation*, Victor Gollancz Ltd., London.

Webb, S. and B. Webb (Potter) (1971), *The Prevention of Destitution*, Longmans, London.

Webb, S. and Freeman, A. (1916), *When Peace Comes – The Way of Industrial Reconstruction,* Fabian Tract No. 181, Fabian Society, London.

Weintraub, E. Roy et al. (1993), 'Mini-symposium: Feminist Theory and the History of Economic Thought', *History of Political Economy*, **25** (1), Spring, pp. 115–201.

Whitaker, John (1977), 'Some Neglected Aspects of Alfred Marshall's Economic and Social Thought', in Wood (1982), I, pp. 453–86.

White, M.V. (1991), 'Frightening the Landed Fogies: Parliamentary Politics and the Coal Question', *Utilitas*, **3** (2), pp. 289–302.

White, M.V. (1993a), 'The Natural and the Social "Science" and "Character" in Jevons' Political Economy', (forthcoming).

White, M.V. (1993b), 'The Irish Factor in Jevons' Statistics: A Note', *History of Economic Review*, **19**, Winter, pp. 79–85.

Wilkinson, T.R. (1871), 'Observations on Infant Mortality and the Death Rate in Large Towns', translations of the *Manchester Statistical Society Session 1870–71*, **4**, pp. 49–55.

Wood, G.H. (1903), 'The Course of Women's Wages during the Nineteenth Century', in B.L. Hutchins and A. Harrison (eds), *A History of Factory Legislation, Appendix*, P.S. King, London.

Wood, J.C. (1982), *Alfred Marshall. Critical Assessments*, Croom Helm, London.

Worsnop, J. (1990), 'A Re-evaluation of the Problem of "Surplus Women" in 19th Century England', *Women's Studies International Forum*, **13** (1/2), pp. 21–31.

Index